Teens in Crisis

Teens in Crisis

HOW THE INDUSTRY SERVING STRUGGLING TEENS

HELPS AND HURTS OUR KIDS

Frederic G. Reamer and Deborah H. Siegel

COLUMBIA UNIVERSITY PRESS NEW YORK

Columbia University Press
Publishers Since 1893
New York   Chichester, West Sussex
Copyright © 2008 Columbia University Press
All rights reserved

Library of Congress Cataloging-in-Publication Data
Reamer, Frederic G., 1953–
Teens in crisis : how the industry serving struggling teens
helps and hurts our kids /
Frederic G. Reamer and Deborah H. Siegel.
    p.   cm.
Includes bibliographical references and index.
ISBN 978-0-231-14462-9 (cloth : alk. paper) —
ISBN 978-0-231-14463-6 (pbk.) —
ISBN 978-0-231-51450-7 (electronic)
1. Youth—Services for—United States—Evaluation.
2. Problem youth—Education—United States.
3. Adolescent psychotherapy—Residential treatment—
United States. I. Siegel, Deborah H., 1951– II. Title.
HV741.R415   2009
362.7083   dc22   2008004360

Columbia University Press books are printed on
permanent and durable acid-free paper.
This book was printed on paper with recycled content.
Printed in the United States of America

c 10 9 8 7 6 5 4 3 2 1
p 10 9 8 7 6 5 4 3 2 1

References to Internet Web sites (URLs) were accurate
at the time of writing. Neither the author nor Columbia
University Press is responsible for URLs that may have
expired or changed since the manuscript was prepared.

For Emma and Leah
We are privileged to be your parents.

CONTENTS

THE INVENTION OF "TROUBLED TEENS"

EVOLUTION OF AN INDUSTRY

SASHA, A *bright, creative, resourceful, and spirited fifteen year old, lives with her parents, who love her deeply. Sasha's parents provide a stable home in a safe, middle-class neighborhood. Sasha and her younger brother enjoy a good relationship with each other. Since first grade Sasha has struggled academically, often forgetting school assignments or leaving partially completed work crumpled at the bottom of her backpack. When she was nine, Sasha was diagnosed with attention-deficit/hyperactivity disorder (ADHD, predominantly inattentive type), depression, and anxiety. She struggles to fit in socially, often feeling different and inferior. In fact, throughout Sasha's school career classmates, especially girls, have ignored, shunned, excluded, mocked, and taunted her.*

Sasha's parents have worked assertively with her school to ensure that her emotional and educational needs are addressed through an individualized education program (IEP). But often school personnel do not meet Sasha's needs. Sasha and her parents have sought help over the years from an array of special education teachers, school psychologists and guidance counselors, social workers, and psychiatrists in the community. Despite these efforts, things began to fall apart in middle school. Seeking acceptance from her peer group, Sasha began to hang out with kids who smoked cigarettes in the school bathrooms. These peers introduced then-fourteen-year-old Sasha to a nineteen-year-old man who convinced her to slip out of school during her lunch period to use drugs and perform oral sex on him. Sasha began lying to her parents about where she had been when she was late getting home from school or returning from walks in the neighborhood.

Increasingly worried and wary, Sasha's parents began to provide more structure and supervision; Sasha rebelled, pulling angrily away from them, becoming sullen, defiant, and uncommunicative. "You just don't want me to have a life!" she howled. Sasha's parents returned to the family therapist who had helped

*them in the past; she coached them skillfully in how to parent a teenager strug-
gling with special needs and normal developmental challenges. Nonetheless,
their concerns grew as Sasha became more defiant, using drugs during school
hours and often locking herself in the bathroom throughout the evening.*

*Late one night, after her parents and brother were in bed, Sasha slipped out
of the house to rendezvous with her nineteen-year-old boyfriend. Her parents
were awakened at 2 a.m. by the phone; it was the police. Sasha and her boyfriend had been arrested for marijuana possession.*

⸫

Struggling teens like Sasha have always been part of the modern landscape.
Most teens wrestle with their emerging maturity and independence; some,
like Sasha, encounter school failure, drug addiction, self-injury, family strife,
pregnancy, and other forms of harm. Some teenagers become known as rebellious, defiant, and troubled, meaning that they struggle mightily with some
combination of mental health difficulties, substance abuse, and academic,
behavioral, legal, and other issues.

Throughout most of history parents and communities dealt with struggling teens by cobbling together various forms of supervision, exhortation,
and discipline. Teachers, clergy, neighbors, family friends, and shopkeepers
might collaborate informally to help parents keep a watchful eye on teens.
Extended family or friends might house a struggling teen for a time to help
the youngster get it together. When all else failed, struggling teens might be
kicked out of their parents' home, placed in foster care, or arrested and managed by juvenile and family courts.

This was almost universally the approach until the 1960s, that is, when the
modern "troubled teen" industry was born. Most experts in the field point
to the opening of a specialty program known as CEDU, the nation's first so-
called emotional growth boarding school, as a pivotal event in Americans'
efforts to respond to struggling teens. CEDU, located in Running Springs,
California, until its parent company filed for bankruptcy in 2005, was founded in the late 1960s by Mel Wasserman, a furniture store owner in Palm
Springs, California. In 1965 Wasserman met and befriended a "down-and-
out" young man who was sitting on the steps of a building across the street
from Wasserman's store. Wasserman and his wife invited the young man to
dinner and, before long, were hosting intense, emotional get-togethers with
a dozen or so area teens. Over time a number of these young people moved
in with the Wassermans, helped with household chores, and formed a small
community (Marcus 2005).

In 1969 Wasserman bought a ranch in the hills east of Los Angeles and relocated there with his family and a number of his adolescent houseguests. Before long a woman approached the Wassermans about the possibility of taking in her teenage son. Other teens followed, and several of the Wassermans' houseguests themselves became counselors for other residents.

The Wassermans called their new program CEDU, since, according to the Wassermans, teens would do well to "*see* yourself as you are and *do* something about it" (Marcus 2005:23). According to the journalist David Marcus, Wasserman

> drew from the humanistic psychology movement that was popular at the time; kids discussed their fears and traumas in frequent group sessions, or raps. The raps often lasted for hours and ended with participants in tears. As word of CEDU spread, social service agencies started paying the Wassermans to take in teenagers who had gotten in scrapes with the police.
>
> A six-foot-three, 250-pound bear of a man, Wasserman often sat in a large chair, sometimes on a riser left over from drama productions. He towered over the counselors assembled around him during meetings. He flew the staff to retreats at his lakefront house in Idaho, which he named Dunrovin' (because he was "done roving" from place to place). As a boss, he alternately praised and ridiculed the staff; when enrollment slipped and money was tight, he bellowed, "We need asses in beds!" (23)

From these relatively humble beginnings the "troubled teen" industry has burgeoned. It is now a largely uncoordinated welter of unevenly regulated programs, schools, and services that adhere to remarkably diverse belief systems, ideologies, and intervention approaches to teens' emotional, behavioral, and educational needs. The industry includes hundreds of different kinds of wilderness therapy programs, emotional growth boarding schools, therapeutic boarding schools, and residential treatment centers. Families of struggling teens use these diverse programs and schools as places of last resort after trying to help struggling teens in community-based programs and services, such as counseling and psychotherapy, special education programs, alternative high schools, day treatment programs, foster care programs, home-based counseling and crisis intervention programs, juvenile and family court diversion programs, specialty drug and truancy courts, and mentoring programs. Programs in the struggling-teens industry vary widely with regard to the professionalism of staff and how well grounded their interventions and protocols are in research. Some programs rely heavily on shame and blame tactics, public humiliation, verbal abuse, and physical intimidation in the form of sleep deprivation, excessive physical exercise intended to exhaust, and physical torture. In contrast, others use only "best practices" that are well grounded in widely regarded professional codes of ethics and theory and research into child development, family systems, education, and medical and mental health. With the exception of a small percentage of independently wealthy parents, most desperate parents pay for these remarkably expensive programs by depleting their retirement, college, and other savings; remortgaging their homes; and taking out hefty loans from companies that specialize in this sort of specialized financing. A fortunate few receive partial or full subsidies from their local school district, public child welfare agency, or health insurer. Too often poor families are ignored or left to their own devices.

One of the most compelling empirical indicators of the magnitude of the industry's growth is the increasing number of specialty schools and programs available to parents who are seeking help and the growth in the number of professional "educational consultants" and resource directories that lead parents to them. Educational consultants earn their living by assessing, screening, and referring teens to specialty schools and programs.[1]

The stunning growth of the "troubled teen" industry has brought significant growing pains. Many professionally and ethically run schools and programs have helped teens and their families in remarkable ways, but a number of schools and programs have proved to be profoundly abusive and harmful, with occasionally fatal results.

What we now have in the United States is a struggling-teens industry that varies tremendously in quality and professionalism. Put bluntly, like the teens and families it serves, the industry is in the throes of its own adolescent turmoil. In order to understand today's struggling-teens industry, it is important to have a historical perspective. How did the industry evolve in the way that it has? To answer this question we begin with the earliest formal efforts in the United States to provide services for so-called troubled youths, particularly those accused of breaking the law.

THE RISE OF CHILD SAVING

U.S. society has a long history of differentiating between the needs of struggling youths and adults. Several key developments occurred in the nineteenth century. In 1825 the House of Refuge in New York became a reformatory, the first residential institution for delinquents in the United States, in an effort to address the unique needs of struggling youths. In 1854 the New York Children's Aid Society began sending poor and homeless youths—most of whom were not delinquents but youths who were living in remarkably unstable and toxic circumstances that sometimes led to mischievous behavior—to rural communities across the United States to shield them from urban ravages. Under the direction of Charles Loring Brace, a young minister, this agency sent more than 100,000 children to new homes in rural America, a foreshadowing of today's foster care system (O'Connor 2004; Whittaker and Maluccio 2002). Brace and his colleagues believed that relocation would provide these at-risk youths with a more wholesome, nurturing environment that would help them cope with life's challenges and prevent delinquency.

By the late nineteenth century the widespread consensus was that minors ought to be "saved" and not primarily punished for their misbehavior. They were to be helped and loved and gently removed from the pernicious and toxic effects of the difficult economic, social, and family circumstances that spawned their misbehavior. For example, the Second International Penitentiary Congress in Stockholm in 1878 resolved that "delinquent children should not be punished but educated so as to enable them to 'gain an honest livelihood and to become of use to society instead of an injury to it'" (Platt 1977:50). Even for youths removed from their homes, the Illinois Board of Public Charities noted in 1879 that "the object of reformatory institutions is well stated; it is not punishment for past offenses, but training for future usefulness" (Platt 1977:106). And in 1898 a delegate to the National Prison Association urged that professionals concerned about misbehaving youths should "point out to the children . . . all that is beautiful in nature and art. . . . Teach them to love mother and the home, and to hope for heaven. . . . Give the little fellows good companionship, decent, comfortable quarters, clean beds and wholesome food. Smile on them, speak to them, and let sunshine into their souls" (Platt 1977:70). That era's pervasive child-saving sentiment was clearly evident in a report issued in 1899 by the Chicago Bar Association hailing the creation of the nation's first juvenile court, which assumed jurisdiction of the most challenging teens, that is, those who broke the law: "The whole trend and spirit of the act [the Illinois State Legislature's Act to Regulate the Treatment and Control of Dependent, Neglected, and Delinquent Children] is that the state, acting through the Juvenile Court, exercises that tender solicitude and care over its neglected, dependent and delinquent wards that a wise and loving parent would exercise with reference to his own children under similar circumstances" (Hurley 1907:47).

A sea change occurred in 1899 when the nation's first juvenile court was created in Cook County (Chicago), Illinois.[2] This development formally acknowledged that struggling teens, particularly those who ended up in trouble with the law, needed help designed especially for them. This recognition was centuries in the making. Distinguishing between the needs of those older and younger than the age of majority is rooted in seventh-century England, where Ine, who was king of Wessex, in the west and south of England, established a code of laws. King Ine made age ten the age of majority for offenses such as stealing: "If any one steal, so that his wife and his children know it not, let him pay LX. shillings as 'wite' [punishment]. But if he steal with the knowledge of all his household, let them all go into slavery. A boy of X. years may be privy to a theft" (Sanders 1970:3). Juvenile probation, considered by many to be a modern invention, was used during the tenth-century rule of King Athelstane of England.

Indeed, even the most ardent proponents of the classical school of criminology—those who regard human beings as rational, calculating creatures responsible for their acts—acknowledged that children should be exempt from the moral standards to which adults are held. The noted British philosopher Jeremy Bentham, in his eighteenth-century classic *An Introduction to the Principles of Morals and Legislation*, describes infancy as a stage during which an individual is not to be regarded as capable of calculated actions (Bentham [1789] 1973). And the British philosopher John Stuart Mill, in his nineteenth-century classic essay *On Liberty*, inserts a disclaimer to his oft-quoted assertion that people have a right to be left alone by the broader society that might be inclined to interfere in people's lives to protect them from themselves: "It is perhaps hardly necessary to say that this doctrine is meant to apply only to human beings in the maturity of their faculties. We are not speaking of children, or of young persons below the age which the law may fix as that of manhood or womanhood. Those who are still in a state to require being taken care of by others, must be protected against their own actions as well as against external injury" (Mill [1859] 1973:484).

The perception of misbehaving teenagers as children not fully culpable for their acts and as victims of miasmic social conditions persisted throughout the first half-century of the juvenile court's life and the early stages of the juvenile corrections field. The mission of the court and the juvenile justice system promulgated in 1899 endured. The contents of the 1949 "Special Issue Commemorating the Fiftieth Anniversary of the Juvenile Court" of the prominent journal *Federal Probation* were entirely in the spirit of the court's late-nineteenth-century proponents. It is also worth noting that the vast majority of the academic literature published between 1899 and the 1950s on juvenile misbehavior and its causes supported the view that juveniles are not responsible for their behavior and are somewhat compelled to act by psychological and environmental forces beyond their control. In the early twentieth century the works of the Italian positivists—Cesare Lombroso, Enrico Ferri, and Raffaele Garofalo—foreshadowed a series of writings that characterized juvenile misbehavior as the product of physiological, psychological, and environmental forces (Quinney 1970). The so-called Chicago School of the 1920s, including Ernest Burgess, Clifford Shaw, and Henry McKay, emphasized ecological factors that were thought to account for juvenile misconduct, as did the famous statement issued by Robert Merton in 1938 on the concept of *anomie*, that is, the disjuncture between the broader society's expectations of youths and the practical means available to youths to reach these goals (Sutherland and Cressey 1966).

During this period—when misbehaving youths were generally viewed as victims of toxic environmental circumstances—one of the earliest organized efforts to help and nurture struggling youths by offering them residential services got its start. In 1917 Father Edward Flanagan borrowed $90 and opened the Home for Homeless Boys in an old Victorian mansion in Omaha, Nebraska, as a small residential program. In 1926 the organization changed its name to Boys Town.[3] Most youths who lived at Boys Town were referred by the court or local citizens or wandered in on their own (Ivey 2000).

This deterministic view of juvenile misbehavior grew during the late 1940s and early 1950s with myriad psychoanalytic explanations of how deprivation during infancy and childhood leads to intrapsychic conflicts that are the roots of juvenile misbehavior. Misconduct was seen as the result of inadequate mothering during infancy and childhood (Berman 1959). The view that youthful misbehavior is determined by circumstance, not choice, was reinforced by the widely publicized work of William Sheldon (1949), who introduced his hypothesis concerning the link between various somatotypes—the endomorph (heavy, soft, and flabby body type), ectomorph (thin body type), and mesomorph (muscular body type)—and varieties of juvenile misconduct. According to this paradigm, one's inborn body type shapes behavior. In addition, the famed sociologist Talcott Parsons (1949) highlighted the supposedly detrimental effects on teens of female-dominated households. In 1955 Albert Cohen published his classic *Delinquent Boys*, in which he sought to explain the causal connection between teenagers' misbehavior and their "reaction formation" against middle-class values.

Toward the end of the 1950s prominent claims emerged in the professional literature about the lack of sufficient roles for contemporary teens, that modern society simply did not offer this age group constructive ways to be productively involved. In earlier times teens would have been full-time workers, not students (Bloch and Niederhoffer 1958). And in 1960 Richard Cloward and Lloyd Ohlin published their influential work, *Delinquency and Opportunity*, which had a profound impact on professionals' efforts to enhance ways for teens to move into legitimate, as opposed to illegitimate or antisocial, roles in the community.

Throughout this period—the first half-century of the juvenile justice system in the United States—the professional and scholarly literature built a clear conceptual foundation:

Struggling teens are not willful, calculating, and mean-spirited actors;

rather, their troubles are the result of a deep and wide array of environmental, economic, familial, and psychological forces. Free-will interpretations of youthful misconduct were overshadowed by determinism (Reamer 1983). For teens in trouble with the law, child saving was in its heyday. This set the stage for society's approach to neglected, abused, and other vulnerable children.

With the baby boom that followed World War II the number of facilities for children with mental health and behavioral challenges saw steady growth (Pappenfort, Kilpatrick, and Roberts 1973). The term *residential treatment* began to gain currency in the late 1940s when a number of factors converged to produce such programs (Leichtman 2006). As Social Security, Aid to Dependent Children, and other New Deal reforms reduced the need to institutionalize children for economic reasons, and as psychiatry and social work grew in influence, homes for dependent children, facilities for delinquents, and schools for children with other special needs were converted into "mental health programs." For example, in this period the Orthogenic School directed by the famed psychiatrist Bruno Bettelheim, and the Southard School at the Menninger Clinic were transformed from programs for children with intellectual and behavioral problems into residential centers treating profound psychiatric disorders. With such changes academic papers began to appear on how psychotherapeutic, and especially psychoanalytic, concepts could be implemented in these facilities and, above all, incorporated in the procedures used by aides and child-care staff (Leichtman 2006).

And then the winds shifted. Clearly, the American public came to feel less charitable toward misbehaving youths, even those who had significant mental health needs. In May 1965 the Gallup Poll showed that, for the first time in the poll's history, "crime" (which, we assume, included juvenile delinquency in the minds of respondents) was perceived as the nation's most important problem (Wilson 1975). The proportion of offenses committed by those younger than twenty-one increased dramatically during the 1960s (Wellford 1973). In part this may have reflected the baby boom generation's arrival at adolescence. With the combination of increasing crime rates in general, an increase in the percentage of offenses committed by juveniles, and a concomitant increase in public concern, the nation's threshold of tolerance for misbehaving youths seemed to drop, along with its child-saving spirit. Americans became less willing to treat kindly the "poor teen who had been through so much." In 1967 the prominent President's Commission on Law Enforcement and the Administration of Justice issued a bellwether statement that clearly reflected the nation's changing view of teens, particularly those who found themselves in trouble with the law. The goals of public safety and protection began to trump rehabilitation and child saving. As the commission put it,

Rehabilitating offenders through individualized handling is one way of providing protection, and appropriately the primary way in dealing with children. But
the guiding consideration for a court of law that deals with threatening conduct is nonetheless protection of the community. The juvenile court, like other
courts, is therefore obliged to employ all the means at hand, not excluding inca-
pacitation, for achieving that protection. What should distinguish the juvenile
from the criminal courts is greater emphasis on rehabilitation, not exclusive
preoccupation with it.   (1967:9)

The commission went one big step further and stated formally that the community should condemn and punish the behavior of its most troublesome
youths, language that represented a radical departure from the child-saving
rhetoric that had shaped rehabilitative efforts and public and judicial policy
for decades.

The cases that fall within the narrowed jurisdiction of the court and filter
through the screen of pre-judicial, informal disposition modes would largely
involve offenders for whom more vigorous measures seem necessary. Court
adjudication and disposition of those offenders *should no longer be viewed solely
as a diagnosis and prescription for cure*, but should be frankly recognized as an
authoritative court judgment expressing a society's claim to protection. While
rehabilitative efforts should be vigorously pursued in deference to the youth of
the offenders and in keeping with a general commitment to individualized treatment of all offenders, the incapacitative, deterrent, and *condemnatory* aspects of
the judgment should not be disguised.   (1967:2; emphasis added)

The 1967 publication of the commission's report signaled a fundamental change in perspective and spawned a proliferation of new programs for
struggling teens. This was the period in which Mel Wasserman's innovation
for struggling teens, CEDU, was born, as popular opinion shifted from child
saving to an emphasis on behavioral control, public safety, and, retribution.
Indeed, CEDU emerged just as two other broad goals came to the fore in the
juvenile justice field: diversion and deinstitutionalization, both of which were
consistent with Wasserman's innovative attempt to provide an alternative program for struggling teens. Diversion includes any attempt to steer struggling
youths away from formal handling by the police or juvenile court. While not
all struggling teens become involved with the police and juvenile court, many
do; the options available for the diverse population of struggling teens are often
shaped by the needs of those who come to the attention of law enforcement
authorities. Diversion programs generally include various kinds of counseling,
vocational training, alternative education, and residential treatment. Their

principal goal is to send the teen a strong message, backed by the court's authority. The intent of diversion is to avoid incarceration, which is expensive, stigmatizing, and not necessarily effective.

Deinstitutionalization was tied closely to diversion, in that it sought to avoid institutional care of struggling teens whenever possible. The deinstitutionalization movement focused its eye on people with mental illness in psychiatric hospitals, inmates in correctional facilities, as well as on struggling teens. When professionals first began waving the deinstitutionalization banner in the late 1960s and 1970s, they had compelling evidence that many juvenile correctional and psychiatric facilities were toxic, abusive, and produced iatrogenic effects. Despite euphemisms such as "training school," "youth development center," "residential treatment center," and "boys' home," those familiar with the daily and nightly workings of these institutional settings knew quite well that they often fell far short of being truly rehabilitative and benign. In the midst of this fundamental shift in worldview—the decline of traditional child saving; increasing demands that misbehaving teens be held accountable; and the emergence of diversion, community-based programming, and deinstitutionalization as key goals—the "troubled teen" industry was invented.

It is also significant that these developments occurred during the 1960s, when wide-ranging therapeutic alternatives proliferated, at times with reckless abandon. The emergence of novel, innovative, and cutting-edge programs also occurred in the midst of the rapid growth of the twelve-step movement (notably, Alcoholics Anonymous) and "human potential" movement in the United States (Derloshon 1982), core elements of which quickly found their way into programs for struggling teens.[4] This remarkable intersection of social and cultural trends—the search for creative, community-based alternatives to institutional care of juveniles, the tolerant "anything goes" climate of the 1960s, greater assertiveness among teens, increased efforts to hold teens accountable for their misbehavior, and the growing prominence of the twelve-step and human potential movements—provided fertile conditions for the nascent struggling-teen industry. Clearly, as people lost faith in the old ways of dealing with struggling teens, they sought creative innovations. Mel Wasserman's CEDU program emerged to fill the void and foreshadowed what has become a remarkably complex, often controversial, industry.

WHO ARE STRUGGLING TEENS?

The contemporary struggling-teen industry has evolved in order to serve a stunningly diverse array of adolescents grappling with many different educational, social, legal, behavioral, and mental health challenges. Some call these youths "troubled teens"; we disagree with that term, as it suggests that the problem lies primarily within the adolescent and is not a result of multiple factors that vary uniquely in each situation, such as fragmented and inadequate services, unresponsive school environments, lack of income supports, racism, homophobia, challenging family circumstances, and mental health issues. The term *troubled* is a negative label that has pejorative overtones. *Struggling* is a less judgmental, more descriptive, and behaviorally neutral term. We prefer the term *struggling teens*, which is now commonly used in the industry, to describe adolescents who have significant emotional, behavioral, and academic challenges. Broadly speaking, a struggling teen may manifest some combination of a long list of common symptoms.

- Isolation and withdrawal. While most teens withdraw from their parents, some sink too far into themselves. They may feel profoundly alone and alienated, unable to connect with any safe adult. While they crave friendships and meaningful human connections with caring, benign adults, these teens feel too demoralized and fearful to reach out to others or respond to friendly overtures. Many have a poor self-image and little confidence. They doubt that they can be competent and successful, and they become increasingly cut off from school, family, and friends. These teens are easy marks for predatory adults or "the wrong crowd" of peers because of their hunger to belong.

> Jonathan, fifteen, lived in a suburban community with his parents and younger brother. He said that he "always felt different from other kids." Ever since preschool Jonathan resisted his parents' efforts to get him to socialize with other children; at family gatherings and social events he often sat by himself in a corner, reading a book, watching television, or, most often, playing an electronic game he carried with him constantly. School teachers described Jonathan as a loner.
>
> As the adolescent years arrived, Jonathan's behavior at home and in school became more and more challenging. His moods seemed to alternate between highs and lows. At times Jonathan would be elated and engaging, talking quickly and animatedly. Within moments, however, his mood sometimes became dark and sullen, surly, irritable, and morose. Jonathan often argued with his parents and alienated many students and teachers at his school. Jonathan's school principal called his parents to discuss whether the school was able to meet Jonathan's needs.

- School failure and truancy. Many struggling teens perform poorly in school. Some were strong students in grade school but became discouraged and alienated from academics in middle school or high school. Other struggling teens have had difficulty with school their entire life because of learning disabilities, mental health issues, a difficult home life, or a school environment that is hostile, unresponsive, and not nurturing.

Lana, sixteen, struggled for years in the local public schools. During her grade school and middle school years, teachers told Lana's parents that she generally was sweet and cooperative but had difficulty staying on task and completing assignments.

By the time Lana reached high school, she was falling further and further behind academically. She and her parents argued frequently about doing homework. Lana resented her parents' efforts to help her structure her time and organize her work: "Stop trying to ruin my life! Stop telling me what to do!" she screamed at them. Whether her parents backed off or tried to help, Lana's grades plummeted. Lana felt stupid, frustrated, and alone. No matter how hard she tried, she couldn't get her schoolwork done. Lana's parents wanted her to see a therapist and get evaluated for special learning needs, but Lana refused. She started talking about how much she hated school and could not wait until she was old enough to drop out.

Lana's distraught parents met with the school guidance counselor, who suggested that Lana might have greater success in a school that was set up to serve underperforming students. In the middle of this ordeal Lana discovered that she was pregnant.

■ Defiance toward authority: Many struggling teens refuse to obey rules laid down by their parents, teachers, the police, and other authority figures. These teens are noncompliant and uncooperative at home; they may cheat on school assignments and become involved in delinquent activity (such as shoplifting, reckless driving, and drug use). They may be suspended or expelled from school, chronically truant, or in trouble with the police.

Christa, fourteen, lived with her parents and younger sister. Christa struggled academically. She had a learning disability and in the fourth grade was diagnosed with ADHD. Christa had difficulty making friends and often felt like she did not fit in. Her parents obtained counseling for themselves and Christa throughout her childhood in order to get extra support and help her develop coping skills. They knew Christa suffered from low self-esteem despite all their efforts to help her feel good about herself.

Christa began hanging out with several teens she met on the Internet through instant messaging and, before long, was skipping school with them, experimenting with drugs, and refusing to be home by her 10 p.m. curfew. The vice principal at Christa's school told her parents that Christa was quiet in school, not disruptive or attention seeking. Christa, always a spirited child, began to argue with her parents constantly and refused to obey basic family rules. She sometimes sneaked out of the house in the middle of the night or stayed up all night talking to her boyfriend on the phone. When her parents began to suspect that she was using drugs, they feared for her safety, could no longer tolerate her rebellious behavior, and felt desperate to find help.

■ Running away from home. Teens may run away from home to escape conflict with their parents, assert their independence, avoid the consequences of breaking rules, or flee their own distressing emotions.

Isaac was a tenth-grader who had always been a feisty child. His mother, a single divorced parent, recalled how challenging he was even as an infant, when he was often irritable and difficult to console. At home and school he was always on the go, often impulsive, breaking things around the house, and injuring himself. Isaac's father, who had little to do with his son, left all the parenting in the weary, stressed hands of Isaac's mother. Schoolteachers frequently called her with reports about how exasperating it was for them to have Isaac in class.

One afternoon Isaac came home from school reeking of cigarette smoke and with bloodshot eyes and dilated pupils. His mother was upset; through her tears she shared her concerns with him and asked if he had smoked pot. Isaac responded angrily and stormed out of the house.

Two months later Isaac's mother found a bag of marijuana while vacuuming under Isaac's bed. When she confronted him, he screamed at her, "Don't you ever go through my personal things again! Stay out of my room! I hate you."

His mother grounded him for a week as a result of the incident, forbidding him to leave the house except to go to school. Isaac laughed in his mother's face. About an hour later his mother returned from a brief trip to the local supermarket to find that Isaac had walked out of the house. He left a note on the kitchen table: "Mom. I can't take it here anymore. All we do is fight. I've decided I'll be better off on my own. Please don't try to find me. This is what I need to do. I'll be okay.—Isaac"

■ Choosing the "wrong" friends. Teens normally seek solace from their peers. Struggling teens have a knack for finding other struggling teens. These friends, who themselves are having a difficult time, engage with the teen in high-risk behaviors, such as drug and alcohol use, sex, and delinquency.

Grady, thirteen, had just enrolled in his eighth school. His parents were both in the army, and, as Grady put it, "I feel like I've spent my whole childhood packing and unpacking moving boxes, changing schools, and losing and finding friends. I hate it."

Grady had a hard time fitting in at his new school in the Midwest. He felt put off by the cliques in the school and was angry that kids made fun of his southern accent.

One Saturday, while hanging out at a local mall that was popular with teens, Grady struck up a conversation with three teenage boys who invited him to join them at one of their homes. Grady was happy to be part of the group and accepted the invitation.

Soon after Grady and the teens got to the home, one teen opened a bag that contained two six-packs of beer. The kids listened to some heavy metal music and drank. Grady began spending much of his free time with these teens. Before long Grady was drinking beer regularly.

One afternoon a teen in the group who had just gotten his learner's permit persuaded the gang to go for a ride in his mother's car. Without the mother's permission, and in violation of the conditions of the learner's permit, the teens took the car. They bought beer using a fake ID and drove to a nearby lake. Just before they reached the lake, the driver, who was speeding and had been drinking beer, lost control of the car and slammed into a tree. Grady, who was legally drunk at the time, broke his pelvis and left femur. Although Grady's parents were primarily concerned about their son's health, they told the hospital social worker that they believed that Grady's life was spinning out of control. They had long suspected that he had been drinking and hanging out with friends who influenced him to take dangerous risks.

■ Impulsive behavior. Teens who hang out with other struggling teens sometimes engage in high-risk and impulsive behaviors, such as speeding, shoplifting, using drugs and alcohol, and having unprotected sex. They may have a devil-may-care attitude and take chances because they feel invulnerable and believe they have everything under control. Teens who abuse drugs and alcohol are even more likely to engage in impulsive behavior because of their substance-induced impaired judgment.

> Darryl, seventeen, lived in a suburban community on the outskirts of a major city. Darryl was a talented guitar player who loved rock music. On weekends he often got together with friends for jam sessions and got high on speed. Before long Darryl was skipping school and spraying graffiti in the town's central commercial district.
>
> One afternoon, while Darryl was wandering the streets of the city near his suburban home, several teens approached him and invited him to join them in a shoplifting spree. Darryl found the invitation exciting—what he later described as "a real rush." In an interview with a social worker after he was arrested and referred to the local juvenile court, Darryl said, "I figured, what the hell? My life at home and in school has been a blooming nightmare. I just decided to go for the gold, you know what I mean? What did I have to lose?"

■ Getting in trouble with the law. Struggling teens may break the law, committing crimes against property (such as spray-painting graffiti, turning over gravestones, stealing cars) or violent crimes (such as assault, robbery, rape).

> Jason, fourteen, lived with his mother and stepfather in a rural area that was gradually becoming suburban. Jason did not like his stepfather and often argued with him. Jason's birth father had abandoned the family shortly after Jason was born; his mother married Jason's stepfather when Jason was eleven.
>
> Jason complained to his mother that his stepfather is "always on my case. All he does is criticize me for the way I look, the way I act, who I hang out with, you name it. I'm sick of it."
>
> To get away from his stepfather, Jason began spending more and more time with two friends whom his mother and stepfather regarded as trouble. Both friends had been suspended from school on several occasions, mostly for school vandalism and cursing at teachers.
>
> Over time Jason's behavior changed. He began wearing black clothing (shirt, pants, belt, socks), wore a large chain that hung from his belt and ran to his pocket, and had his hair shaved on the sides with a spiked, red-dyed Mohawk down the middle. Jason's stepfather was particularly upset, often enraged, by Jason's appearance and refused to be seen with him in public.
>
> One night Jason refused to come home by his curfew time. He chose to hang out with several friends. The group stole some beer from an outdoor store display and went on a rampage around town, smashing rural mailboxes, vandalizing cars, and spraying graffiti. Jason and his friends were arrested by the police when someone reported seeing the group rocking a car parked on the street.

■ Depression. A significant percentage of struggling teens show signs of depression. Common symptoms include either poor appetite or overeating; difficulty with sleep (difficulty falling asleep and staying asleep, early morning awakening, or sleeping too much); low energy; fatigue; low self-esteem; poor concentration; difficulty making decisions; feelings of hopelessness, guilt, and worthlessness; and irritability.

> Alma, fourteen, lived with her adoptive parents and two younger sisters in a medium-sized city. In grade school Alma had been a good student and had several friends. But when she reached high school, she began to isolate herself more and more. She was often irritable and, according to her teachers, chronically quiet and withdrawn at school.
>
> Alma's parents found it increasingly difficult to communicate with her. Usually, she grunted or gave one-word answers and isolated herself in her room, refusing to join in family meals or activities. She cut herself off from peers as well. Her school grades deteriorated; Alma sometimes refused to get out of bed in the morning, sleeping until noon. Her parents often found collections of junk food stashed in Alma's dresser drawers, under her bed, and behind her desk. They arranged for Alma to meet weekly with a counselor for psychotherapy, who helped Alma connect with a psychiatrist for medication for depression. But there appeared to be no change in Alma's mood or behavior.

■ Abusing alcohol or drugs. Many struggling teens experiment with or abuse alcohol or drugs, such as marijuana, methamphetamines, ecstasy, cocaine, heroin, or medications. Teens who are abusing alcohol or other drugs may experience some combination of a persistent desire for the substance; difficulty cutting down or controlling consumption despite negative consequences from use; frequent intoxication; withdrawal symptoms; impaired school, job, or social functioning; and a need for increased amounts of the substance to achieve a high.

> Dillon, sixteen, was arrested by police for cocaine and ecstasy possession. For about a year he had been using and selling drugs to friends so he would have money to support his own drug habit. Dillon's heavy drug use started shortly after his parents divorced and his father remarried. Dillon was often truant, defiant at home, and involved with the police and juvenile court.
>
> Alarmed by his growing drug problem, Dillon's parents sent him to an after-school teen substance-abuse program in their community, and the whole family attended several counseling sessions there. But Dillon's drug problems continued. Dillon kept slipping out of school during the day, occasionally sneaked out of bed in the middle of the night to talk on the phone and use the computer, and was chronically combative, hostile, and oppositional at home and school. He was suspended from school several times. Dillon's parents became afraid for him. They didn't know what to do to stop his downward slide.
>
> The lawyer representing Dillon on the drug charges told his parents that together they should try to find a therapeutic boarding school for Dillon. The lawyer explained that a judge might be willing to order Dillon to the school as an alternative to sentencing him to a juvenile correctional facility.

■ Eating disorders. Some struggling teens show signs of an eating disorder, such as anorexia nervosa, bulimia, or compulsive overeating. They may seriously undereat or binge and purge (by vomiting or laxative use).

> Shania, sixteen, never knew her father, and her mother was in prison for a drug-dealing conviction. As a result Shania lived in foster care. Three foster placements ended because the foster parents found Shania's behavior too defiant, controlling, manipulative, and angry to handle.
>
> During the past year Shania's weight dropped precipitously; her pediatrician was alarmed and referred Shania to a clinical social worker, who learned that during the previous eighteen months Shania had been bingeing, purging, and using laxatives to help her lose weight.

■ Self-injury. Some teens in distress hurt themselves by cutting, burning, branding, bruising, and hitting themselves. Mental health professionals generally agree that teens who engage in these behaviors are trying to cope with emotional pain; the self-injury temporarily releases unbearable psychological tension.

> Until she was fifteen, Juanita got along reasonably well with her parents and two brothers and was a "B" student. Recently, however, Juanita had become sullen and withdrawn. Her grades slipped and, on several occasions, she cut her arms with a blade and burned the backs of her hands with cigarettes. Juanita's school social worker referred her to a psychiatrist, who began treating her for severe depression. Then Juanita attempted suicide twice. The psychiatrist suggested that Juanita's parents find a residential treatment center that might help. However, Juanita's parents did not have comprehensive health-care coverage to pay for the services she needed.

Current data provide ample evidence of the number of teens experiencing serious mental health, behavioral, economic, and health risks. Data from various sources show the breadth of the issue and help explain the impressive growth of the struggling-teen industry (McWhirter et al. 2007). The Annie E. Casey Foundation's KIDS COUNT project (2007), which regularly collates national data on the well-being of minors, reports that

■ Seven percent of teens are high school dropouts. The rates vary from a high of 14 percent for Latino teens to a low of 3 percent for Asian/Pacific Islander teens. Eight percent of African American teens and 6 percent of white teens are high school dropouts.

■ Eight percent of teens are not in school or working. The highest rates are for Native American teens (16 percent), black teens (12 percent), and Latino teens (12 percent). The lowest rates are for white (6 percent) and Asian/Pacific Islander teens (5 percent).

■ Eight percent of female teens aged fifteen to nineteen become pregnant. The pregnancy rate for black teens is 15 percent; it is 14 percent for Latino teens and 6 percent for white teens.

The Youth Risk Behavior Survey (YRBS), a widely cited, ambitious national assessment of students in grades nine to twelve sponsored by the U.S. Centers for Disease Control and Prevention (2006), documents the extent to which teens engage in a wide range of high-risk activities or manifest significant symptoms of risky behavior. Among the key findings were that during the thirty days preceding the survey, 9.9 percent had driven a car or other vehicle one or more times when they had been drinking alcohol, 18.5 percent had carried a weapon (e.g., a gun, knife, or club), and 4.5 percent of students had vomited or taken laxatives to lose weight or to keep from gaining weight. In addition, 7.5 percent of students had been physically forced, at some point in their life, to have sexual intercourse when they did not want to, and 7.6 percent of students had used a form of cocaine (e.g., powder, crack, or freebase) one or more times during their life. In the year before the survey 16.9 percent of students had seriously considered attempting suicide.

Clearly, many adolescents in the United States struggle with complex social, behavioral, substance abuse, and mental health issues.

COMMON MENTAL HEALTH AND BEHAVIORAL CHALLENGES

Many struggling teens live in stressful circumstances that contribute to their challenges. They may be coping with intense poverty, divorcing parents, parents who struggle with psychiatric or substance abuse issues, incarcerated parents, significant loss (for example, the death of a parent), histories of physical and sexual abuse, learning differences, sexual orientation and gender identity issues, and various forms of trauma.

Many struggling teens have been assessed at some point by psychiatrists and other mental health professionals who have made formal psychiatric diagnoses. Among the most common diagnoses given to struggling teens are anxiety disorders, depression, bipolar disorder, ADHD, oppositional defiant disorder, conduct disorder, eating disorders, posttraumatic stress disorder, and substance abuse. Accurately diagnosing a child or a teenager can be extremely difficult, as symptoms of different disorders may overlap, and different youths who have the same diagnosis may present different symptoms. Nevertheless, the National Mental Health Information Center (2003), an arm of the U.S. Department of Health and Human Services, has summarized prevalence data for these major diagnoses. The descriptions provided here are brief. For a more complete description of each disorder, see American Psychiatric Association (2000).

ANXIETY DISORDERS

Struggling teens with anxiety disorders experience excessive fear, worry, or uneasiness. Anxiety disorders are among the most common of childhood disorders. According to one prominent study, as many as thirteen of every hundred young people have an anxiety disorder that, by definition, causes significant distress and impairment in social, educational, or occupational functioning (U.S. Department of Health and Human Services 1999). Anxiety disorders include

Phobias, which are unrealistic and overwhelming fears of objects or situations

Generalized anxiety disorder, which involves a pattern of excessive, unrealistic worry that cannot be attributed to any recent experience

Panic disorder, which includes terrifying "panic attacks" accompanied by physical symptoms, such as a rapid heartbeat and dizziness

Obsessive-compulsive disorder, characterized by a pattern of repeated thoughts and behaviors, such as counting or hand washing

Posttraumatic stress disorder, which is typified by flashbacks, nightmares, hypervigilance, an exaggerated startle response, and other symptoms following a distressing event, such as abuse, witnessing violence, or exposure to other traumas such as war or a natural disaster

MAJOR DEPRESSION

Studies show that approximately 10 to 15 percent of adolescents may experience major depression (National Institute of Mental Health 1999). The disorder is marked by changes in

Emotions—sadness, irritability, guilt, worthlessness, hopelessness

Motivation—apathy, fatigue, loss of interest in pleasurable activities, decline in quality of schoolwork

Physical well-being—changes in appetite or sleeping patterns, physical complaints such as headache and stomachache

Thoughts—distorted cognitions, negative cognitive schemata (an organized pattern of thinking that focuses on negative interpretations of events)

BIPOLAR DISORDER

While mood swings are normal in adolescence, some teens experience extraordinary highs (mania) and lows (depression), symptoms of bipolar disorder (sometimes called manic depression). Typically, periods of moderate mood occur between the extreme highs and lows. During manic phases adolescents may talk nonstop, need little sleep, and show unusually poor judgment. Bipolar disorder can recur throughout life and usually begins in late adolescence and early adulthood (Leahy and Johnson 2003; National Institute of Mental Health 2006).

ATTENTION-DEFICIT/HYPERACTIVITY DISORDER (ADHD)

Teens whose ADHD is predominantly the inattentive type may have difficulty consistently sustaining their focus on tedious, boring tasks, organizing their schoolwork, following directions, and completing tasks. Those whose ADHD is predominantly the hyperactive type may be fidgety, always on the go, impulsive, and risk taking. Those who have a combination have both sets of symptoms. Attention-deficit/hyperactivity disorder occurs in as many as five of every hundred minors (U.S. Department of Health and Human Services 1999). Symptoms must be evident in at least two settings, such as home and school, for a legitimate diagnosis of attention-deficit/hyperactivity disorder.

CONDUCT DISORDER

Teens diagnosed with conduct disorder repeatedly violate the basic rights of others and the rules of society, acting out their feelings or impulses in destructive ways. The behaviors in which they engage include fire setting, breaking and entering, stealing things of nontrivial value (such as a car), and vandalism. Estimates of the number of minors with this disorder vary, ranging from one to four of every one hundred children aged nine to seventeen (U.S. Department of Health and Human Services 1999).

OPPOSITIONAL DEFIANT DISORDER

Teens who have been diagnosed with oppositional defiant disorder (ODD) typically engage in an ongoing pattern of uncooperative, defiant, and hostile behavior toward authority figures that seriously interferes with the teen's day-to-day functioning. Symptoms of ODD may include frequent temper tantrums; excessive arguing with adults; active defiance and refusal to comply with adult requests and rules; deliberate attempts to annoy or upset people; blaming others for one's own mistakes or misbehavior; often being touchy or easily annoyed by others; frequent anger and resentment; mean and hateful talking when upset; and seeking revenge. The symptoms are usually seen in multiple settings but are generally more noticeable at home or at school.

Five to 15 percent of all schoolage children meet the criteria for ODD (Busta-mante 2000; Christophersen and Finney 1999; Evans et al. 2005). ODD is sometimes a precursor to conduct disorder. In contrast to teens with conduct disorder, the behavior of teens with ODD does not involve serious violations of others' rights. It does, however, impair the teen's family, academic, and social functioning.

EATING DISORDERS

Adolescents who do not recognize that they are underweight and who are intensely afraid of gaining weight may have an eating disorder that can be life threatening. Those with anorexia nervosa, for example, severely restrict their calorie intake and experience significant weight loss. Anorexia affects one in every one hundred to two hundred adolescent girls and a much smaller number of boys (National Institute of Mental Health 1999).

Adolescents with bulimia nervosa eat huge amounts of food in one sitting and then purge in order to prevent weight gain. Purging may entail self-induced vomiting, excessive laxative use, taking enemas, or exercising obsessively. Reported rates of bulimia vary from one to three of every hundred young people (National Institute of Mental Health 1999). Many adolescents compulsively overeat in order to self-soothe. Their obesity jeopardizes their physical health and incurs social opprobrium.

SUBSTANCE ABUSE AND DEPENDENCE

Substance use and dependence puts millions of adolescents at increased risk for alcohol-related and drug-related traffic accidents, potentially dangerous sexual practices, poor academic performance, and juvenile delinquency. Substance abuse is any pattern of substance use that results in repeated adverse social consequences related to drug taking, for example, interpersonal conflicts; failure to meet work, family, or school obligations; or legal problems. Substance dependence, commonly known as addiction, is characterized by physiological and behavioral symptoms related to substance use. These symptoms include the need for increasing amounts of the substance to maintain its desired effects, withdrawal if drug taking ceases, and a great deal of time spent in activities related to substance use.

Many teens who have academic, behavioral, and emotional challenges self-medicate with alcohol and other substances. The substance abuse and other challenges then exacerbate each other. An estimated 19.5 million Americans aged twelve or older were current users of an illicit drug in 2003. More than half (51 percent) of America's teenagers have tried an illicit drug by the time they finish high school. Nearly 30 percent of high school students were offered, sold, or given an illegal drug, often marijuana, on school property at some point during the year preceding one prominent survey (Johnston et al. 2007; McWhirter et al. 2007).

Clearly, teens struggle in many ways. In recent years a wide variety of specialty programs and schools have emerged to address these challenges. The population of struggling teens is large and complex. In the next chapter we provide a comprehensive overview of the current range of options, along with typical examples.

2

THE STRUGGLING-TEENS INDUSTRY

A COMPLEX LANDSCAPE

The struggling-teens industry now includes a bewildering, largely uncoordinated, and disconnected array of specialty services, programs, and schools. Thoughtful analysis of the industry requires a descriptive overview of the kinds of schools and programs one finds in the United States today. Many are highly respected, reputable, and competently managed by credentialed professional educators and licensed mental health specialists who follow best-practice protocols based on empirical research published in professional literature. Other programs, as we document in chapter 3, are highly controversial, use unconventional methods, and have documented records of abuse and scandal. Many of these programs have been founded or are run by charismatic people who rely primarily on ideology and beliefs unsupported by solid research evidence of what works.

In this chapter we focus primarily on the range of mainstream programs and schools. Some programs for struggling teens provide relatively short-term crisis intervention, and others provide long-term care and treatment. It is useful to think about these services and programs as a broad spectrum of options, recognizing that the spectrum is multidimensional rather than linear. One key dimension has to do with the degree of emphasis that the schools and programs place on education versus mental health needs. A second key dimension has to do with the extent to which the school or program serves teens and families in the home community as opposed to serving them in a residential placement some distance from the home community. Although we have organized the spectrum along these two principal dimensions, we recognize that in important ways these are artificial distinctions. This simplified conceptual framework helps to organize a complex welter of programs and schools that, in reality, do not fall neatly into distinct conceptual categories. Stated broadly, at one end of the spectrum are services and programs that place primary emphasis on educational issues but also, in addition, attend to teenagers' emotional needs. Many such schools and programs are located in teens' home communities. Examples include traditional public and private high schools and specialized community-based high schools that provide counseling and special education services through individualized education programs (IEPs) or the so-called 504 plans to supplement the academic curriculum. At the other end of the spectrum are programs that focus primarily on struggling teens' psychiatric, emotional, and behavioral needs and, in addition, provide academic and educational services. Some of these schools and programs are located in teens' home communities; however, many are located some distance away. Examples include therapeutic boarding schools and residential treatment centers. In the middle of the spectrum are schools and programs—such as "emotional growth" boarding schools—that focus simultaneously and relatively equally on youths' mental health, personal growth, and educational needs.

Professionals who work with struggling teens generally agree that it makes sense as a first line of response to serve many struggling teens in their home communities instead of sending them to schools and programs away from home. The least intervention that produces the desired outcome is often the least expensive, financially and emotionally. Use of the least restrictive environment is a widely supported educational and mental health intervention guideline. However, in some instances the best way to meet struggling teens' needs is to enroll them in residential schools or programs. This may be necessary when the teen's needs cannot be met in the home community, either because the services needed do not exist or because the teen needs a completely new social environment, away from negative influences and distractions.

It is important to note that teens and families in low-income, economically distressed communities face special challenges, including high rates of poverty and crime. Oppression and discrimination permeate their lives. The challenges that typical adolescents face can be especially severe for low-income teens who are of color, immigrants, or refugees. Because of racism and prejudice the needs of these youths may be ignored or responded to punitively rather than therapeutically. These teens may be singled out, bullied and taunted, victimized in racially charged incidents, and harassed by educators, local merchants, neighbors, or police who target teens of color, assume they are "trouble," and lack compassion for the challenges these youths face. Racial and ethnic tensions contribute to the behaviors that sometimes get these teens in trouble.

Affluent families may be able to pay for programs and services or have health insurance that covers some of the costs, but many families cannot afford needed programs and services, do not have adequate insurance, and are unable to obtain funding from their public school district or public child welfare agency. In some instances parents who cannot afford needed services agree to give legal custody of their teen to the local public child welfare agency, which then funds the services or programs (in several states the public child welfare agency will fund services without requiring that parents relinquish legal custody). In still other circumstances desperate parents may turn to the juvenile or family court and formally request that the teen be declared "wayward" or "ungovernable," thus enabling the court to require the child to accept intervention. In those cases the public child welfare agency typically pays for needed services and programs.

What follows is a comprehensive overview of services, programs, and schools for struggling teens that will provide the context for our subsequent discussion of both scandalous practices and "best practices" in the field. We limit this overview to program and school models that are widely accepted and generally regarded as appropriate options for struggling teens. The overview is presented on a continuum, starting with home-based and community-based services and moving to residential programs and schools. As we move along this continuum, we see schools and programs with different degrees of emphasis on teens' academic and mental health needs.

The differences between and among programs of the same type may be profound, given different philosophies, models, policies, staffing patterns, and procedures. In addition, programs in different categories may look similar. It may be, for example, hard to distinguish a day treatment program from a partial hospitalization program, or an emotional growth boarding school from a special education boarding school or therapeutic boarding school. An emotional growth boarding school located many miles from a teen's home community may assertively and conscientiously involve the teen in the community surrounding the boarding school and include family members in school programming. Hence, the overview of program and school options provided here does not suggest pure, discrete types. Nonetheless, this is a useful way to think about the enormously complex array of programs and services for struggling teens.

CRISIS INTERVENTION

A broad range of professionals and agencies offer crisis intervention and follow-up counseling services to teens and families in their home communities. These services may be available through family service agencies, community mental health centers, hospital outpatient clinics, public child welfare departments, and psychotherapists in private practice (such as clinical social workers, clinical and counseling psychologists, mental health counselors, pastoral counselors, psychiatric nurses, and psychiatrists).

Many communities offer comprehensive counseling and family intervention programs specifically for teens and families in crisis. These programs— known by such names as "comprehensive emergency services" or "children's intensive services"—provide home-based assessment, counseling, information, and referrals to prevent out-of-home placement in foster care, juvenile correctional facilities, psychiatric hospitals, and other residential programs. Some programs have staff members who work with families in their home to observe family members' interactions in the natural environment and coach families on the spot to help them strengthen their communication, child-rearing, problem-solving, coping, and other skills.

Typical crisis intervention programs for struggling teens that provide home-based services reach client families within twenty-four hours of referral. Most services take place in the client's home or the community where the problems are occurring. Therapists may be on call to their clients around the clock to monitor potentially dangerous situations, intervene as needs arise, and teach the skills necessary for the family to remain intact. Therapists in these programs often carry only two or three cases at a time, so they can be accessible and provide intensive services when needed. Therapists provide a wide range of services, from helping clients obtain such necessities as food, clothing, and shelter to providing individual and family therapy. Therapists teach families basic skills such as how to use public transportation, budget, and deal with the social services system. They also educate families about child development, parenting skills, anger management, emotional self-regulation, stress reduction, communications, and assertiveness. Teaching strategies involve modeling of positive behaviors, descriptions of skills, role-playing, and rehearsing newly acquired skills. Staff may use skills-based videotapes and audiotapes, workbooks, handouts, articles, and experiential exercises. Therapeutic interventions include using behavioral principles and techniques, motivational interviewing, relapse prevention, rational emotive therapy, and other cognitive strategies.

SPECIALTY COURTS

Many communities have developed specialty courts to intervene early when youths become truant or involved in alcohol or other drug use.

SUBSTANCE ABUSE COURTS

These courts (sometimes known as drug courts) are for youths whose substance use has brought them to the attention of law enforcement officials. A teen may have been apprehended for underage drinking, selling marijuana, or other substance use and abuse. These specialty courts are designed to take a supportive and nurturing approach rather than a punitive one. Using case management, counseling, tutoring, mentoring, and parent education, the courts' goal is to prevent future problems and further, more intensive, and extensive involvement with the juvenile justice system. Their aim is to nip the teen's substance abuse in the bud.

Substance abuse courts integrate alcohol and other drug treatment services and judicial monitoring. Using a nonadversarial approach, prosecution and defense counsel attempt to simultaneously address the teenager's substance abuse issues and promote public safety while protecting the youth's due process rights. Typically, eligible participants are identified early in the judicial process—usually soon after arrest—and promptly placed in the substance abuse court's program. Substance abuse courts require that the teen enroll in alcohol, drug, and related treatments, and they are monitored by frequent alcohol and drug testing. When feasible, parents are required to attend substance abuse court hearings and participate in their child's substance abuse treatment. Successful completion of the program can lead to dismissal of the delinquency charges.

TRUANCY COURTS

Many communities sponsor truancy courts for teenagers who have skipped significant numbers of school days. Research shows that truancy is often a correlate and predictor of other substantial problems in a teenager's life (Quinn 2004). These specialty courts are designed to use a supportive and nurturing approach rather than a punitive one to help struggling teens. Using case management, counseling, tutoring, mentoring, and parent education, the court's goal is to prevent future problems and more formal involvement with the juvenile justice system.

Truancy courts, like substance abuse and drug courts, integrate counseling and other social services with judicial monitoring. Using a nonadversarial approach, prosecution and defense counsel attempt to simultaneously address the teenager's truancy while protecting the youngster's due process rights. Truancy courts provide access to mental health, case management, educational, and substance abuse services. Teenagers enrolled in the program are monitored by truancy court staff and are required to reappear in court to provide frequent updates on their progress.

During typical truancy court sessions the judge focuses on the student's attendance record, academic performance, and school behavior. Teachers of students in the program periodically complete a form that provides the court with feedback on the youth's progress. If the student's performance does not improve, the student may be required to attend an after-school program for a specified period. Some truancy courts include an aftercare phase in which staff members monitor the youth's attendance after leaving the program.

NONRESIDENTIAL SCHOOLS AND PROGRAMS

Parents of struggling teens naturally want to place their child in a school or program in their local community that provides the structure, services, and discipline needed to keep their child safe and on track academically. Many communities offer a range of options.

COMMUNITY-BASED ALTERNATIVE HIGH SCHOOLS

Alternative high schools in the home community provide education, including special education services, to teens who have floundered academically or socially in traditional high schools. These schools may be freestanding or sponsored by a community mental health center, family service agency, school district, or a regional "collaborative" comprised of several social service and educational programs.

Alternative community-based high schools vary widely. Most offer smaller and more individualized academic programs than are typically available in traditional high schools. Alternative schools may provide frequent opportunities for students to express themselves creatively through music, art, drama, and writing. Some encourage students to do community-based internships in local organizations, agencies, and businesses. These schools may emphasize student-led initiatives and encourage relationships between students and mentors or coaches. Creative, nontraditional, multisensory, hands-on, experiential, and interactive approaches are also used to engage students by, for example, encouraging students to use video equipment or dramatic presentations to communicate their ideas.

These alternative high schools tend not to arrange classrooms in rows of desks facing a teacher who stands at the front of the room, favoring instead seats around tables that facilitate discussion. In many alternative high schools, rather than assign students traditional grades, teachers write detailed narrative assessments of students' work and progress, summarizing their successes, challenges, and learning needs. Some school districts offer nontraditional options designed specifically for teens who are eager to complete their high school education with a diploma from the local school rather than a GED (general educational development) diploma.[1]

YOUTH DIVERSION PROGRAMS

Youth diversion programs typically attempt to help struggling teens who have had contact with the police avoid more formal involvement with the juvenile courts and correctional facilities. Typical youth diversion programs offer first-time offenders individual and family counseling, access to other services (such as psychiatric medication), and education. Eligible offenses often include shoplifting, petty theft, trespassing, destruction of property, curfew violation, alcohol violation, and running away from home. A juvenile enrolled in a diversion program typically meets with a probation officer who provides the court with periodic progress reports. The diversion plan may require individual, family, or group counseling; educational workshops (for example, on substance abuse issues or domestic violence); volunteer work at a nonprofit agency in the community; restitution; and participation in an employment program. The primary goals of the diversion program are to encourage at-risk teenagers to engage in more positive and constructive behavior; intervene at an early stage and avoid progression toward more serious offenses; avoid the negative connotations associated with formal referral to juvenile court; and provide the teenager and family with appropriate social services. Teens who comply with youth diversion program requirements may be able to avoid formal adjudication.

"Outreach and tracking" is one type of diversion program used in many communities. The staff of these programs initiates face-to-face contact with the struggling teen several times a day, seven days a week, in order to provide close monitoring. The goal is to keep a watchful eye on the teen in order to keep the youngster safe in the community, family, and school and out of trouble.

MENTORING PROGRAMS

Mentoring programs provide struggling teens with trained, caring adults who provide support, guidance, advice, and friendship. Mentoring programs encourage teens to stay focused on their education; provide support during crises; offer constructive ways to spend free time; and expose teens to career paths and options. Mentors seek to enhance but not replace the roles of parents, guardians, and teachers. The mentor and teen may begin their relationship by participating in a variety of activities. Depending on the type of mentoring program—and the program's rules and regulations—a mentoring pair may begin getting to know each other by going to a local gym, playground, museum, restaurant, athletic event, or rock concert. Mentors and mentees might also meet at the child's school once a week where they might talk or work on schoolwork together. In many mentoring programs mentors are included in group programming, family sessions, and, often, home visits conducted by caseworkers and social workers.

DAY TREATMENT PROGRAMS

Day treatment programs provide teens with nonresidential services to help them address their mental health and substance abuse issues. Typical programs require youths to participate in individual, group, and, when feasible, family counseling. Psychiatric evaluation and medication are also provided. Day treatment programs usually address such issues as severe mood swings; school problems; defiance issues; frequent rage, outbursts, or threats; isolation or withdrawal; alcohol and drug problems; ADHD; depression; and anxiety. Adolescents meet individually with staff members to develop an individualized treatment plan. Treatment may consist of several types of therapy, such as individual counseling; group therapy; family therapy; experiential and expressive therapies, such as recreation, art, music, and drama therapy; cognitive-behavioral therapy; and medication management. Educational services may be included to help teens stay on track academically. A day treatment program may engage the teen every weekday or for a portion of the week; teens may participate for full days or portions of the day, depending upon their clinical needs and program funding, family finances, and insurance coverage.

PARTIAL HOSPITALIZATION PROGRAMS

Like day treatment programs, partial hospitalization programs are for teens with serious mental health issues. The programs—which, unlike day treatment programs, are affiliated with hospitals—are an alternative to inpatient hospitalization. Partial hospitalization programs are designed to fill most of the teen's daytime hours Monday through Friday and provide a therapeutic milieu that includes psychiatric medication management; individual, family, and group therapy; psychoeducational therapy; and occupational and recreational therapy. Usually, teens attending a partial hospitalization program sleep at home or live in a group home or foster home and go to the partial hospitalization program during regular work hours on weekdays.

RESIDENTIAL PROGRAMS AND SCHOOLS

A variety of residential therapeutic schools and treatment programs serve teens who struggle with significant behavioral, emotional, mental health, substance abuse, and educational issues. Many of these schools and programs, such as residential treatment centers, therapeutic boarding schools, and wilderness therapy programs, focus primarily on mental health, emotional, and behavioral issues while including an educational component. Emotional growth boarding schools address mental health, emotional, behavioral, and educational issues simultaneously.[2] Other boarding schools focus primarily on learning disabilities while also paying attention to the whole student. In short, different programs and schools give different degrees of emphasis to personal and academic issues.

Some of these schools and programs—such as some military boarding schools and those that advertise their mission as "character education"—may not provide the mental health services and other special education services that many struggling teens need. These schools and programs may focus primarily on "attitude" and view special education and mental health challenges as mere character flaws that the teen can overcome by will. Such schools and programs minimize or discount the impact that disabilities may have on the teen's behavior and achievement. Therefore we have not included them in the review that follows.

GROUP HOMES AND SHELTERS

Group homes provide teens with structured, supervised out-of-home care. Teens are placed in a group home when living with their family is not realistic or appropriate. In addition to housing, many group homes provide individual and group counseling, health care, educational services, independent living skills, and follow-up services. The program staff may teach residents interpersonal relationship skills and how to plan, shop, and prepare meals, find and keep a job, and manage money. Lengths of stay vary considerably depending upon the teen's needs and family circumstances; some shelters provide short-term respite and diagnostic and assessment services, while others provide longer-term care with many supportive services.

WILDERNESS THERAPY PROGRAMS

Wilderness therapy programs (also known as outdoor behavioral health programs) offer highly structured intensive short-term (usually six to ten weeks) therapy in remote locations that remove adolescents from the distractions available in their home community (cell phones, television, radio, portable music players, electronic toys, computers, cars, drugs and alcohol, movies, delinquent peer groups) and from negative peer influences and stressful family interactions. The natural challenges of living full-time outdoors and developing wilderness survival skills help teens take responsibility for their choices, experience the natural consequences of their behaviors, and develop confidence, problem-solving skills, and social skills under the guidance of therapeutic staff members.

Typical teenagers enrolled in wilderness therapy programs are coping with a variety of emotional, behavioral, and educational struggles such as depression, substance abuse, oppositional defiant disorder, and learning disabilities that negatively affect school performance and interpersonal relationships. The teens may isolate themselves, expect instant gratification, or act entitled, demanding, and self-centered. They may be self-medicating with alcohol and other substances, constantly battling their parents, and failing to respond to limits and rules.

Typical wilderness therapy programs provide counseling, education, leadership training, and wilderness survival skills that strengthen the teenager's ability to function in a community of people. Programs foster interdependence and seek to enhance the teenager's honesty, self-awareness, openness, accountability, and responsibility. Common wilderness therapy activities include education about outdoor and wilderness survival, team-building exercises, structured daily activities, some academic coursework (sometimes coordinated with the teen's home school to help the teen stay at grade level), individual and group counseling, hiking, rock climbing, and expeditions.

A key goal of wilderness therapy programs is to remove teens temporarily from their "comfort zone" and give them opportunities to experience the natural consequences of their decisions and actions. For example, if a defiant teen refuses to learn how to build a campfire without matches, he will be cold as the sun sets and will have only raw food to eat. If an oppositional teen refuses to put plastic under her sleeping bag, she will be uncomfortably wet when it rains heavily during the night. These experiences help defiant teens learn what can and cannot be controlled in life. That is, one cannot control the rain, but one can control how one copes with the rain. Ideally, teens transfer this understanding to their life following completion of the wilderness therapy program.

Another goal of wilderness therapy is to give teens the opportunity to develop self-confidence by mastering outdoor challenges, such as starting a fire without matches or a lighter, that require persistence, patience, frustration tolerance, and skill. The teen's enhanced, earned sense of competence can encourage more positive behaviors at home and school. Ironically, many teens whose behavior is controlling or oppositional actually feel deeply discouraged, demoralized, and out of control when they are sent to the wilderness therapy program. A good wilderness therapy experience can help the teen to recognize this dynamic and begin the process of changing it.

Often, families are advised to send their struggling teen first to a wilderness therapy program and then to a therapeutic or emotional growth boarding school. This sequence—wilderness therapy first, followed by an emotional growth boarding school, therapeutic boarding school, or residential treatment center—accomplishes two objectives. First, the wilderness experience, ideally, readies the teen to take full advantage of the help available in the next placement; teens who have experienced wilderness therapy tend to be less resistant, more open to intervention, and more cooperative with program staff members. Second, youths who leave wilderness therapy and return immediately to their home environment are more likely to regress because they are returning to the peers and family dynamics already embedded in their problematic behaviors. Following a wilderness therapy experience up with another program away from the environment where the teen's problem behaviors emerged and flourished allows the therapeutic gains experienced in the wilderness to solidify and be reinforced.[3]

In many wilderness therapy programs teens progress through several phases. Upon arrival they receive a physical examination, clothing, and backpacking gear. Then the teens are transported to the small group with which they will be living in the wilderness during their program stay. During the first twenty-four to forty-eight hours teens in many programs are physically separated from their group; they may sit under a nearby tree watching the group but are not allowed to participate. This gives the teen an opportunity to withdraw from any illegal drugs, allows the teen to observe the group rules and procedures, allows staff to observe the teen's coping style, and helps the student feel more ready to join the group rather than isolate and withdraw. During this time the teen may be asked to complete individual assignments, observe group dynamics, and decide to comply with the program.

This introductory phase gives teens an opportunity to feel their emotions (anger, fear, sadness); adjust to their loss of freedom and contact with family, friends, and modern conveniences; and let the reality of their new peer group and wilderness environment set in. During this stage teens may be asked to write their life story, write letters to parents acknowledging the impact of their behaviors on the family and others, and learn about camping and backcountry skills (such as tying knots, building fires and shelters, and how to meet one's nutritional and hygiene needs in the wilderness).

During the second phase of many programs teens focus on how their past and current behaviors affect their short- and long-term options. They learn basic communication skills, the value of personal responsibility, and the importance of relationships. Writing assignments and group discussions during this stage are designed to motivate the teens to accept responsibility for their actions, express themselves both verbally and in writing, and begin to separate from friends and family.

During the next phase of many wilderness programs teens are expected to assume greater leadership responsibility. For many this is their first opportunity to mentor, lead by example, and guide others. A teen may lead a group hike through the forest and mentor a new teen while she continues to work on her personal and family issues. Teens who have made considerable progress are assigned more and more responsibility for the group and given additional privileges. They may be asked to join the staff in planning activities, develop their own therapy assignments, and help the group resolve issues.

The final "transition" phase of a wilderness program typically focuses on the next steps in the teen's life. During this period teens receive more freedom and privileges as they demonstrate leadership, personal responsibility, appropriate interactions with others, problem-solving skills, effective communication skills, awareness of strengths, and reconnection with family. Staff members work with teens and their parents to develop appropriate aftercare plans, which may include a residential treatment program, therapeutic boarding school, or emotional growth boarding school.

BOARDING SCHOOLS FOR TEENS WITH LEARNING DISABILITIES

Boarding schools for teens with learning disabilities offer structured academic programs that focus on teens' learning disabilities while providing counseling services for the emotional and behavioral issues that often arise with learning disabilities. After years of academic and social frustration in school, teens who have learning differences may also have depression and anxiety and feel profoundly disheartened, inadequate, ashamed, isolated, and excluded. Hence, a boarding school can provide a positive social opportunity as well as academic and emotional supports that enable the youth to succeed academically.

The typical boarding school for students with learning disabilities provides students with special education services tailored to each student's learning differences and special needs. Students live in dormitories with resident counselors. In addition to the academic program, students are offered social, recreational, cultural, and athletic activities that are sensitive to the range of students' strengths and challenges.

EMOTIONAL GROWTH BOARDING SCHOOLS

Emotional growth boarding schools offer structured college preparatory programs and focus on emotional development and personal growth but do not provide the intensive treatment services offered by therapeutic boarding schools or residential treatment centers. While these schools typically provide some special education services for youths who have learning differences, these schools may not be appropriate for students whose disabilities make college an infeasible goal. Typical emotional growth boarding schools cater to students struggling with a mix of behavioral, emotional, and mental health issues. Typical students have a history of academic and personal underperformance; in traditional school settings they may have acted out and posed behavioral challenges. Many students who enroll in emotional growth boarding schools resemble students who attend alternative high schools.

Emotional growth schools are similar to traditional boarding schools in some respects, with their structured and supervised daily schedules, afternoon and weekend activities, cultural events, and athletics. However, unlike a more typical boarding school, an emotional growth boarding school strives to create a milieu that provides the structure and support struggling teens may need to take responsibility for their actions, develop self-awareness, and cope with their special challenges. Some emotional growth boarding schools offer group and individual therapy; others arrange for students to receive counseling from a therapist in the local community. Emotional growth boarding schools that do not provide on-site group treatment may instead run peer support, self-exploration, and psychoeducational therapy groups. For example, students may gather for regularly scheduled staff-led discussions about healthy relationships, sobriety, sexuality, and personal responsibility or conflict resolution and problem-solving skills. These schools actively provide students with emotional support and guidance; students receive frequent messages that their contributions are valued and that they are important members of the community. At the same time the schools hold students accountable for their choices and behavior, providing structured, ethically administered discipline and ongoing feedback about the student's coping skills and the effects of the student's behavior on others. Faculty and counselors may use naturally occurring experiences and events in the classroom and dormitory to help students improve their self-awareness, as well as their decision-making, problem-solving, and interpersonal skills. Some emotional growth boarding schools follow a traditional academic calendar year (September to June); others operate year round.

THERAPEUTIC BOARDING SCHOOLS

Some struggling teens need more intensive around-the-clock mental health care than is available in an emotional growth boarding school. Therapeutic boarding schools focus more on students' mental health, substance abuse, and behavioral needs while also providing a college preparatory education. Therapeutic boarding schools provide regularly scheduled mental health and, when necessary, substance abuse counseling and treatment. They may also include periodic family therapy sessions. Students admitted to therapeutic boarding schools typically have a diagnosis of a mental health problem, including depression, bipolar disorder, dysthymia, ADHD, oppositional defiant disorder, conduct disorder, anxiety, posttraumatic stress disorder, substance abuse or dependence, or an eating disorder. Many teens who enroll in therapeutic boarding schools are described as impulsive, underachieving, defiant, and oppositional, and they may have struggled with substance use and sexual acting out. Many therapeutic boarding schools require that the student first complete a wilderness therapy program before enrolling.

RESIDENTIAL TREATMENT CENTERS

Residential treatment centers offer highly structured treatment in a twenty-four-hour therapeutic milieu that addresses substance abuse, family, and other mental health issues. Residential treatment centers are more like a psychiatric facility than a school, although they may have an academic/educational component to their program. Some offer ambitious academic programs, including a college prep curriculum. Teenagers admitted to residential treatment centers must receive a diagnosis of a mental disorder. Their behaviors are most likely a threat to their own or others' safety. They may have the same diagnoses as youngsters in emotional growth boarding schools and therapeutic boarding schools, but the symptoms may be more intense, persistent, and severe.

Some teenagers enter residential treatment centers following brief psychiatric hospitalization. Lengths of stay vary considerably depending upon the nature of the teenager's clinical and behavioral history and needs and the availability of appropriate follow-up services and programs, such as therapeutic boarding schools and emotional growth boarding schools. Lengths of stay are also influenced by insurance coverage. Sometimes a teen follows a "step-down" path, beginning with acute short-term hospitalization, followed by a residential treatment center, then therapeutic boarding school, then emotional growth boarding school. A wilderness therapy program may be helpful at any point along the path. Before embarking on this out-of-home series of placements, the youth's family ideally would have used the full array of home- and community-based options.

3

A LEGACY OF SCANDALS

EXPOSURE OF A TROUBLED INDUSTRY

Until recently, programs and schools for struggling teens—many of which are reputable, ethical, and professionally run—operated with scant scrutiny by government agencies. Anecdotes about shoddy and abusive practices remained just that—anecdotes—until around 2003, when the media, especially regional media outlets, publicized crises associated with the World Wide Association of Specialty Programs and Schools (WWASPS) that we detail later in this chapter.[1] WWASPS was an umbrella organization of interconnected companies, programs that provide residential services to struggling teens (Szalavitz 2006). The *New York Times* cast considerable light on the brewing controversy, exposing abuses at a WWASPS-affiliated school, the Academy at Dundee Ranch in Costa Rica (Weiner 2003a):

> A torrent of teenage rage, hard and fast as the tropical rain on this Pacific coast, washed away the Academy at Dundee Ranch this weekend.
>
> Dundee Ranch, the latest foreign outpost in a far-flung affiliation of behavior modification programs that promises to convert troubled American teenagers into straight arrows, lasted 19 months before the students rose up in revolt and overthrew their masters.
>
> The rebellion erupted after Costa Rican officials visited the ranch—an old hotel on a rutted red-dirt road—and told the children of their rights after complaints about the program from a former director.
>
> "They told us you have the right to speak, you have the right to speak to your parents, you have the right to leave if you feel you've been mistreated," said Hugh Maxwell, 17, of Rhode Island. "Kids heard that and they started running for the door. There was elation, cheering and clapping and chaos. People were crying."

According to the *New York Times* report, the academy's owner, Narvin Lichfield, was jailed for thirty hours. Dundee Ranch was a program within a Utah-based business called the World Wide Association of Specialty Programs and Schools, or WWASPS, that generated yearly revenues of $60 million or more. The *Times* further reports that a Utah prosecutor, Craig Barlow, brought a child abuse charge against the director of one WWASPS-affiliated school and quoted Barlow as saying that WWASPS programs are "a lateral arabesque with no hub except for these connections in Utah" built on a network of interlocking directorships based on family and business ties.

Out of this report and an exposé by Maia Szalavitz (2006) have emerged several ambitious attempts to examine the broad struggling-teen industry, focusing especially on quality controls and oversight mechanisms designed to prevent abuses (Leichtman 2006; Pumariega 2006). Especially prominent is the Alliance for the Safe, Therapeutic, and Appropriate Use of Residential Treatment (ASTART), established under the auspices of the University of South Florida and the Bazelon Center for Mental Health Law (Friedman et al. 2006). ASTART began operation in 2004 to address growing concern about abusive residential programs for struggling teens. According to the organization,

> A concern about a growing number of reports from youth, families and the public media regarding the exploitation, mistreatment, and abuse of youth in unregulated, private residential treatment programs has given rise to an alliance of individuals and organizations that are working together to address this problem.
>
> Over the past decade in the United States, hundreds of private residential treatment facilities for youth have been established, described as a $1 billion to $1.2 billion industry that serves 10,000 to 14,000 children and adolescents. This increase in residential programs is alarming because research has established that community-based treatment and support is effective and indicated for most youth and families, even those with serious problems who need intensive support.
>
> Some residential programs self-identify as "therapeutic boarding schools," "emotional growth academies" or "behavior modification facilities," and market to families of youth with psychiatric diagnoses, claiming expertise in treating a variety of serious conditions. Many of these new programs are not currently subject to any state licensing or monitoring as mental health facilities. Currently, the only information available about most of these programs comes from their own marketing efforts and there is no systematic, independently collected descriptive or outcome data on these programs. Highly disturbing reports have been published in the public media and provided by youth and families describing financial opportunism by program operators, poor quality

education, harsh discipline, inappropriate seclusion and restraint, substandard psychotherapeutic interventions conducted by unqualified staff, medical and nutritional neglect, and rights violations in a number of unregulated facilities. Multiple state investigations have been conducted and lawsuits have been filed in response to reports of abuse, neglect and mistreatment of youth in unregulated residential programs. In numerous cases the lawsuits have led to convictions or high cost settlements. In many states there are limited to nonexistent regulations and there is a lack of federal legislation supporting oversight of private residential treatment programs.   (ASTART, n.d.)

After surveying the wide array of residential programs for struggling teens throughout the United States, ASTART concluded that many programs are negligent and abusive, using a severe and rigid approach to discipline and activities of daily living (Friedman et al. 2006). For example, some programs do not allow teens to have contact with their parents both initially—sometimes for months—and subsequently when youth do not comply with rules. Programs may use youths to monitor and discipline their peers, a particularly questionable practice since all youth sent to the program presumably have special challenges themselves and certainly lack professional training and credentialing for working with struggling teens.

ASTART further reports that therapy within these programs is often provided by staff members who have not received formal clinical training, and Friedman and colleagues (2006) documented descriptions of interventions suggestive of gross incompetence. Psychiatrists are not routinely included as treatment team members; dosing errors, as well as inappropriate medication or overmedication of youth, have been reported. ASTART concludes that this substandard treatment is especially troubling because programs often quite explicitly direct their marketing efforts to families of youth with psychiatric diagnoses and often claim expertise in treating a variety of mental or behavioral health challenges.

A second major effort to expose abusive programs led to the publication of *Help at Any Cost: How the Troubled-Teen Industry Cons Parents and Hurts Kids*, a scathing critique by Szalavitz (2006), a freelance journalist and former television news producer. In *Help At Any Cost* Szalavitz explores the modus operandi of many schools and programs for struggling teens that use a "tough love" approach, programs that "share the belief that difficult teens are always acting deliberately, even those who have been diagnosed with mental illnesses—and that through harsh confrontation and deprivation of privileges, they can be broken and resocialized to better conform with parental and societal expectations" (2006:5). Szalavitz closely examines "tough love" schools and programs—a subset of a much broader group of schools and programs—and reaches a hard-hitting conclusion: "What all this boils down to is that tough love programs are sold on false premises, exaggerating both the risks to untreated teens and the benefits of residential treatment. It also means that any claim that a program 'saved' a kid needs to be taken with a grain of salt—unless there was a control group followed who had the same level of initial problems and who received no treatment or different treatment" (12).[2]

Szalavitz focuses especially on abusive and "get tough" practices made famous, or infamous, by a substance abuse treatment program known as Straight, Inc. Straight was founded in the mid-1970s by Mel and Betty Sembler. Approximately fifty thousand teens are believed to have spent time in Straight, which operated until the early 1990s (Szalavitz 2006). Sembler, a multimillionaire who chairs the Sembler Company, which develops shopping centers, served as U.S. ambassador to Italy from 2001 to 2005, during the George W. Bush administration, and as U.S. ambassador to Australia and Nauru from 1989 to 1993, during the George H.W. Bush administration. According to the Sembler Company's Web site:

> Although best known as a leading shopping center developer, Sembler is also renowned for his activism in the anti-drug movement. In 1976, Sembler and his wife Betty founded STRAIGHT, an adolescent drug treatment program. During its 17 years of existence, STRAIGHT successfully graduated more than 12,000 young people nationwide from its remarkable program. He is nationally recognized as an activist in the anti-drug campaign and as a staunch, long-time supporter of the Republican Party and its candidates.[3]

The rise and fall of Straight is emblematic of the most controversial programs for struggling teens. Nearly all of the most controversial programs fall into the broad category of "tough love" programs, that is, programs into which teens are typically enrolled against their will and that are widely believed to use angry confrontational tactics, intimidation, shaming, humiliation, enforced sleep deprivation, lack of privacy, constant haranguing, exercise to the point of exhaustion, denial of private conversations with one's parents, and demands that one maintain physically difficult positions for long periods of time. Among the programs and organizations that have received the greatest scrutiny are the Seed, Straight, SAFE, North Star Expeditions, and WWASPS. The oldest is the Seed, which served as the model for Straight. An overview of these programs illuminates the controversies that have engulfed them and many of the abusive practices that continue today in some programs for struggling teens.

THE SEED

The Seed, a chain of controversial drug rehabilitation programs, was started in 1970 with the support of federal funding from the Law Enforcement Assistance Administration. A comedian named Art Barker founded the Seed in Fort Lauderdale, Florida. Teenagers enrolled in the Seed had been using drugs or were believed to have been at risk of doing so. They were required to spend ten- to twelve-hour days seated erectly on hard-backed chairs and to wave their arms furiously to catch the attention of staffers, most of whom were former participants themselves. Faced with these conditions, the teens begged to confess their bad behavior (Szalavitz 2007).

Upon admission to the Seed, each youth was placed in a "host home" where he would spend each night—the house of parents of other program participants. Each host home had been specially prepared to prevent Seed clients from leaving at night. If these "newcomers" didn't give convincing confessions in group sessions held during the day while attending the Seed program, they were not allowed to "progress" in the program and return to their own home.

In 1974 Senator Sam Ervin, the North Carolina Democrat best known for heading the congressional committee that investigated Watergate, presented a report to Congress entitled *Individual Rights and the Federal Role in Behavior Modification* (1974). Ervin and other members of Congress were concerned about federal funding for efforts to change people's behavior against their will. The federal report cited the Seed as an example of programs that "begin by subjecting the individual to isolation and humiliation in a conscious effort to break down his psychological defenses" (*Individual Rights* 1974:15). It concluded that such programs are "similar to the highly refined brainwashing techniques employed by the North Koreans in the early 1950's" (1974:15). Ervin's report led Congress to cut off the Seed's funding.

Marc Polonsky, whose parents enrolled him in the Seed, has written a widely distributed, compelling first-person account of his experience in the program. Polonsky's detailed description is included here because it is an especially precise, clear, and articulate statement about policies, procedures, and practices that laid the groundwork for some current programs for struggling teens.[4]

MY STORY

I was fourteen and a half years old. It was October 1972, and I had just begun the ninth grade. My experience with drugs consisted of having tried marijuana about ten times and drinking wine perhaps five. My parents were concerned about the company I was keeping and my disrespectful attitude toward them. My sister too, a year and a half my senior, was a source of worry to them for her use of drugs and her rebellious attitude.

I was in my science class one afternoon when a note arrived, summoning me to the dean's office. When I got to the dean's office, my sister was there also. "Mommy needs us," she said, and I could tell by her eyes that this was the message she'd received, that she knew no more about it than I, and that she too felt vague apprehension—perhaps of some family tragedy. I certainly sensed something ominous. I imagined my grandmother might be very sick or perhaps even dying.

My sister and I sat outside in front of the school for a few minutes until my parents pulled up. There were two other adults with them, a couple who were introduced to us as Mr. and Mrs. J. I knew immediately, from my parents' pleasant, jovial air, that my grandmother had not died nor had any other terrible thing occurred. I was relieved.

My sister and I got in the backseat, and I don't think either of us noticed anything unusual about Mrs. J's taking the window seat next to my sister and Mr. J's getting in on the other side next to me. This was of course a precautionary measure by the four adults in case one of us should try to escape from the car before we reached the Seed. I later learned that Mr. and Mrs. J already had two sons in the Seed who had previously met with and impressed my parents with their politeness and their good-natured, clean-cut appearance. The type of assistance the J's were giving my parents in this instance was standard for fellow Seed parents.

In any case they had nothing to worry about. My sister and I had lightened up considerably upon seeing our parents' cheerful attitude. Our parents let us try to guess where we were going. About halfway there my mother gave my sister a hint: "Remember that news story we saw on TV the other night?" My sister replied, "Oh, the Seed," and it was confirmed.

My sister and I weren't the slightest bit alarmed, because we were both quite ignorant of what the Seed really was. All we had heard was that it was a drug rehabilitation center. My conception of a drug rehabilitation center was a place where people came when they were addicted to drugs, a place that helped people who were unfit to function in the world. I pictured arts and crafts lessons, cooking, etc. We imagined that we were merely being taken to see this place for some reason. Maybe our parents wanted to scare us away from experimenting with drugs by showing us what the addicts looked like. I mentioned to my father that I was planning to go to a chess club that afternoon with a friend and did not want to be detained for too long.

We arrived at the Seed. It was an old warehouse building surrounded by a chain link fence. There were two young men sitting on chairs by the driveway who halted us for a moment, exchanged a word or two with my parents, and then let us drive in and park.

In the reception office a middle-aged woman named Betty sat down with my parents, my sister, and me. She addressed my sister first, asking her age, grade, and the kinds of drugs she had used. My sister answered frankly. There followed a peculiar conversation between the two of them during which my parents and I were silent (except for my parents' interjecting a word or two). This conversation essentially consisted of Betty's aiming insulting remarks at my sister about her character and her lifestyle, for no apparent reason other than to goad her. My sister's first reaction was astonishment, and then reciprocal hostility. It is hard to say what the point of it was except perhaps to prepare my sister for what was in store or—and this I strongly suspect—to provide an opportunity for this woman to "play the Seedling." Let me explain what I mean by this.

Betty was a Seed mother who had been, I suppose, exceptionally enthusiastic and consequently assimilated into the organization. She knew the attitude the Seed always took toward newcomers and this was her opportunity to represent that attitude.

Here and there, people were coming in and out of the office: other Seedlings. Perhaps one of them would call out a greeting to Betty or simply convey a brief message to her. At the end of each of these tiny interactions Betty said in a singsong voice, "I looove you." "I love you" was said by Seedlings to each other, always, after each and every interchange, and the way Betty said it, in a chirpy but unmelodic singsong, was one of the standard ways it was often said.

Toward the end of this prickly conversation between Betty and my sister, it was revealed to my sister and me that we would be staying at the Seed for a while and that we had no choice. I was shocked, but I imagined we would certainly get out soon, once the Seed saw we were not "druggies." I simply had no conception of what was really happening. I even said to my sister, who was quite upset, "It's okay. We'll just agree with what they say and then we can go," thinking they would tell us drugs were bad and we shouldn't use them.

Betty finally got around to me. When she asked me what drugs I had used, and I told her, she said sweetly, "Don't bullshit me," and looked me sharply in the eye in a way that seemed meant to inspire fear and awe. I replied, thinking myself clever, "I wouldn't baloney you." I was soon to learn just how clever it was to get clever in the Seed.

While Betty was "doing my intake," my sister had to use the bathroom. She was accompanied there by a female Seedling. A few minutes later a female Seed "staff member" approached my parents and regretfully informed them that my sister's initial attitude was "really rotten." She explained: "We have a rule here that when a newcomer goes to the bathroom someone must be there to hold her hand. Your daughter didn't accept this so she swung at the other girl."

My sister and I were each taken to a room to be searched. I had to strip and I was relieved of keys and money, which were turned over to my parents. Shortly thereafter we were led to the room where all the Seedlings were (commonly known as the *group*)—a long stark white cement room with a gray floor. The windows were all eight or nine feet above the floor, and the two doors were well secured by Seed staff. A sign on the wall proclaimed, "You're not alone anymore," and the only other ornaments were signs listing the "three steps" and the "seven steps" (which will be explained later).

About three hundred young people, ranging in age from about twelve to twenty-six (with a mean age of sixteen to seventeen), sat in rows of hard-backed fold-out chairs, facing the "rap leader," who sat on a high stool, holding a microphone. Boys and girls (always referred to as "guys and chicks" in the Seed) were separated by a wide aisle down the middle of the room. Around the room Seed staff members stood against the wall—male staff members on one side, female staffers on the other.

A "rap" was in progress when my sister and I entered. The rap leader would make comments into the microphone, whereupon everyone in the group would raise their hands enthusiastically, and then someone would be called on by the rap leader to "participate."

The rap was briefly interrupted upon our arrival. We were led to stand in front of the group and we were introduced: "This is Judy. She's done pot, hash. . . . And this is Marc. He says he's only done pot." Then the group greeted us in unison with a resounding "Love ya, Judy and Marc!" and we were led to seats in the front rows of our respective sections.

This is how newcomers were always introduced and welcomed into the Seed.

I do not remember much of that first rap I ever sat through. The rap leader was a staff member named Danny. (Raps were always led by staff members.) At first my sister and I exchanged glances every few minutes, but this was soon put a stop to. Each of us was approached by a friendly male staff member who explained we were not to do this. At the very outset, one was treated somewhat gently in the Seed. This generally lasted a day or two.

I think the subject of this particular rap was probably "happiness" because I vaguely recall someone standing and gushing "and then we can all be like Art Barker and go out there and change the world!!" It was generally in the "love" and "happiness" raps that such ebullient declarations were heard.

Art Barker is the ex-alcoholic who founded the Seed. He was revered in the group as "the strongest." He rarely came before the group himself. Whenever he did, as soon as he was spotted in the room, ecstatic shouts of "Love ya, Art!!" erupted throughout the room. Barker, a former stand-up comedian and recovering alcoholic, was a charming, energetic, often vulgar, thoroughly charismatic man.

As for "raps," there were ten to twelve standard subjects. Some were "love," "happiness," "games," "old friends," "the three steps," "the seven steps," "conning," "analyzing and justifying," and "honesty." (The nature of "raps" will be further elucidated a bit later in this account.)

The rap and the Seed day ended in the usual manner, which I shortly got used to. First, when the rap concluded, a few songs were sung. There was a limited repertoire of songs sung in the Seed, innocuous stuff such as "Zippity-do-dah." While songs were sung, everyone put their arms around the shoulders of the two people next to them and sang with great gusto.

After a few songs the rap leader asked, "Who wants to say why we sing 'Jingle Bells'?" and everyone's hands flew up, many Seedlings making eager inarticulate sounds as their arms pumped the air. When the lucky person was chosen, he got to stand up and shout, "We sing 'Jingle Bells' because every day we're straight it's like Christmas!!" whereupon the group applauded wildly and roared into a chorus of the song.

After this came the announcements. Some announcements served to inform certain Seedlings that they had reached the next stage in the program. This was done in the following manner:

The rap leader might say, "John Jones, Kate Green, Molly Smith—stand up." A pregnant pause. "You all go back to school tomorrow." Hearty applause followed and the fortunate few were patted, hugged, and congratulated by those sitting around them.

The other announcements were to tell newcomers whom they would be going home with. For example:

"Martin Ivory, stand up." (He stands.) "You're going home with Jack Potter." (Jack stands and waves to the newcomer. The group says, "Love you, Jack." They both sit down.) And so on, one by one.

Then everyone stood and joined hands to recite the Lord's Prayer.

Then the rap leader said, "Okay, all old-comers picking up newcomers, pick 'em up." The Seedlings who were living at home and had newcomers in their charge would come around to where their newcomers were sitting. The corresponding newcomer got up and the old-comer placed a hand on a male newcomer's shoulder or took a female newcomer's hand. In this manner the old-comers with newcomers were filed out the door. Then everyone else was allowed to go.

My first night, I went home with a young man named Aaron. Aaron was fifteen and had only been in the Seed a little over thirty days himself. I tried to explain to him that I was not a druggie, but he insisted I was a druggie, by the Seed's definition, even if I had only smoked pot once. Or, for that matter, even if I only had what they called "a druggie attitude." Aaron was not abusive; it was my first night and I had a lot to learn. In fact, Aaron was a kind individual who did not really want to get tough. The toughest thing Aaron ever said was when I told him I thought my attitude was fine and he replied, "Your attitude sucks. Listen. Don't argue with me. Your attitude sucks." "Your attitude sucks" were watchwords in the Seed. They applied to all newcomers.

I slept on the floor of Aaron's bedroom that night, in his parents' house. He had removed the handles from the windows and he slept with his bed across the door. All newcomers are similarly imprisoned in the first stage of the program, with varying degrees of security. At this point I still felt it was all a mistake and was entertaining hopes of getting back home and to school very soon. I thought that the Seed was probably a good place for some people but that I obviously did not belong there.

THE STAGES OF THE SEED PROGRAM

I will now digress from my own story and describe the different stages of the Seed program, followed by a description of what generally took place at the Seed during the day. There was no time limit for any stage; one did not progress forward in the program until the Seed staff determined that one was ready. There were, however, time minimums.

The first stage of the program was "newcomer-living-away-from-home." During this stage the newcomer was at the Seed, in the group, from 10 a.m. to 10 p.m. six days a week and from 12 to 10 on Sundays. He (or she) was never allowed to be alone, even to use the bathroom. He lived with an "old-comer" whose duty, before and after Seed hours, was to persuade the newcomer on intimate terms that his previous life was characterized by dishonor, dishonesty, pettiness, insecurity, and meanness and that he should henceforth adopt the Seed's philosophy and become "straight" (a term that signified a great deal more than merely refraining from drug use). It was also the old-comer's responsibility to give his newcomer(s) a place to sleep that would not afford an opportunity to run away, and to feed him/them when appropriate.

When Seed staff decided, after a minimum of fourteen days (or a minimum of thirty days for those sent to the Seed through the courts), that a newcomer could be trusted on his own, and had been sufficiently persuaded that he was wrong and the Seed was right, the newcomer was allowed to go home and live with his parents. But he still had to report to the Seed all day every day.

Next he was allowed to go back to school, but he continued to report to the Seed immediately after school and stay there until 10 p.m. every day.

Finally, he was put on his "three months" and was now called an "old-comer," as opposed to merely a "newcomer living at home." (At any stage during which he was living at home, though, he was eligible to take home newcomers—and be their "old-comer.") This stage was called "three months" because three months was the *minimum* amount of time it had to last. (For those sent to the Seed by the courts, the minimum time was six months.) During this stage he needed to report to the Seed only three evenings a week, for the evening rap from 7 to 10, and for one full weekend day. In his free time, if he wished to go out to a movie or to go out anywhere without his parents, other than to school, he had to first obtain permission from the Seed.

This permission was usually granted if it involved going out with another Seedling of the same sex or an extracurricular activity at school. Other kinds of permissions, such as one I requested once to attend a youth group meeting, were generally refused. Most Seedlings knew not to ask for them.

Finally, the Seedling was allowed "off his program" and had achieved the status of "old-timer."

At any of these stages, however, for a variety of real or imaginary transgressions, a Seedling could be demoted back to an earlier stage of the program for a "refresher" or even started over at the very beginning.

THE SEED DAY

The Seed day began at 10 a.m., by which time everyone was seated in the large warehouse room that I described earlier. The first activity, barring possibly a few songs, was the "morning rap," which lasted a little over two hours. The rap leader sat on a stool in front of the group and called on people to stand, "participate," and sit down again. Everyone who had been in the Seed more than three days had their hand raised to participate at all times (except when someone else was already talking). This was because everyone was told as a newcomer, "You should always have something to say or else you're just copping out."

During the first three days of one's program, one was not allowed to actually participate but had to simply sit in the group and listen. By the end of these three days one was expected to understand what was going on.

Staff members were stationed around the room. They made sure everyone was paying attention to the person speaking—not talking, daydreaming, or sleeping. If someone had to use the bathroom, he had to raise his hand and wait for the nearest staff member to call on him. Staff members could easily tell whether someone was raising a hand to participate in the rap or raising a hand for the bathroom. One who had to go to the bathroom was looking at the nearest staff member and raising his hand toward that staff member. Usually, although the staff member would notice him right away, he would have to wait at least a few minutes. Often he would have to wait much longer if the staff member did not feel he had been "working," i.e., paying 100 percent attention to the rap and participating "honestly."

If a newcomer living away from home had to use the bathroom, the staff member would also have to pick someone to take him there. That is, someone who had been around for a while had to place a hand on the newcomer's shoulder, walk him to the toilet, and walk him back.

Incidentally, staff members were all people who had been through the Seed themselves.

THE RAPS

Some of the standard "raps" were these:

■ "Old friends"—also known as "old druggie friends." This rap was about the ways in which you and your old friends "used" each other (for drugs, money, status, etc.) and how you pretended to be friends while secretly despising each other and talking behind each other's backs. There were no two sides to this. No one ever stood up to say, "Well so-and-so was really a good friend, and we really loved each other and helped each other out." If anyone had said such a thing, he would have been cut down immediately by the rap leader and possibly made to stand for a while to be abused by the group also. Such a comment was obviously not "honest."

■ "Honesty"—The first and most important rule in the Seed was honesty, and the Seed defined what you were thinking if you were honest with yourself. Honesty meant admitting you were "into acceptance" before coming to the Seed, that you were "full of shit" before coming to the Seed, that all your relationships had been "bullshit," that you had been horrible to your parents who loved you—that you were a dishonest, insecure, unkind, thoroughly worthless mess before you were fortunate enough to have landed in the Seed. A frequent subtheme in this rap was "honesty vs. truth," i.e., how you used the truth to distort honesty by taking facts out of context and painting dishonest pictures for people, usually your parents.

■ "Love"—This rap would normally start out with comparisons of what you used to think love was to the *real* love that you had found in the Seed. Then it would proceed to "how real love makes you feel," whereupon people would begin to get very happy and excited. There would be many ecstatic comments about the "vibes" in the room.

■ "The three steps"—The three steps were *think think think, first things first,* and *easy does it.* Each of these steps was examined one at a time, with people participating as to what "think think think," or one of the other steps meant to them.

■ "The seven steps"— These steps were adapted from AA's twelve steps. The first step, "We admitted we were powerless over drugs," usually evoked comments like, "When someone offered me a joint, I could never refuse because I wanted to be accepted."

■ "Conning"—If someone was merely parroting the Seed philosophy, saying what one was supposed to say without really subscribing to it, this was conning. During this rap everyone would participate about how they had once tried to con the Seed. But this was, of course, impossible because "everyone knows just where you're at." Seedlings were simply too supremely "aware," and they could spot a con a mile away. Seedlings were, in fact, the most aware people in the world—much more aware than even their parents. Of course we were not supposed to let on to our parents that this was the case, but Seedlings were "superior human beings." All of this was stated *explicitly.*

■ "Analyzing and justifying"—These two bad habits, though an inseparable pair, were discussed one at a time. Analyzing was taking things apart, mixing them up so as to make them confusing. Justifying was what you achieved by doing this. You analyzed your past actions to make it seem as if you had had good or honest intentions. Or you analyzed what the Seed was telling you and tried to construe it in such a way that the Seed was wrong and you were right, although you knew in your heart it was vice versa and that you were an asshole. (Everyone was an asshole before they came to the Seed. Most everyone had to proclaim it in the group at least once before they got to go home.)

■ "Games"—Everyone, if they were honest, had to admit they had played all sorts of games: "attention games," "prove-you-love-me games," and others. I cannot remember them all; there were about four or five basic ones. The ones I have listed are self-explanatory.

■ "Happiness"—basically a rap about what happiness is and what makes you happy. When this rap came up, it was, in a sense, a break. Like "love," happiness raps elicited exuberant participation and frequent rejoicing in "the vibes."

■ "Potential"—basically a rap on using it, now that you are a Seedling, rather than letting it stagnate as you did "when you were a druggie." (Other common references to one's pre-Seed days: "When I was on the streets," "on the outside.")

■ "The Serenity Prayer"—is of course, "God grant me the serenity to accept the things I cannot change, the courage to change the things I can, and the wisdom to know the difference." This was another one-line-at-a-time rap, with special focus on the words *serenity, courage,* and *wisdom.* For example, courage to tell your old friends you don't want to talk to them.

❖

As I have mentioned, sleeping and daydreaming during these raps was strictly prohibited. Sleep (although virtually everyone was deprived of it) was deemed unnecessary; it was merely a way of "copping out of the rap." If you saw someone sleeping nearby, you were supposed to shake him awake, as he would unfailingly do for you. Daydreaming, or "getting into your head," was also pounced on immediately. If someone was caught looking like he was not paying attention to the rap, the rap leader or a nearby staff member would shout, "Hey! Get out of your head!"

"In your head" was, in fact, considered a very bad place to be even if you were not in the middle of a rap, even if there was nothing specifically calling for your attention in a given moment. Just by the look on your face, any other Seedling would be able to tell if you were "getting into your head" and would say, "Hey, get out of your head!"

"Getting into your head" really meant any kind of introspection, and the giveaway was an inward, perhaps even zoned-out, facial expression. Private reflection and introspection were counterproductive, because they inexorably led to "analyzing and justifying" and also to "fantasizing" (another watchword), which was deemed a perilous waste of time.

During any of these raps special events could occur. One person, whom the rap leader disliked or who was exceptionally unwilling to be "honest," might be "stood up." This person would be made to stand while the group raised their hands to take turns telling him how appalling he was, with abusive language, name-calling, derision, sneering, and much profanity. Profanity was common, and even implicitly encouraged, in the Seed.

Sometimes the stood-up person would be an old-comer who, in the rap leader's judgment, had been acting suspiciously. In many cases this old-comer would be sentenced to a "refresher" or even started over, right then and there.

Or a brand-new newcomer might arrive. Or someone who had "split"—run away from the Seed (either escaped while living away from home or defected while living at home, the latter offense being by far the more serious)—might be brought in, often struggling and kicking and screaming. An intense "come-down" session would follow.

On my second or third day a young man named Jerry was made to stand in front of the group. Apparently, he had turned eighteen and was legally able to choose to leave the Seed. (It seems strange in retrospect because I recall that many eighteen- and nineteen-year-olds who were not from the courts were nevertheless being held against their will.) And Jerry had made the choice to leave. A staff member introduced him, briefly explained the situation, and said dryly, "I think we should try to talk him out of it."

One by one, members of the group told Jerry what they thought of him and what would happen to him if he tried to make it "back on the streets." The males said things like, "If I had met up with a guy like you on the streets, I would have used you for what I could get from you, walked all over you, and then beat the crap out of you." Many of the females emphasized that he was pathetic and ridiculous and unmanly, and at one point the rap leader asked, "How many of you chicks would have had anything to do with a guy like this when you were on the streets?" And of course no one raised her hand. This was a common routine in the Seed: collectively asking all the members of the opposite sex if they would have had any respect for the person currently being "come down on." Everyone knew not to raise their hands.

When the group was finished with Jerry, he was crying and pleading to be allowed back in the group. The rap leader contemptuously gave Jerry precise words to say, instructing him to beg the group to allow him back and to apologize for his misbehavior. Jerry dutifully repeated the prescribed words through his tears.

Everyone knew the kinds of things they were supposed to say in all of the raps—the gist being the denigration of their former selves and celebration of "getting straight" through the Seed. If one wished to make progress in the program, it was what one had to do—and make it convincing lest one be accused of "conning" or giving "pat answers."

An ironic aspect of "raps" was that the rap leaders repeatedly warned the group: "I don't want to hear any pat answer!" which placed many Seedlings in a double-bind. They were expected to always say the same types of things but in a different way, and this was taxing on the imaginations of some. It was especially difficult to avoid pat answers in the nightly "rules raps," which I will explain shortly.

BACK TO THE SEED DAY

After the morning rap a few songs and then lunch. A line was formed at the back of the room and each person picked up his or her sandwich and a cup of Kool-Aid and returned to his or her seat. (Sandwiches were always either peanut butter and jelly or baloney and cheese.)

Most of the songs, as I mentioned before, were innocent ditties such as "I've Been Working on the Railroad," but a few had their words altered a bit to fit the spirit of the Seed, e.g., "Straight Christmas," "If You're Straight and You Know It Clap Your Hands." And then there was the "Seed Song," sung to the tune of "Greensleeves":

> *Chorus:*
> The Seed indeed is all you need
> To stay off the junk and the pills and the weed.
> You come each day from ten to ten
> And if you screw up then you start again.
>
> *First Verse:*
> Faith, love and honesty will prevail
> And if you can't dig it you'll go to jail.
> Old friends and phone calls you can't make
> And if you do, your leg I'll break

I have forgotten the second verse.

Lunch was about one half hour. Sometimes during lunch an old-comer would "introduce himself" before the group. He would sit on the rap leader's stool, say his name and the drugs he did, and proceed to relate his personal story of how miserable and phony he had been in his old life and how happy and fulfilled he had become in the Seed.

Somewhat arbitrarily, the Seed defined a hierarchy of drugs: marijuana, hashish, barbiturates, mescaline, LSD, amphetamines, cocaine, and heroin, in that order. Presumably, this was the natural progression in which everyone tried the different drugs. So if someone said, "I've done pot to speed," this included LSD but excluded cocaine.

After lunch came the afternoon rap, lasting until 3. Then everyone was filed out into the parking lot for a half hour of exercises. The males and females remained separated at all times.

Then "guys and chicks" gathered at opposite corners of the parking lot for "boys' raps" and "girls' raps." I cannot say for certain what went on in the girls' raps but I can guess. In the boys' raps we talked about "chicks," how they used and manipulated us, and how they always had us "by the balls" even though we did not know it. (I could not participate too well in these raps since I had never really had a girlfriend, but I found things to say all the same.) One frequently delivered pronouncement was, "Chicks are so slick, man!" usually following a story of how someone had been manipulated by his girlfriend. There was also contrite acknowledgment of what *we* had really wanted "chicks" for after all; it always came down to sex and ego gratification, not necessarily in that order.

The boys' and girls' raps lasted until 5 at which time everyone was filed back inside. Next came the rules rap, which lasted about an hour every evening. Each of the Seed's rules was discussed, and a few people would be called on to "participate" for each rule, that is, they had to say something about why the rule was there. The first rule cited each night was honesty. "Honesty is our first and most important rule." This sentence, verbatim, was stated every single night. The other rules followed in no particular order:

No boy-girl relationships while on your program—the reason being that you had to get straight first before you could take on any kind of relationship with the opposite sex that was not "bullshit." In fact, a lot of jargon was tossed around in the Seed, particularly in the boys' raps, about waiting for "that one good relationship."

No old druggie friends or old druggie hangouts—for obvious reasons. In fact even talking to an old druggie friend was a capital offense and if someone was caught doing so, say, in school by another Seedling, one could be started over, or at least severely "come down on" in the group and intimidated into not doing it again. In fact, it was every Seedling's responsibility to watch over each other when they got back to school.

No hitchhiking or picking up hitchhikers—People who hitchhiked or picked up hitchhikers were invariably druggies.

No stopping at the store on the way home if you have newcomers in the car—Stores, such as 7–11, were "druggie hang-outs" and could conceivably "push buttons in the newcomer's head." It was also dangerous because it could offer a newcomer a chance to escape when no one was looking.

No newcomers talking to newcomers—Newcomers were full of shit and had nothing to say anyway. They could only hold each other back by talking to one another.

No automatically moving ahead in the program—Each individual worked at his own rate. The Seed, with infinite understanding, could best say when the time was right for an individual to progress to the next stage.

Protect each other's anonymity—This was an interesting one because, once you were back in school, everyone knew you had been to the Seed anyway. But the gist of what people said night after night was, Don't ever mention the name of a Seedling and tell an outsider that this person was in the Seed. You never know, someone might want to run for office some day, and it could hurt his chances.

As the reader might imagine, it was not easy to avoid "pat answers" when this rap took place every single night.

Supper was served in the same way as lunch, with a few songs before, during, and after. It generally consisted of "sloppy Joe" or dubious chow mein. The drink was the same: a cup of Kool-Aid or powdered milk. During the rules rap and supper those who were back in school but still going to the Seed every day until 10 were allowed to sit apart from the group and do their homework.

At 7 was the evening rap, which lasted until about 9:45. Then a few songs, announcements (already explained), and the end of the Seed day.

OPEN MEETINGS

"Open meetings" took place at the Seed on Monday and Friday evenings. Therefore, on Mondays and Fridays the boys' and girls' raps were superseded by "homes raps."

The boys and girls had separate homes raps. The purpose of the homes raps was to see how the group as a whole felt about each individual who was eligible to go home (those newcomers living away from home who had been at the Seed fourteen days or more—or thirty days or more for those sent by courts). These individuals were stood up one by one. The rap leader would then call on a few people to participate as to how they felt this newcomer was doing, how much progress he had made so far. It was usually a scathing process because most newcomers were still full of shit and had not really started "working." Evidence of this was the quality of the newcomer's participation in the general raps, which was usually not too sophisticated or enthusiastic at first.

Sometimes there were cutting personal insults. There was always profanity. A couple of lines which were tossed about every homes rap were "Grow a set of balls!" and "Get your head out of your ass!" Another standard comment was, "I don't think he's really being honest yet." But favorable opinions were voiced, too. "I think he's trying." "He's working some." "He's changing." And sometimes benevolent but stern: "He's working but not for the right reasons." "I think he's still got a way to go." The staff member leading the rap would be the last to speak to each newcomer that stood up, sometimes with vicious, angry condemnation, sometimes with soothing, encouraging words, and sometimes something in-between. As each newcomer would sit back down, the group would intone, "Love ya [the newcomer's name]."

But newcomers did not find out in the homes raps whether or not they could go home. This was revealed during the open meetings, and there were often big surprises. ·

The open meeting started at 7:30. It usually lasted far past 10, often past midnight. It was called an open meeting because parents, family, and sometimes others were allowed into the Seed. No one could just walk in off the street, however. Everyone who came had to be cleared through the Seed staff.

The parents were filed into the room and seated in rows of chairs opposite those of their children. Sometimes there were a few songs at the beginning. Art Barker himself was usually on hand to say a few opening words of comfort and assurance to the parents. It was by no means a solemn occasion. Everyone had cause to be happy. The kids were in the best place they could possibly be and—sure, it might take some bumps and hard knocks—but every one of these kids was on his or her way to getting straight. There could be no doubt about that. And no matter what anyone said or did, the Seed was just gonna keep on saving kids. Art Barker used that phrase every time: "save kids." Especially in times of adversity, such as when the Seed was attempting to obtain a license to open a second Seed in Miami and was encountering resistance in the community there. "Screw 'em all! We're gonna *save kids*!!"

Then a Seedling, an old-comer or old-timer, would introduce himself (or herself) to the assembled parents and to the group. When this short presentation was over, each newcomer who had been in the Seed from four to fourteen days was made to stand, tell his name, the drugs he had done, and say a few short words about what he had learned so far in the Seed.

Then it was the parents' turn to speak to their children. The microphone was passed from parent to parent, and each in turn could stand and say a few words to their child, who would also stand, across the room. Parents could take as long as they liked, which was the reason for the length of the open meeting. Usually, parents would say things like, "Keep working. You gotta get straight," and "We all have faith in you and we miss you." But once in a while a vindictive parent stood up and said something like, "We got your message through the Seed that you needed some more clothes and some cigarettes. Well, we brought your clothes, but we didn't bring cigarettes. You don't deserve any and we don't like you smoking anyway!" The crowd—kids and parents—invariably applauded such words. Any public censure of a child by a parent was applauded on principle. That was, after all, why the kids were there: to learn, among other things, respect. (Cigarette smoking was permitted in the Seed at all times; there were no rules about smoking in the group. Cigarettes were supplied through one's parents.)

But the exciting thing about the open meetings was this: it was the *parents* who first learned, at the door, whether or not they could take their child home with them that night. And they would be the ones to let their kid know, when they stood up with the microphone. It would happen something like this:

"Hi, John."

"Hi, Mom."

"How ya doin', honey? We miss you. You working?"

"Yeah. I know I gotta work harder, though."

"Hmm. Well, you must be doing something right because . . . YOU'RE COMING HOME TONIGHT!!"

Wild applause. John is hugged, patted, congratulated, has his hair tousled by everyone within two or three chairs of him.

There were many variations on this theme, of course, but basically that was it. The drama and emotion of it were spectacular. Of course there were those of us who stood up, open meeting after open meeting, waiting expectantly for the magic words which did not come. This was no fun.

After the open meeting was over, announcements made, final words to parents said, and songs sung, many of the newcomers were permitted to walk over and talk to their parents for a few minutes. Newcomers were informed before the open meeting if they were to have this privilege. Then they would say, when they stood up during the meeting to speak to their parents, "I'll get to talk to you after the meeting." Often came the reply, "All the way home."

THE SEED EXPERIENCE AFTER HOURS

Having described the nature of what took place at the Seed every day, I will return to my own story to focus on what happened outside the building itself. I believe my experiences were not atypical.

I spent my first night at Aaron's house still feeling that I should shortly be back home and in school as soon as the mistake was cleared up. In the morning Aaron and I were picked up by other Seedlings who lived nearby, and in a car full of Seedlings and their newcomers we drove to the Seed. Upon arriving and getting out of the car, a train of young men was formed, each with his hand upon the shoulder of the next one. In this manner we walked to the door and gave our names to the person who was signing us in. Every morning that I was a newcomer, the procedure was similar.

But despite this and other precautionary measures, many newcomers did attempt to split at certain moments when they felt they had a chance. Usually, they were caught immediately and restrained by physical force. As for those who did get away, very few had places to run to. They were usually retained later. Of course "splitting" could occur at any stage of the program—sometimes even an old-comer would run away from home and the Seed. It was primarily the newcomers, however, who made the attempt. An old-comer had more to lose; if you split and were brought back, you were made to start your program all over again from Day One.

The one thing I remember distinctly about my first full day at the Seed was that the morning rap was on "conning." It was a horrifying and awakening experience for me because, when people stood up and said things like, "I thought I could con the Seed by just saying everything they wanted me to," I realized that the Seed was after a very different, more fundamental, kind of change than I had thought. I was scared.

That night I tried to explain to Aaron that, although the Seed was obviously a wonderful place, I did not belong there. But Aaron adhered to the Seed's dogma, which said that if someone had smoked a joint even once, then that person belonged in the Seed. In fact, everyone could use a hitch in the Seed. Still, Aaron was admirably (in retrospect) unfirm. In fact, in response to my persistence and my distress, he said he would try to get me a conference with a staff member, although he did not think I would be able to convince a staff member either.

But this was an extremely unusual thing for an old-comer to say to his or her newcomer. All newcomers thought they didn't belong in the Seed. I don't think Aaron ever really acted on it—I don't think it would have looked good for him, as an old-comer, if he had made a request to staff for such a conference for no good reason. But as it turned out, I got my conference anyway, on my third day, because my sister had escaped from the Seed.

I was called out of the group to speak privately with Gloria, a nineteen-year-old staffer. Gloria wanted to see if I had noticed Judy's absence and what my reaction had been if I had. She began by saying, "As you probably know, your sister split this morning." We talked for an hour or so. At one point, as I was trying to explain that I did not have a "druggie attitude," Gloria asked me, "Have you ever been inside Raiford [State Penitentiary]?" I said I had not, and she said, "It's an *awful* place. People use you. They use your *body*." The implication was, if I did not get straight through the Seed, I was likely to end up in Raiford. The specter of prison was often held over the heads of resistant Seedlings, especially the youngest ones ("You wouldn't last very long at Raiford, smart-ass").

I wound up crying during this interview and, needless to say, I did not convince Gloria that I was straight and should be sent home. I must have, however, made some sort of impression because that night I was sent home with a different old-comer. He was a little older than Aaron, had been in the Seed longer (he was on his three months), and was a really "strong" Seedling. His name was Stan.

Stan had three Seedlings besides me living with him at the time. There were two other newcomers, and there was Joe, who was on his newcomer-living-at-home stage and who acted as a sort of assistant old-comer to Stan. (Joe's parents lived in St. Petersburg and so he could not return home before completing his program.)

The lineup at Stan's home was to shift during my four-week stay there. The other newcomers would get to go home before I would, and Joe was to be placed in another "foster home." At one point, for about a week, it was just Stan and me. Then, a couple of days before I was allowed to go home, he took another newcomer.

Stan lived with his father in an enormous house in Coral Gables, an hour and fifteen minutes' drive from the Seed. This distance was one factor that made sleep particularly sparse for his newcomers; Stan was the other. There were two adjoining rooms upstairs, a large bedroom and a small parallelogram-shaped room. It was these two rooms that the five of us shared, with Stan sleeping in his bed, and mattresses on the floor provided for the rest of us (including Joe). There was also a bathroom adjoining the bedroom, the door of which remained always open.

These two rooms each had one entrance door, other than the door they shared. Both of the entrance doors had security locks on them to which Stan alone had the keys. So at Stan's house I was under stricter security than I'd been at Aaron's house. Each night Joe slept in the small bedroom with two of the newcomers, while Stan slept in the big bedroom with the remaining newcomer—generally the one who was currently most in favor.

It is difficult to summarize my relationships with Stan and Joe and the other newcomers.

Newcomers were not allowed to talk to each other anyway, strictly speaking, so there was not a tremendous amount of conversation between us. But we were permitted to speak to each other in front of the old-comers. At breakfast and at certain other times there would often be light discussion of things, such as popular music, which were of no consequence. At these times everyone was allowed to talk to one another and it could be quite pleasant. (Exception: one twenty-four-hour period during which Stan sentenced me to absolute silence. He told me that I was not to utter one word to anyone, until he said I could, except in the group at the Seed.)

These were not the only opportunities we newcomers had to speak to each other, though. Often we would be driven back to Stan's house at night in a van full of Seedlings all going home to the same area. And sometimes two of us would be sitting together in the back unnoticed or ignored in all the conversation and song singing. Mostly, we simply talked about things we enjoyed, like music, but this was special because we could speak as equals in a peer relationship—a luxury in our situation. But sometimes we also spoke of the Seed or our old-comers or of our lives outside the Seed. These conversations were usually cut short by one newcomer for the sheer paranoia that such conversation induced, knowing as we did how thoroughly prohibited it was. Each one of us was vacillating between acting like human beings toward one another and trying to look good in the eyes of our old-comers (trying to become real believers in the Seed) so that we would get to go home. So the newcomer who said first, "Hey, you know this is bullshit and we shouldn't be talking to each other anyway!" obtained a kind of psychological advantage and felt safer, even if no one (no old-comer) was really listening in at the time.

So the newcomers were alternately in relationships of trust and distrust, support and competition with each other. If an old-comer saw any signs of two newcomers' forming a real bond, he made sure they were separated at all times.

The newcomer-old-comer relationship, on the other hand, was supposed to be intimate. It was the old-comer's responsibility to get his or her newcomer straight, and to do that the old-comer had to get to know his newcomer and highlight his newcomer's weaknesses and inconsistencies so that the newcomer would be willing to accept his old-comer's judgment and become a new person through the Seed.

Many times Stan screamed at me, "You don't argue with what I say! You just *accept* it!" Disputing the old-comer's word was high insolence and a sure sign of being full of shit, not honest, not working, etc. And one had to please one's old-comer if one were to entertain hopes of going home since the old-comer could (and sometimes did, though we never knew how often) report to the Seed staff on the newcomer's progress.

The things Stan told me, and insisted I must accept, were essentially the same things the Seed told everyone, but it was more personal and intense. I would mention that I had had two best friends, and Stan would state flatly that they were not my friends, nor had they ever been, nor had I ever been a friend to them. Stan insisted that I was completely insecure and unhappy before coming to the Seed. And he loved me too much to let me deny it.

Stan was a young man with an immense ego. Although we were not supposed to talk about our old druggie lives, at least not in any but the most derogatory terms, Stan insidiously bragged about his. He would recount to his newcomers numerous tales of all the LSD he had taken, girls he had bedded, and smashing parties he had thrown—and how through it all he had been secretly miserable. Although he had been undisputed king of his druggie world, inside he had been suffering, and late late at night when the parties were over, he would throw himself on his bed and cry. Poor Stan. Lucky thing he got straight. He also made sure to point out, especially to me, that he had always been an A-student with a genius's IQ, just in case I should make the error of imagining that I was smarter than he was.

Beginning on one's fourth night at the Seed, one had to write a "moral inventory" each night. This meant listing all the good things you did that day (e.g., "I participated honestly in the morning rap about my friends"), listing all your bad points of the day (e.g., "I was getting into my head during the afternoon rap"), and then explaining why you had your bad points (e.g., "I was copping out of the rap because it was blowing my image of myself"). The moral inventory I wrote each night had to satisfy Stan before I was allowed to go to sleep. Often he would have me do it over two or three times until it was "honest." "You should always have at least four or five good points and bad points," he said when I had trouble thinking of different ones to put down every night. Often he or Joe would think of a bad point that I should list, such as "false pride," and tell me to list it.

We newcomers got an average of five to six hours of sleep a night. Stan turned sleep into a privilege that was never granted before extracting a price of some sort. That price was usually a lie, a concession, a chunk of dignity—at the very least, a satisfactory moral inventory. Sleep was the carrot at the end of the stick; the newcomers never had enough of it. Stan knew it was his chief instrument of control, and he seemed to enjoy it. (Stan himself, being on his three months, did not have to spend twelve hours at the Seed the next day.)

Often I would be the last newcomer allowed to retire because I was arguing with Stan or Joe on some point about myself, my friends, or my sister—or things like whether or not I had read books like *Siddhartha* for pleasure or just to impress people. This kind of thing was often a heated point of argument because I had read much and had a good vocabulary. If I would mention a book I had read, or unwittingly use a word like *spontaneous,* I was vehemently accused of "playing the heavy intellectual." It was just a game I was playing, they said, the "heavy intellectual" game. I knew this was absurd, and it took me a long time to give in on this point, but I eventually did, since it was not one of the more important points, and my stubbornness only earned me more scorn and rage. It hurt, though, to say they were right, as it hurt to eventually agree that even my friendships had been worthless. Stan was bent on driving home that I was an absolute fool to think anything in my life before the Seed had had any value or validity whatsoever. Everything druggies did was for the purpose of appearing "cool." And I had been a druggie. It was as simple as that. No matter how many times I had actually smoked pot, the point was that I was "into acceptance" and a druggie. Stan was utterly furious and sometimes astonished at my unwillingness to be honest. He told me often that I was the "biggest asshole" of all the newcomers he'd ever had.

"What are you thinking?" he would demand, quite often, as if opening my head like a jar full of jelly beans were his natural right. Most of the time I would tell him truthfully. I wouldn't dare not answer, and I knew he could tell if I lied, because it would take me a moment to make something up or twist what I was thinking into something more acceptable to him. So I'd usually tell him precisely what I was thinking, and then he would pronounce it "bullshit" and tell me what I *should* think instead.

In one way, however, I must credit Stan. When his newcomers got home from the Seed each night, he fed us all wonderfully—things like little pizzas and most anything we wanted. There were a few nights, though, when he was especially angry with me and I was not allowed to eat anything. Still, I cannot say I was deprived of food. It was sleep that was drastically reduced.

There were many times when I was simply unable to last the day at the Seed without dozing off (a common predicament), and sometimes I could get away with it for fifteen minutes or so during the rules rap before being shaken awake. I also learned how to sleep with my eyes open. I believe many (perhaps most) newcomers did.

There was one night when Stan had a special guest sleep over. His name was Lloyd and he had been Joe's old-comer. Lloyd was eighteen and a very "strong" Seedling. He was venerated by both Stan and Joe, and of course he had words of wisdom to bestow on each of the newcomers. He told each of us that a haircut would help our attitudes greatly. (Stan eventually gave me a haircut. Almost all male newcomers submitted to haircuts before being allowed to go home.) And there was one point in the evening when he and Stan and Joe were all working on me at once, sitting on the floor in the small bedroom, and Lloyd leaned back for a moment and commented softly, "If you had not come to the Seed, you would not have ended up in prison. You would not have wound up dead or a junkie. *You* would have gone insane and wound up in a mental institution." And he looked me solemnly in the eye.

Joe nodded wisely. "Yes. I see that in him, too."

According to the Seed, there were only three roads a person could hope to travel after his first puff on a joint: death, prison, or insanity—unless he was saved by the Seed. Newcomers were told repeatedly, "You were just one step away from sticking a needle in your arm!"

Another heated point of debate between Stan and Joe and myself was their insistence that, had I met either one of them before any of us were in the Seed, I would have looked up to them for being better, "cooler" people than me, and they could have "used" me for whatever they had wanted. I maintained that I would have had nothing to do with people like them.

But for some reason, the only point on which I did not eventually give way to Stan was that I was happy before I came to the Seed. This was enough to enrage him. He would demand, "What about those nights when you lied awake in bed, wishing things were different somehow because you knew you just didn't feel right?" and I would reply that there had been no such nights. And he would tell me what an asshole I was and so on. It was in fact this very argument that, on the night before I was finally allowed to go home, led him to comment, "You've made some progress, but you're not even in the same *ballpark* as being allowed to go home."

But that progress I had made had already cost me dearly. I felt like I had betrayed my friends and my sister and that I was no longer the same person. Even if I were to be completely pulled off the program at that point, I could not go back to being the person I had been. I could no longer think clearly or reflect on things in the privacy of my own mind, the way I had used to. My mind was too cluttered and confused and reflexively frightened of being invaded. Stan had always been asking, "What are you thinking?" when I had least expected it. This "What are you thinking?" ploy of Stan's had been very effective in breaking down my resistance and cutting me off from my internal resources.

Of course, like all Seedlings, Stan only did what he did because he "loved" me. In fact, although it is possible that Stan may have been more zealous than most, I believe what old-comers did and said to their newcomers was all basically the same. (I never took a newcomer myself.) I heard many stories—some better, some a lot worse, than the kinds of things I went through at Stan's house.

I think that Stan was a genuine true believer in the Seed. Once, after a night of arguing with me, he sighed and said softly, "You know, even though you're so full of shit right now, I know you're gonna make it. You'll be another Seed success story." And once I heard him remark reverently to Joe, "The Seed will change the world. The Seed'll *be* the world some day."

For that was the mythology of the Seed into which we were all indoctrinated. The Seed would keep growing until there were Seeds in every city on the globe, and the Seed would transform the world. The Seed possessed ultimate, perfect wisdom, and the Seed was not merely the one drug program that worked (all other "rehabs" were "bullshit"); it was also the primary source of enlightenment to the entire world. In fact, any other belief system or activities that one might investigate to broaden one's mind, such as meditation or yoga, were categorically deemed "bullshit." There was no higher consciousness than that of the Seedling.

Art Barker talked often about "Seed City," which was certain to manifest in the not-too-distant future. And once, in an "old-timers' rap" (for Seedlings who had completed their programs), the rap leader was disgruntled at a few of the old-timers and remarked angrily, "This is *supposed* to be the top echelon of people in the *world*." Old-timers were, after all, consummated Seedlings.

BACK HOME

On my thirty-second day, a Monday, I was allowed to go home. I walked out the gate that night with one arm around each parent. When we got home, I told them how wrong I had been to them, how happy I was they had brought me to the Seed, and, many times, how much I loved them. There were smiles all around and I was fed all my favorite foods to my heart's content. (My parents had been stockpiling them for my return.) And I could walk around, take my dog out, play my records, use the toilet . . . all by myself. The freedom I experienced was heavenly, and I cannot say I was unhappy on this night. But underneath all the jubilance there was, deep down, a sick feeling. I had said to my parents all the things I knew I was supposed to say and which would make them happy. But as much as I tried to believe them, I knew in my heart that I did not feel these things. The brand new son that my folks were so pleased with was not who I really was.

A day or two after coming home I wrote a letter to my sister. She was now living in Miami in a drug rehabilitation/psychotherapy center called Genesis House. In this letter I told her all about the new person I was. I wrote eloquently about how wrong we had been to our parents and how fortunate I was to have stayed in the Seed. I disparaged my previous relationship with her. Months later I was to learn how deeply and harshly this letter had affected her. But at the time I wrote it, I only felt that it must at some point be intercepted and read by the Seed and that would be good for me since it would amount to proof of my loyalty.

I don't think it was really ever intercepted, but at the time I had a very fuzzy concept of the Seed's relationship to the U.S. mail. I felt they could somehow get a hold of anything. This was because of a few incidents which had taken place in the group while I was living away from home, when a rap leader had mentioned, or even read aloud to the group, intercepted letters.

One story sticks vividly in my mind (though not all of it took place when I was a newcomer):

Two Seedlings—Donna, an old-comer, and Leo, a newcomer living at home—had run away together. When they were caught and brought back to the Seed, they were made to stand in front of the group for a verbal lashing. He was a twerp, a pussy. And she—where could she hope to be in a few years?—standing on a street corner waiting for the next trick to come along! (When girls were stood up, they were almost invariably told that they were destined to become prostitutes if they didn't shape up.)

After the group finished with these two unspeakable ingrates, they were made to take their seats in the front row and start their programs over again. A few weeks later Leo escaped again and was heard from no more. But Donna stayed on her program and was well into her three months when the following event occurred.

One of the female staffers, Gloria, came out to lead the evening rap. Instead of announcing a familiar topic, she said, "I'd like to talk about some of those mushy things we used to do and say with our old druggie boyfriends and girlfriends, to make ourselves think we were really in *love*."

No one knew exactly what to say at first since this was so unusual. It was not a familiar theme. But people offered statements such as, "Well, my old boyfriend and I used to exchange little love notes. It made us feel like we were Romeo and Juliet or something."

After ten minutes or so of this Gloria said, "Donna Stratton, stand up."

From her seat in the group Donna stood.

Then Gloria produced a sheaf of letters that Donna had written over the months to Leo (who was now either in jail or reform school). The essence of what Donna wrote was that they were still in love, she was saving money, and when Donna got out of the Seed they could be together again. The group laughed uproariously at each sentimental word or phrase, and assorted snickers punctuated the rest. Then, after a brief come-down session, Donna was led up to the front row and started over yet again.

The funny thing about staff members like Gloria was that they could be quite kind and sympathetic to those whom they liked, and yet they were positively vicious to those whom they disliked. Most of the staffers fell into this category, which is why it was advantageous to be liked by them. Of course some were just generally vicious and some generally kind. Some, if you caught their eye during a rap, would give you a terrible hard look as if to say, "What are you looking at me for? Pay attention!" Some would ignore you. And there were one or two who would smile at you.

A week after arriving home I was allowed to go back to school, and two days after that I was on my three months.

There were about thirty-five Seedlings in my high school. They had all seen my face in the group and I was recognized immediately. I was instantly a member of their society. There were other Seedlings in two of my classes, and they both came right up and introduced themselves to me [on] my very first day back in school. One of them later showed me where the "Seed lunch table" was in the cafeteria, so I could sit with the other Seedlings. There was even a spot where the Seedlings gathered at the end of the school day, to chat or arrange rides to the Seed.

Everyone was extremely friendly and I felt welcomed. At the end of the day one or two of them would ask me if I'd had any hassles. This was a way of showing concern and interest to the newcomer back in school. Hassles were one of two things: come-ons from your old druggie friends who were trying to make you talk to them or simply people harassing you because you were a Seedling. It was easy to see that you were a Seedling if you had been absent from class for an extended period of time, had a haircut, hung out with the other Seedlings, and refused to talk to anyone else. Many students enjoyed hassling Seedlings. The proper response was to say, "I love you," and ignore them.

As far as my old druggie friends were concerned, I had only one in school, and he, like me, had done very little to earn the title "druggie," at least as far as drugs were concerned.

George was in my first period class and I sat immediately behind him. My first day back in school, when he looked up and saw me, I said nothing but simply took my seat. He turned around, looked at me, and asked, "Same as you were?"

I smiled an arrogant Seed smile. "A little different," I said.

"I liked the way you were."

"Turn around. I can't talk to you."

I was already afraid that, if another Seedling was in the class, I had already said too much by answering George's first question.

Of course I learned that day just which of my classes did have other Seedlings, and it did not take more than a day or two before I decided that George was really straight after all, and it would be okay for me to talk to him.

But George "looked like a druggie," and when another Seedling spotted me talking to him one day, he pointed this out and asked if George was an old friend. Yes, I replied. But he was straight.

No, he was not straight. He was "dry," perhaps, but just by looking at him you could tell he was a druggie.

There was a category known as "dry druggies"—people who had gotten high before but were currently not using any drugs. Part of the Seed catechism was that there was absolutely no way to "get straight on your own"—these attempts were always doomed to failure. Even such drastic measures as the "geographical cure"—moving away from the area where your druggie friends lived—could not succeed because you were still "into acceptance."

In school someone had to look *very* straight for it to be all right to talk to them. George, with hair pronouncedly over his ears, did not meet this criterion.

So within a week of being back in school, I was in trouble. At the lunch table I was the sole object of discussion that day. I must say, however, it was *not* a come-down session. There was no name calling or threats (although the threats were implicit). Everyone seemed genuinely concerned with showing me, by argument, that talking to George was "dangerous." (Druggies in general were "dangerous" to talk to because they could lead you back into your old ways. Old friends and ex-Seedlings—those who had been "pulled off" the program by their parents and were no longer straight—were the most dangerous because they knew how to "push buttons in your head.") Hadn't George once been a part of the life I had led before the Seed? He was a dry druggie at best—and how did I know he wasn't using drugs now? He could be lying to me.

Fortunately for me, and to the credit of the Seedlings at my high school, I don't think this incident was ever reported back to the Seed. I certainly would have heard about it if it had been. Other Seedlings had been put on refreshers or even started over for less serious offenses. "Talking to old druggie friends" was a cardinal sin.

I told George the next day that I could not talk to him. When I reported this to a fellow Seedling he good-naturedly corrected me: "You should say you don't *want* to talk to him. Not you *can't*." So that is what I said the next time George tried to talk to me.

Seedlings were supposed to keep an eye on each other in school (although some followed this directive much more enthusiastically than others). If someone was even missing from the Seedlings' lunch table, it was cause for deep suspicion. School officials and teachers were in no way part of this arrangement, although now and then the school did cooperate with the Seed in small ways (such as the way my sister and I were called to the dean's office to go to the Seed). Many teachers, however, expressed open disapproval of the Seed.

Seedlings were forbidden to talk to reporters about the Seed, and once, when a group of teachers in a couple of schools suggested open after-school discussion sessions about the Seed—with Seedlings, ex-Seedlings, and former friends of Seedlings—this was also strictly forbidden. These were offenses punishable by as much as starting over, or so it seemed from the dire warnings we all received at the Seed. The rationale was that all these people merely had a "con" they wanted to perpetrate.

I eventually worked out an arrangement with George whereby I talked to him only one period a day, in gym class. The reason I gave George for this was that although I was still committed to the Seed, I did not think it would harm me to talk to him just one period per day.

The real reason was that I felt safe because gym class was held outside, and there was no chance of another Seedling's walking by, as in a classroom. Of course I did not admit to myself that this was the reason. I dared not admit to myself that I felt anything but fierce loyalty to the Seed.

Of course my relationship with George was never quite the same.

I spent a total of exactly three months, two weeks, and four days on my "three months." I graduated from the Seed nine days after my fifteenth birthday. For a few weeks it was still mandatory for me to come to the "old-timers' raps" on Tuesday and Saturday nights. But when I started missing them here and there, and no one said anything, I gradually got the idea that I could come or not come as I pleased. Over the months I attended them less and less, as did most Seedlings.

A year or so after completing my program I was excommunicated from the Seed community at school for talking to druggies, growing my hair long, and showing various other signs of attitude disintegration. I was not the first. About half the Seedlings I had been on my program with had already gone back to drugs and their old friends. Within a year I was to see all but one or two of the other half do the same.

I would like to insert an anecdote that pertains to the apparent loyalty all Seedlings had to the Seed:

When I was still a newcomer living at Stan's, the Seed was trying to obtain a license to open up in Dade County (Miami). During this period of time a song was introduced and sung frequently in the group. It was called "When the Seed Comes into Dade," and it was sung to the tune of "When the Saints Go Marching In." During renditions of this song we would all wave our hands above our heads in a hallelujah-type gesture and sing more and more exuberantly with each repetition of the verse. (There was only one.)

And there was one time when, in the group, the rap leader asked who would like to go down to the courthouse (or wherever it was the whole matter was to be decided) to support the Seed, and everyone eagerly raised their hands. The lucky ones who were permitted to go got to spend the day sitting around the courthouse singing songs.

And finally, when, in the middle of an open meeting one night, Art Barker strode into the room and announced that the Seed had won its license, I was among the three-minute standing ovation that ensued. And despite my adversarial relationship with Stan, despite the fact that I was there unwillingly, despite my general misery—I somehow felt included in the victory.

THE AFTERMATH AND MY INTERNAL PROCESS

Shortly after my experience in the Seed, I did use drugs again—many more drugs, in fact, than I had used prior to the Seed. My relationship with my parents deteriorated severely; it became far more fraught with hostility than it had ever been before the Seed. My school grades fell and I failed classes for the first time in my life.

I knew and spoke with many ex-Seedlings during the first couple of years after I graduated the program. Some, like me, were deeply bitter about the experience. But most were indifferent; they seemed to have gotten over it quickly, and they wondered aloud why I couldn't do the same. One or two even contended that it had been good for them to have received a little shaking up at the right time. They felt that, although they were basically back to the lives they had led before the Seed, they were now somewhat more in control.

I have no explanation for these differing perspectives, and I do not know what these individuals might say today. I have long lost contact with all of them. There is a Web site for Seed survivors, where the great majority of participants feel that the Seed did them terrible, traumatic harm. But of the thousands of children who were forced into the Seed and who went through the program, only a hundred or so have posted to this Web site.

It took me well over a decade to understand what had happened to me, what the Seed had done to my psyche, and what I'd done to myself while I was in the Seed. I strongly suspect that my internal process was very similar to that of many other Seedlings, though I cannot speak for others.

In a nutshell the Seed forced me to "mean things that were not true." Under the combined pressures of sleep deprivation, lack of privacy, and constant haranguing—both at the Seed and in Stan's charge—I eventually, with my words, betrayed everything that was sacred to me at that time in my life. I felt that if my friends on the outside still had any good feelings for me, then I no longer deserved them.

The obvious question, though, is *why did I have to mean it?* Why couldn't I simply say what I was being forced to say but hold the words more lightly? Why couldn't I—or anyone else, for that matter—simply "con" the Seed?

I think many kids actually did con the Seed. But I couldn't, and I imagine most other kids couldn't either. The strategy I believe most Seedlings adopted (including me) was to try and persuade themselves that the Seed had to be right. Maintaining a consistent lie, a conscious subterfuge, under such stressful conditions was a tall order for an unsophisticated young teenager. Also, I saw other Seedlings getting busted for conning right and left in the group. (I have no idea how many of those accused of conning were actually deliberately conning, any more or less than the rest of us.)

I remember a moment of horror, on the evening of my seventh or eighth day, when I realized that I was unable to "think" any longer. I had lost the ability to retreat into the sanctuary of my own mind and think things through, because I had grown so accustomed to being intruded upon without a moment's notice. It was as if I'd had a sealed-off room in my head that had previously been accessible only to myself, and now even I could not enter. (I think I may have known even then, in my heart of hearts, that I would regain access to this room at some point in my life, but it would be a long time, much longer than I could accept at age fourteen.)

During my time with Stan, I put a great deal of energy into resisting him. I set up a psychic force field, as it were, between us. To keep from being devoured I had to maintain a certain tension, a precarious balance between overt resistance and total surrender. So I emerged at last from his dominion with a certain meager sense of myself intact. But still, I felt horribly guilty and empty, as if I had been pillaged and broken.

At some point shortly after being allowed to go home, I was sitting in the large warehouse room, in the group, at the Seed, pondering how I still believed myself to be "different" from everyone else there and wondering what good it did me to feel this way. I could see how it was causing me pain. I could not see how it would ever serve me. My fate, as far ahead as I could see, was locked. There was nothing for me but to be a Seedling. I might as well be one, then, and wholeheartedly embrace whatever attendant rewards there were. There were some: I could feel a part of something larger than myself. I could be part of an (albeit self-proclaimed) elite. I could have friends, a community, an identity. Why hold out for some other ambiguous set of rewards that I had already sold myself out of anyway?

And here is where I made a strange decision. I decided to make myself a true Seedling. All the energy I had put into resisting Stan, I now directed at my own resistance. I now became my own primary oppressor, working to deny and even to *change* my genuine feelings. After all, I already felt that I *had* betrayed myself (and all of my friends), I was already lost; one step further would not make a difference. I could not see the light at the end of the tunnel.

In one sense this "strategy" worked brilliantly. I moved through the rest of the program very quickly. Perhaps it was only an extension, really, of what I'd been doing in the Seed all along up until then—nothing fundamentally different in kind. Whenever the tension between what I really thought and felt and what I was "supposed to" think and feel became too apparent and unbearable to me, I had to deny the conflict and push it out of mind. I was unable to "ride out" the discomfort of being divided. My choices were either to consciously live a lie or start working internally against my own emotions. I didn't feel myself capable of the former.

The ultimate consequence of this process for me was a profound loss of self-respect, a sickening self-disgust that lingered for years, and piercing emotional pain.

As a result of my experience in the Seed, everything seemed a mockery of itself. I fundamentally doubted the authenticity of any conviction, any emotion—my own or anyone else's. The Seed, in my psyche, had crapped all over everything. Nothing stood apart, unsullied by the shadow of the Seed's judgment. I had acquiesced in adopting that judgment as my own for a time, and I could not easily disown it. It had sunk in deeper than my rational mind.

The process of putting things back into their proper perspective vis-à-vis the Seed—that is, learning to see and *feel* the Seed as just one tiny, narrow-minded, self-aggrandizing pocket of fear in the world, as opposed to a fundamental frame of reference—corresponded to the process of learning to *forgive myself* for what I had done, for the part I had played in my own undoing.

First, I had to realize that, rightly or not, I did hold myself accountable; I did blame myself. From there I needed to look at the fourteen-year-old kid I had been in 1972, and understand the pressures he was under, and have compassion for the choices he made, and accept that I hadn't been perfect, or maybe just not as heroic and invulnerable as I would have liked to have been. These insights crystallized in my mind just about fourteen years after the Seed, when I was twenty-eight. I think of this as the time when my emotional healing really began to take hold.

CONCLUDING THOUGHTS AND OBSERVATIONS

I was younger than most Seedlings and had had less experience with drugs than most Seedlings. Still, *the vast majority of Seedlings—over 95 percent—were not addicts. They were teens experimenting with drugs who had been forced into the Seed against their will.*

The Seed was a highly publicized and controversial program. Everyone talked about it. There were news reports and articles about it. The Seed thrust *itself* into the public eye; Art Barker was an incorrigible grandstander, and there were even Seed license plates proclaiming, "The Seed Loves You." But too much attention proved damaging to the Seed. In 1974 the United States Senate published a study that accused the Seed of using methods similar to North Korean communist brainwashing techniques. The Senate stated that the Seed's teenage clients were "subjected to experimental and potentially harmful treatments." This type of bad press, in conjunction with legal pressure from the National Institute on Drug Abuse, coupled with withdrawal of federal funds, forced the Seed out of Dade County and caused the Seed to scale back its operations dramatically. By the 1980s it had shrunk to a small fraction of its former size and was officially taking kids and adults only on a voluntary basis. The Seed endured in this diminished capacity until it closed in 2001.

Successor programs to the Seed, including the notorious Straight, Inc. (which was founded by fanatical Seed parents), have been, by all accounts, much more savvy and meaner than the Seed. Most of these programs have avoided publicity; they have flown under the public radar. They are also far more tightly controlled, and their teenaged "clients" are subjected to levels of physical and emotional stress that make the Seed seem mild by comparison.

The fact that certain elements in the Seed were *uncontrolled*—for example, what took place between old-comers and newcomers in the old-comers' homes—represented a risk for unmonitored abuse but also an opportunity for breaths of fresh air. For example, the fact that my fellow Seedlings at school did not turn me in for talking to George—this was an occasion on which the redemptive and unpredictable human element quietly expressed itself. Even at Stan's house there was often an unstructured, genuine conviviality around mealtimes. These uncontrolled moments and unsupervised dynamics were important threads of sanity. The Seed, in some ways, was loosely structured, and I believe this was a saving grace for some of us.

By contrast, in hundreds of "residential teen treatment centers" today, children are imprisoned *at the facility itself* twenty-four hours a day, for months at a time. In these programs ongoing psychological and verbal abuse is accompanied by the threat and administration of severe physical abuse. There are many documented accounts of these horrors on the Internet and elsewhere. The organization ASTART (Alliance for the Safe, Therapeutic, and Appropriate Use of Residential Treatment), an association of mental health professionals concerned about teen abuse, has compiled numerous first-person reports like this one. Most of them describe events far more disturbing than those that took place at the Seed.

Based on what I have read—the testimony of program survivors—it remains the case that the vast majority of the TENS OF THOUSANDS of teens currently incarcerated in these cruel and abusive programs *are not drug addicts.* These teens did *not* pose an imminent danger to themselves or others before being committed and locked up. They were merely doing what millions of other teens do, namely, experimenting with drugs and sex.

I call on parents to weigh the possible consequences of committing their child to a "therapeutic facility" whose day-to-day operations are mysterious. If you are worried that your child is in danger, there are licensed, reputable alternatives to coercive behavior modification.

I am very dubious about the value of coercive persuasion. There are some program graduates who will testify that such treatment saved their lives. While I cannot dispute anyone else's personal testimony, it is nonetheless hard to imagine that such treatment can have long-term benefits for any but the most desperately troubled and self-destructive drug users and addicts. Such treatment certainly does NOT improve long-term relations between children and parents. On the contrary, an ordeal of this kind can sever the parent-child bond permanently.

I call on parents to consider that what they are purchasing, when they turn their children over to such programs, is a "product," not a "process." What I mean is that parents are *not* buying a course of therapeutic treatment for their children; they are buying the "end product" that the program promises: a well-behaved, well-groomed, drug-free, grateful, and obedient child.

The Seed was a harmful and traumatic episode in my life, and it took me years to heal from it. Given that I've had a lot of luck and a lot of help, and also given that the Seed was a gentle program compared to most analogous programs operating today, I am extremely concerned for the well-being of teenagers in today's behavior modification/coercive thought reform "treatment centers." Were the Seed still in existence, I would advocate that it be closed. I feel that much more strongly about the unregulated "teen help" industry that now exists in frightening proportions.

I offer this testimony in hopes that it may contribute to larger organized efforts to curtail the reprehensible activities of those who profit from inflicting systematic abuse and misery on vulnerable children.

STRAIGHT, INC.

Out of the Seed grew Straight, Inc., a program that was very similar to the Seed. Founded in 1976 by Mel Sembler, Straight was staffed by former Seed parents and program graduates, some of whom had also worked at the Seed. Earlier Sembler had enrolled one of his sons in the Seed.

Controversy swirled around Straight until its demise. Sembler and his colleagues were lightning rods for critics who claimed that Straight staffers engaged in abusive, controlling, and brainwashing tactics (Barstow 1991; Burgess 1983; Finkel 1987; Hurst 1990; Latimer 1984; Rivera 1990; Zibart 1983). According to a recent article in *Mother Jones* magazine:

Sembler knows a thing or two about the humiliations of involuntary confinement. For 17 years, he directed Straight, Inc., a substance-abuse rehab and behavior modification program that treated American teens like terrorism suspects. Sembler's official bio boasts that the "remarkable program"—where children had to flap their arms like chickens or else face shaming as "sluts" and homosexuals—treated 12,000 kids. President George H.W. Bush hailed it as one of his "thousand points of light." But in the early '90s, amid state investigations and suits filed by clients claiming physical and mental abuse, his clinics were dismantled. Hundreds of Straight alums now claim they were scarred for life, among them Samantha Monroe, who was enrolled in 1980 at age 12 and claims she was starved, raped, and confined in a closet.   (Gorenfield 2006)

Straight was controversial from the beginning. Within a year of its creation several ex-counselors complained to authorities that Straight was abusing children (Szalavitz 2006). The *St. Petersburg Times* quoted one former counselor as saying, "The program was getting . . . so bad that I felt it was hurting more kids than it was helping" (Nottingham 1978, quoted in Szalavitz 2006:53). Nonetheless, between 1981 and 1989 Straight expanded its operations to Atlanta, Cincinnati, Boston, Detroit, Orlando, Virginia, and California. Before long, lawsuits alleging abuses were filed and investigations were launched. An official of the American Civil Liberties Union dubbed Straight "a brutal program" and "a concentration camp for throwaway kids" (Moore 1982, quoted in Szalavitz 2006:54).

Central figures in the Straight controversy are Fred Collins, Leigh Bright, and Richard Bradbury, former Straight clients who decided to make public their claims of widespread abuse. Collins grew up in Alexandria, Virginia, and was in his first year of college at Virginia Tech when he encountered Straight. His parents were concerned about his drug and alcohol use, as well as his brother's substance abuse, and arranged to enroll both in Straight. Fred Collins eventually fled Straight and sued the program for false imprisonment, intentional infliction of emotional distress, and assault and battery. The case was heard in the federal court for the Eastern District of Virginia and covered extensively by the *Washington Post*, Florida newspapers, and the television program *60 Minutes* (Szalavitz 2006). In addition to presenting evidence of Straight's abuse of Collins, Collins's attorney called another Straight client, Leigh Bright, to the witness stand. Szalavitz (2006) provides a compelling description of Bright's testimony:

Leigh Bright testified about a series of events that began with her punishment for refusing to participate in exercise. She was thrown face-first to the floor repeatedly by girls making her do "push ups." Toe-touches were simulated by grabbing her by the hair, yanking her head back violently, and then forcing her forward. "They did that so many times that my head went numb," Leigh said.

Then, she was carried "like a pig on a skewer," into the open meeting room. Soon thereafter, angered by her continued defiance, Straight's national clinical director, Miller Newton, grabbed Bright by the hair, dragged her to the floor, and cursed at her, ordering that she be kept awake and "marathoned" for three days. For over seventy hours at her "host home" and in the Straight building, Leigh was shouted at and doused with water: anything to keep her eyes open. She was even slammed into a concrete wall. At one point, she was dragged off the toilet while having a bowel movement and made to clean feces from the toilet bowl with her bare hands and a paper towel. . . . Eventually, she began to hallucinate.   (49–50)

The jury in the Collins case quickly returned a verdict in his favor, concluding that Collins had been falsely imprisoned by Straight (Szalavitz 2006; Zibart 1983).

And then there is Richard Bradbury's saga with Straight. According to Leonora LaPeter (2006), a reporter for the St. Petersburg Times, Bradbury says a fire fighter molested him when he was eleven, abuse that continued for three years with a high school principal and other men acquainted with the fire fighter. Bradbury dropped out of school; he claims he was not addicted to drugs when his parents brought him to Straight.

According to Bradbury, as reported by LaPeter and Szalavitz, other teens enrolled in Straight forced him to sit up in a plastic chair for ten to twelve hours a day. If he leaned back, he was thrown to the floor and others sat on his arms, legs, and chest. Bradbury says he was physically beaten and sometimes forbidden to use the bathroom.

Bradbury eventually graduated, joined the Straight staff, and physically beat other teens. He left Straight in 1985; Bradbury reports that he discovered other counselors were sexually abusing teens and tried to report it, only to be told to keep quiet or be returned to the program as a client. According to Szalavitz,

What Richard had learned about how Straight used [sexual humiliation] made him increasingly uncomfortable. He says he kept hearing that some of the female counselors had moved beyond verbal taunts and into physical sexual molestation. The verbal stuff alone was pretty horrifying: boys were constantly called "cocksuckers" and "faggots" while girls were labeled "sluts" and "whores."

By late 1985, Richard had decided to quit. He wrote a six-page resignation letter, complete with names of those he believed to be the perpetrators of sexual abuse. He distributed it to the entire staff and left. A few days later, Richard says, he received a phone call from one of Straight's top executives, who asked him to come in for a talk. He says that when he arrived, he was baited and attacked. The leadership didn't want to change the program, Richard learned— but they did very much want to keep him quiet. When he noticed that the program's consulting psychiatrist was lurking in the hallway, he began to think that Straight staffers were trying deliberately to anger him, in hopes that he would get physical and give them a reason to have him committed. (2006:42–44)

Bradbury put considerable time into his efforts to expose abuses at Straight. He completed all the forms required by federal privacy law to gain release of his files from Straight, files that Bradbury believed would document the abuses he suffered, but he met with limited success. Bradbury was also frustrated in his attempts to convince state regulators to investigate Straight (Szalavitz 2006). Bradbury said he eventually decided to break into Straight offices in an attempt to steal the files of Straight's clients to prove his allegations. On the night of January 26, 1988, Bradbury dropped in on a rope hung through the skylight. He heard sirens and ran out the back door empty-handed. He turned himself in, was sentenced to five years' probation for burglary, and was ordered to stay away from the Semblers.

In 1989 Bradbury organized an anti-Straight group with chapters around the country. Dozens of former clients accused Straight of kidnapping, beating, and other abuses. Bradbury reached out to dozens of families that had been sued by Straight because they owed the program money. Bradbury eventually contacted an NBC affiliate, and its news staff taped interviews with Straight participants.

One of the most dramatic episodes in Bradbury's persistent efforts to expose Straight occurred in December 1991 (Szalavitz 2006). Bradbury had organized a number of protesters to picket outside Straight's headquarters in St. Petersburg, Florida. In the midst of the protest four teenagers fled the program, chased by angry staffers. Shortly thereafter an area television talk show, *Eye on Tampa*, devoted a program to the Straight controversy. Bradbury produced graphic photographs of Straight clients who claimed to have been physically abused. The Florida inspector general began an investigation and found in 1993 that "despite 'a propensity for abuse or excessive force,'" Straight kept getting licensed: "It appears that pressure may have been generated by Ambassador Sembler and other state senators" (LaPeter 2006). By the end of the year all the Straight programs had been closed. A *St. Petersburg Times* editorial on Straight bearing the headline "A Persistent Foul Odor" began: "Straight, Inc. is dead and buried in Florida, and well that is" (Szalavitz 2006:59).

But the day after Straight shut its doors in Orlando, a new program, SAFE

(Substance Abuse Family Education), opened in the same building with the same staff and model (Billman 2003; Szalavitz 2006).

SAFE (SUBSTANCE ABUSE FAMILY EDUCATION)

In January 2003 reporter Jeffrey Billman of the *Orlando Weekly* shocked central Florida with yet another scandal involving a program for struggling teens. Billman told the harrowing story of Jeffrey Henschel, a teen whose parents had enrolled him in SAFE:

> The Henschels' problems began when Barbara found what she thought to be pills in her son's room. (She learned later that she'd found vitamins.) Barbara consulted the private counselor that she hired to treat her son's behavior problems. The counselor said Jeff didn't have a drug problem. But she pressed, and the counselor referred them to Kids Helping Kids, an eight-month rehab program in Milford, Ohio, close to the Henschels' Cold Springs, Ky., home.
>
> Barbara called and got the stiffest sales pitch she'd ever heard. "If he doesn't get help right away he'll die," the receptionist told her. Barbara hung up the phone an hour later, convinced Jeff was in trouble. . . .
>
> A representative from Kids Helping Kids called Barbara almost daily for two weeks, assuring her that insurance would cover 80 percent of the cost, and that Jeff could attend a similar program, SAFE, in Orlando. Barbara was sold. Her son was a drug addict and his life was on the line. She cut the initial $5,000 check and had her husband Claude fly with Jeff to Orlando. He enrolled at SAFE May 2, 1999.

According to the *Orlando Weekly* report, when Jeff's parents removed him from the program four months later, he was a different kid. His mother said that Jeff was pale and acne-ridden after being denied sunlight his entire stay. He had more than ninety infected, self-inflicted scars on his body, many of which are still visible today. He was thirty pounds lighter, and had high levels of an attention-deficit disorder drug in his system; doctors later told Barbara that he would have died if he stayed longer. Jeff later spent two weeks at Wellspring, an Albany, Ohio facility that specializes in deprogramming brainwashed ex-cult members.

SAFE has since closed its doors.

NORTH STAR EXPEDITIONS

Thus far we have reviewed how SEED evolved into Straight, which morphed into SAFE, and how all three iterations used abusive tactics as core program practices. Sadly, unsafe practices in a wilderness program called North Star Expeditions also resulted in tragedy.

Aaron Bacon grew up in Phoenix. During his high school years he began using drugs and, according to his parents, hanging out with the wrong crowd. His parents became very concerned and, based on a friend's recommendation, enrolled him in a wilderness therapy program for struggling teens, North Star Expeditions (Szalavitz 2006). According to Szalavitz, on March 1, 1994, Bacon was awakened at 6 a.m. by two strangers, one of whom told Bacon, "You're coming with me. If I detect any resistance, I'll assume you are trying to get away and I'll take the appropriate action. Do I make myself clear?" (2006:81). Bacon was driven to the local airport and flown in a small plane to Escalante, Utah. After they arrived, Bacon was strip-searched and driven deep into the desert to begin the program. Almost immediately, Bacon showed signs of distress, documented in his journals. He complained of severe hunger, gastrointestinal discomfort, and emotional trauma. As he recorded in his journals,

> I can tell already that it is going to test my physical limitations and broaden them. I am pretty scared of the next couple of weeks. I've been sick all day with a horrible stomachache. It's been heck hiking as much as we do. We are on "impact" getting rid of all the toxins in our bodies by not eating. I suppose it won't be bad because I don't know how to cook well enough yet. I feel really bad after eating. . . .
>
> I feel like I am losing control of my body. I've peed in my pants every night for the last three nights and today when we started our little hike, I took a dump in my pants. I didn't even feel it coming, it just happened. I told Jeff, because I thought he might be more sympathetic and easy on me, but he yelled to Craig, "Hey, he took a dump in his pants." All the other students started to laugh. . . . I've been telling [the staff] that I'm sick for a while and they say I'm faking it. . . .
>
> All I can think about is cold and pain. . . . I miss my family so much. My hands, my lips and my face are dead. (Szalavitz 2006:84, 87–88)

By March 29, only four weeks after his arrival, Bacon was in deep physical and emotional distress. According to Szalavitz (2006), "Aaron was so sickly that he could walk no farther. The other campers carried him back to base camp. He vomited all over them, babbling incoherently about seeing purple stars in a purple sky. Again, he asked for medical attention and again, despite obvious evidence to the contrary, he was called a faker by program staff. The other campers—who'd seen Aaron naked when they'd done 'full body hygiene' and stripped to wash both their bodies and their laundry—were already describing Aaron as 'weak and brittle' and like 'a skeleton' or an 'old man' or someone 'from Ethiopia'" (89). Shortly thereafter Bacon collapsed and died. Bacon's story and his experience with North Star Expeditions were featured prominently in the media (Krakauer 1995; Morgenstern 1995; Smith 1995). Jon Krakauer (1995), writing in *Outside* magazine, described the sad end to Aaron's life:

> The long-distance connection was good, but as Sally Bacon stood in her Phoenix kitchen, she couldn't make sense of what she was hearing. A month before, she'd sent her 16-year-old son, Aaron, to a Utah wilderness school called North Star Expeditions. Now a disembodied voice from North Star was telling her, "Aaron is down. We can't get a pulse."
>
> "What does that mean, you can't get a pulse?"
>
> "Aaron's been airlifted to the hospital in Page, Arizona," came the reply. "Call your husband. He's been given the hospital phone number." Sally frantically dialed Bob Bacon at his office. Sounding numb, he repeated what he knew: Aaron had collapsed in the desert. It was a freak accident. There was nothing anyone could do. Their son was dead.

According to the autopsy, the cause of Aaron's death was acute peritonitis resulting from a perforated ulcer. The contents of Aaron's gastrointestinal tract had leaked through two holes in his small intestine, spreading a massive infection throughout his abdominal cavity (Krakauer 1995).

North Star Expeditions has since closed, but it has a compelling legacy. William Henry, owner of North Star Expeditions, pleaded guilty to negligent homicide in Aaron's death and was given three years of probation (Schemo 2007; Gordon 2000). Aaron's father, Bob, shared his personal anguish and plea for reform in the struggling-teen industry when he addressed the U.S. House of Representatives, Committee on Education and Labor, in 2007:

> Speaking for my wife, and Aaron's mother Sally, his brother Jarid and his sister Kia Sullivan; and speaking on behalf of the many families not at this table whose lives have been shattered by these fraudulent programs, we deeply appreciate your efforts to put a stop to this country's growing industry of institutionalized child abuse.

During our search for the best alternative to the remaining three months of Aaron's sophomore year in high school, my wife and I spoke with therapists, counselors, pastors and doctors until we were eventually referred by friends to North Star Expeditions, a now defunct, but formerly licensed Utah-based program that billed itself as a "wilderness therapy program for troubled teens."

After reading their very compelling brochure, speaking to their office by phone, and finally meeting the owners for a personal interview, we thought we had found the perfect situation: Caring people who were experienced in counseling kids who were struggling with drugs and social pressure—and to top it off—writing in a daily journal we were told was an integral part of their "counseling" program. As a writer, we felt journaling would help Aaron to sort things out; and we were certain that, as a poet Aaron would find the awesome beauty of southern Utah to be inspirational and spiritually healing.

Of course, being normal, trusting and honest people ourselves—we assumed we were being told the truth. We were dead wrong. His mother and I will never escape our decision to send our gifted 16 year old son to his death at North Star. The guilt of our apparent naiveté was crippling. We were conned by their fraudulent claims, and will go to our graves regretting our gullibility.

Adding further to our regret, we were talked into using their escort service. Aaron was taken from his bed at 5:00 AM on Tuesday morning, March the 1st, 1994 by two burly strangers who announced to Aaron with a tone of authority that any resistance on his part would be countered with whatever physical force was necessary. He was not allowed to speak to us, or put on any shoes.

His eyes expressed a strange mixture of anger, despair, fear and loving sadness. I was able to manage only the briefest of hugs which, being restrained, he could not return. In the trauma of this surreal instant I offered words of comfort without thinking of their potentially ominous meaning when I said, "Aaron, I know you will find God in the wilderness." Little did I know that these would be the last words I would ever speak to my youngest son!

His mother managed only a fleeting moment to cradle his face in her hands and utter her spontaneous words of love and the assurance that he would later see that this was really for the best.

I cried inconsolably from the depths of my soul as the escort van backed out of our driveway with our terrified son silently pleading with his sad eyes for us not to send him away. This excruciating scene would have to serve for the rest of our lives as the last living memory of our beautiful son.

Aaron arrived in the Escalante Wilderness Area of southern Utah that same night and waited a few days for a brief intake exam, indoctrination into the rules of the program, and the issue of ill-fitting shoes and clothing. This picture of him was taken on March 8th, when he was noted as weighing 131 pounds on a lanky 5'-11" frame.

Aaron's bloody and tattered journal would contain no poetry, but would record in his own words an unbelievable account of torture, abuse and neglect; a horrific tale that is corroborated by the journals of the so-called "counselors", along with the journals and sworn testimony of his troubled young cohorts.

This calendar was assembled by criminal investigators from program records and chronicles 21 days of ruthless and relentless physical and psychological abuse and neglect. Aaron spent 14 of his 20 days on the trail without any food whatsoever, while being forced to hike 8–10 miles per day. On the days he did have food it consisted of undercooked lentils, lizards, scorpions, trail mix, and a celebrated canned peach on the 13th. On top of this, with temperatures below freezing, he endured 13 of 20 nights with only a thin wool blanket, plus 5 nights without warmth or protection of any kind. Aaron complained of severe stomach pain and asked to see a doctor as early as the third day of hiking, and by the tenth day had lost all control of his bodily functions; but unbelievably, as he got weaker and lost nearly 20% of his body weight they repeatedly refused to send him to a doctor. Taken from what appears to be the industry handbook, their policy had predetermined that these kids are all liars and manipulators and therefore "Aaron was faking."

[Slide #3] This grotesque skeleton is what Aaron looked like when he was seen the evening before he died by Georgette Costigan, the registered EMT who, still insisting that he was faking, didn't even take his vital signs, but instead took the occasion to barter a meager piece of cheese in return for his promise to try harder and hike the following day. This company-employed EMT, and relative of owner Bill Henry, dismissed his final desperate plea to see a doctor who could prove he wasn't faking and made a conscious decision to prove a point rather than render aid, thus effectively killing our son rather than saving him.

What you cannot see in these photos are the bruises, cuts, lesions, rashes, blisters and open sores that covered Aaron's body from head to toe. These scars of abuse and the dried skin stretched taut over his bones are what his mother and I were left to discover without any warning when the sheet was pulled back at the mortuary. This, we screamed, could not be our son as we grabbed each other and collapsed to our knees, but the scar above his now sunken right eye told us that it was. It was in that one shocking moment of proof that our lives changed forever.

The stories of Aaron's death and the others who have died, or survived the abuses of these programs, are chilling reminders of the dangers of absolute power, and point out the extremely high risks in allowing these programs to operate without strict regulation and oversight.

This country, this congress and this committee are faced as never before with several urgent and critically important choices.

If we choose economic growth over human rights; if we choose no-growth-in-government over the safety of our children; and if we continue to place our faith in the self-regulation of private enterprise over the mandate of our government to protect our nation's health, safety and welfare, we are choosing to fail in our sacred obligations to our children, our families, and our future.

I implore you, as I know Aaron would, to PLEASE stop paying lip service to "family values" and start placing "value-in-families." We can do this in part, by investing the resources of the American people in our children who will soon inherit our challenging legacy; and we can START NOW by putting a stop to these fraudulent and destructive programs of institutionalized child abuse. (Bacon 2007)

WORLD WIDE ASSOCIATION OF SPECIALTY PROGRAMS AND SCHOOLS (WWASPS)

The World Wide Association of Specialty Programs and Schools (WWASPS), founded by Robert Lichfield, was an umbrella organization of interconnected programs that provided residential services to struggling teens. Programs affiliated with WWASPS have included the Academy at Ivy Ridge, Carolina Springs Academy, Casa by the Sea, Cross Creek Programs, Darrington Academy, Dundee Ranch Academy, Majestic Ranch Academy, Paradise Cove Academy, Spring Creek Lodge Academy, and Tranquility Bay, among others. Before he founded the group in 1998, Lichfield had been the director of residential services at a Utah program for struggling teens, Provo Canyon. Until recently, WWASPS operated as an association of residential treatment programs for troubled and at-risk teens. The various programs to which WWASPS referred inquiring parents were located inside and outside the United States. WWASPS provided marketing support and referral services for its associated programs and dealt directly with parents, government agencies, other residential treatment facilities, and industry professionals. WWASPS did not manage any of the programs but maintained an extensive network of relationships and contracts with them (Bolton 2007; Szalavitz 2006).

Lichfield has close ties to Mitt Romney, the former governor of Massachusetts and presidential candidate. In June 2007 Lichfield was named as a defendant in lawsuits alleging that programs for struggling teens that he owned or operated engaged in abusive practices:

Former Massachusetts Gov. Mitt Romney (R) has collected hundreds of thousands of dollars through the fundraising efforts of a supporter targeted by several lawsuits alleging child abuse.

In a lawsuit filed in the U.S. District Court for the District of Utah, 133 plaintiffs have alleged that Robert Lichfield, co-chairman of Romney's Utah finance committee, owned or operated residential boarding schools for troubled teenagers where students were "subjected to physical abuse, emotional abuse and sexual abuse."

The complaint, which plaintiffs amended and resubmitted to the court last week, alleges children attending schools operated by Lichfield suffered abuses such as unsanitary living conditions; denial of adequate food; exposure to extreme temperatures; beatings; confinement in dog cages; and sexual fondling.

A second lawsuit filed by more than 25 plaintiffs in July [2006] in the U.S. District Court of the Northern District of New York alleges that Lichfield and several partners entered into a scheme to defraud them by operating an unlicensed boarding school in upstate New York. The suit does not allege physical or emotional abuse. (Bolton 2007)

WWASPS, as an organization, has been the target of widespread allegations claiming that its member programs engaged in abusive practices. A mere sampling of news headlines from around the country and in Latin America about WWASPS and its affiliates tells the story:

- *Missoula News*, June 16, 2005, "Spring Creek's Short Leash: Montana's Behavior Modification Programs Watch Their Troubled Charges Like Hawks," by John S. Adams
- Fox News, June 11, 2005, "Tough-Love Schools Are Both Loved and Hated," by Carol McKinley
- *Deseret (Salt Lake City) News*, April 9, 2004, "N.Y. Probing Utah-based Youth Programs," by Ami Joi Bryson
- *Daily (Provo, Utah) Herald*, September 20, 2004, "Investigation Shows Troubled School May Be Buying Interest with Lawmakers"
- *Tico (Costa Rica) Times*, January 17, 2003, "Officials to Investigate 'Tough Love' Facility Here," by Tim Roger
- *New York Times*, November 5, 2003, "Plea for Inquiry on School Network," by Tim Weiner

Controversy surrounding WWASPS led U.S. Representative George Miller of California to seek federal legislation requiring more oversight of such organizations:

The World Wide Association of Specialty Schools (WWASPS) founded by Robert Lichfield of La Verkin, Washington County, . . . uses behavior modification tactics to curb rebellious behavior in kids and often establishes schools in rural, out-of-the-way areas to deter notions of running away. Monthly tuition is several thousand dollars, on top of admission fees. . . .

It was Miller, the senior Democrat on the Education and Workforce Committee, who demanded in 2003 that then–Attorney General John Ashcroft investigate WWASPS.

The request, made again last year, never gained much traction, so Miller is now pushing for passage of the "End Institutional Abuse Against Children Act," which among other things, would establish federal civil and criminal penalties for abuse against children in residential treatment programs and expand federal regulatory authority to overseas programs operated by U.S. companies. (Bryson 2005)

WWASPS no longer operates under that name. The WWASPS Web site (www.wasp.com) now refers users to seven "enrollment services" and their toll-free telephone numbers: Teens in Crisis, Teens Soulutions [sic], Teen Help, Cross Creek Admissions, Help My Teen, Lifelines Family Resources, and Parent Resources Hotline. On March 10, 2008, and March 17, 2008, we called several of these telephone numbers to obtain information about the services offered. We spoke with representatives of five of these services; each said that her or his organization represents a large number of residential programs for struggling teens. When we checked the Web sites of the programs to which the services refer parents, we learned that many of these programs once were affiliated with WWASPS. One representative explained that the organization he represents no longer uses the WWASPS name because of negative publicity associated with it. Another representative said that her organization is a "marketing program" for schools for "troubled" teens. Two representatives acknowledged that their staffers are not trained mental health professionals; they said that the schools they represent provide them with a list of screening questions to use to make referrals. Another representative explained that her son graduated from one of the programs eleven years ago and she would recommend it for a teen who has problems with "detachment disorder." She was not aware that there is no such disorder in the *Diagnostic and Statistical Manual of Mental Disorders* (American Psychiatric Association 2000), which is the standard compendium of mental health diagnoses. This representative explained that her organization does not employ mental health professionals to assess teens' needs: "We don't have a Ph.D. psychologist or anything like that," she said.

The controversy swirling around WWASPS has been cataclysmic for the struggling-teen industry. It has received considerable media attention, which, unfortunately, has led many to assume that WWASPS programs and practices are emblematic of programs for struggling teens; many reputable and professionally administered programs and schools have been tainted by the WWASPS stain. As regrettable as this is, one useful by-product has been greater scrutiny within the industry.

ADVOCACY AND WATCHDOG ORGANIZATIONS

As a result of the scandals and allegations surrounding some programs for struggling teens, a number of advocacy and watchdog organizations have emerged. These organizations seek to expose abusive practices and organize efforts to confront the programs. These advocacy organizations have Web sites that typically include descriptive information about alleged abuses in programs and schools for struggling teens, commentary, and critiques. Some of these organizations and Web sites have existed for years; others are transitory. Some Web sites critique the broad struggling-teens industry; others feature critical commentary about specific schools and programs (among those that are frequently mentioned are the Seed, SAFE, Straight, KIDS of New Jersey, WWASPS, and the Hyde Schools).[5] We are not in a position to verify the claims and allegations of these watchdog and advocacy organizations. Our point here is that the intense controversy surrounding some programs and organizations has given rise to these watchdog and advocacy organizations. Also, we are not saying or implying that all programs and schools are abusive or negligent or that all watchdog organizations are accurate in their criticism.

The impressive collection of scandals and controversies surrounding some programs for struggling teens may create the impression that the industry is saturated with abuse, neglect, and misconduct. Fortunately, that may not be the case. While there is no denying that some programs and schools for struggling teens have been notoriously abusive and harmful, the industry also features many competent, professional, and ethically run programs and schools that scrupulously avoid any form of abuse, intimidation, or coercion.

No program or school can guarantee success, of course, however measured. Programs and schools for struggling teens are destined to have mixed results that include success stories and disappointing outcomes. There are no miracle cures or quick fixes for the behavioral and clinical challenges that many struggling teens bring with them to programs and schools—intensely defiant behavior and, often, protracted histories of mental illness and substance abuse. Under the best of circumstances progress may be incremental, slow, and uneven. The mark of competent, professional, and ethical programs and schools is that they seek to serve teens based on the best knowledge available, doing everything possible to increase the odds of success. We now turn to our review of the current status of that knowledge.

4

HELPING STRUGGLING TEENS

The most reputable programs and schools for struggling teens are those that base their services on research that has been published in peer-reviewed professional journals. The peer review process offers some assurance that the research satisfies widely accepted scientific standards. Although that research knowledge is imperfect and incomplete, the empirical evidence of effective (and ineffective) ways to help teens who struggle is extensive. Programs that ignore this evidence imperil their adolescent charges. In addition to depriving teens of the most effective services and interventions, and sometimes endangering the youngster, the programs expose themselves to malpractice and negligence claims. While using research-based interventions does not guarantee effectiveness, failure to use these approaches may increase the risk of harm.

EVIDENCE-BASED PRACTICE

Those who provide services to struggling teens and their families have a responsibility to use the best available research-based knowledge. As the first three chapters suggest, basing programs and practices primarily on belief systems and charismatic personalities can endanger teens emotionally and physically, particularly when these belief systems and practices fly in the face of what methodologically rigorous research data suggest help and hurt teens and their families.

Evidence-based practice as we know it today emerged from the field of evidence-based medicine, the origins of which can be traced to nineteenth-century France.[1] According to the original concept, a specific set of medical practices properly administered would ensure the greatest likelihood of recovery. Since the mid-1980s mental health and social service professionals also have made extensive efforts to implement evidence-based practices (Corcoran and Vandiver 2004; O'Hare 2005; Roberts and Yeager 2004, esp. chap. 1; Stout and Hayes 2005; Thyer 2004; Vandiver 2002).[2]

Delivering evidence-based services to struggling teens and their families means that providers

- Rely on the findings of published research from multiple studies
- Draw on a continuum of empirical and nonempirical databases (for example, systematic reviews of research) to guide interventions
- Implement interventions for which research evidence is sufficiently persuasive to support their effectiveness in attaining desired outcomes
- Review the literature on what works, with whom, and under what conditions, and individualize intervention approaches accordingly
- Use clinical interventions that have been (1) evaluated by well-designed clinical research studies, (2) published in peer-reviewed journals, and (3) consistently found to be effective or efficacious for a specific problem upon consensus review
- Blend the best researched evidence and clinical expertise with the values of the client and the professional

Evidence-based practice includes several core processes that inform and shape the efforts of professionals to intervene with struggling teens and their families:

A comprehensive, organized, purposeful assessment of the teen and family, completed and continuously revised, so that interventions target relevant issues and challenges

Selection of the most appropriate intervention from information from multiple sources (for example, systematic reviews of research and published practice guidelines derived from a consensus of experts)

Research in the professional literature for cutting-edge developments and practice-based articles when no empirically based guideline is available for a particular issue or challenge

ASSESSING THE QUALITY OF AVAILABLE RESEARCH: THE CONTINUUM

The quality of research evidence pertaining to struggling teens and their families varies enormously. Researchers typically make distinctions along a multilevel continuum of quality ranked by level of methodological rigor (Rosenthal 2004; Vandiver 2002).

Level 1 is the highest level of evidence. It includes systematic reviews of relevant studies using meta-analyses or two randomized controlled clinical trials. Meta-analysis is a research technique that combines the results of a large number of studies in an effort to identify patterns across different studies that ask the same or very similar questions using comparably rigorous research methods (Lipsey and Wilson 2001). The appeal of meta-analysis (for further information about this and other terms used in this chapter, see the glossary) is that it combines all the research on one topic into one large study with many participants. Drawing on meta-analyses enhances the likelihood that the conclusions drawn are more accurate than those of any one individual study.

The Cochrane Collaboration, publisher of what are known as Cochrane Reviews of research, and the Campbell Collaboration, an international nonprofit dedicated to disseminating cutting-edge health-care information, both publish widely cited meta-analyses related to the human services. Cochrane Reviews, sponsored by the Cochrane Collaboration and published in the quarterly *Cochrane Library*, are based on the best available information about health-care interventions.[3] The reviews explore the effectiveness and appropriateness of specific health-care treatments in specific circumstances. Cochrane Reviews investigate the effects of such interventions as medication, education, and therapies for prevention, treatment, and rehabilitation in a health-care setting. Most Cochrane Reviews are based on randomized controlled trials, but other types of evidence may also be taken into account, if appropriate. A randomized clinical trial is considered the gold standard. In it, people are randomly assigned to an experimental treatment group, a control group that does not receive the experimental treatment, and, when possible, a placebo group. The random assignment controls for differences among the different groups' members that might influence the outcomes independent of the intervention. Thus differences among the groups with respect to the outcome measures can be attributed to differences in the effects of the experimental treatment, the absence of treatment, and placebo.

Cochrane Reviews are designed to facilitate professionals' choices. A structured format helps the professional to find her way around the review easily, while a detailed methods section allows the professional to assess whether the review was conducted with suitable methodological rigor to justify its conclusions. The quality of clinical studies to be incorporated into a review is carefully considered, using explicit predefined criteria. In addition, a thorough and systematic search strategy, including searches for unpublished and non-English records, aims to provide as complete a picture as possible to try to answer the question considered. Multinational editorial teams also try to ensure that a review is applicable in different parts of the world.

If the data collected in a review are of sufficient quality and similar enough, they are summarized statistically in a meta-analysis, which generally provides a better overall estimate of a clinical effect than the results from individual studies. A meta-analysis also makes it possible to explore the effect of specific research design characteristics (for example, study quality) on the reported results (for example, does exclusion of nonrandomized studies change the overall result?). It also allows one to explore the effects of an intervention on subgroups of research participants (for example, does the intervention have a different effect on older or younger teens or on male versus female teens?).

Review authors and editors try to make the reports relatively easy to understand for nonexperts, although a certain amount of technical detail is always necessary. To achieve this, Cochrane authors and editors like to work with people who are likely to use the reviews or be affected by them; these individuals also contribute by pointing out issues that are important for people receiving certain interventions. Additionally, the *Cochrane Library* provides glossaries to explain technical terms.

Finally, the reviews can be updated. Results from newly completed or identified clinical trials can be incorporated into the review after publication. Additionally, readers may send comments and criticisms to any review, and reviews may be changed accordingly to improve their quality.

The Campbell Collaboration (www.campbellcollaboration.org/) is an independent, international, nonprofit organization that tries to help people make well-informed decisions about the effects of interventions in the social, behavioral, and educational arenas. The Campbell Collaboration seeks to improve the quality of public and private services internationally, by preparing, maintaining, and disseminating systematic reviews of existing social science evidence. The collaboration's substantive priorities include, but are not limited to, education, social welfare, and criminal justice.

A protocol known as a Campbell Systematic Review synthesizes evidence on social and behavioral interventions and public policy related to these priorities. The primary concern is to evaluate evidence about the effectiveness of an intervention or policy and how variations in process and implementation, intervention steps and recipients, as well as other factors, influence that effectiveness. Campbell Collaboration Reviews are designed to provide high-quality evidence of "what works." They are published electronically so that they can be updated promptly as relevant additional evidence emerges or in light of criticisms and advances in methodology. A typical Campbell review on a topic relevant to struggling teens and their families includes overviews of the topic being reviewed; the research question, including its theoretical, practical, and methodological history; and what professionals and researchers have learned from past research efforts, including inconsistent findings and methodological strengths and weaknesses. The review also provides a conceptual discussion of the problem being explored and a statement of the problem's significance, a description of the qualitative and historical debates surrounding the research question, and a discussion of previous reviews of the research topic. It thoroughly details the criteria for including and excluding studies, and for determining independent findings; the search strategy for identifying relevant studies; a description of research methods used in the studies included in the review; statistical analyses and conventions, and analysis of qualitative research; principal conclusions; and implications.

Below Level 1 are various categories of research findings based on less rigorous research methodology. Level 2 includes circumstances where no meta-analyses are available but one randomized clinical trial has been conducted or a national consensus panel has endorsed a conclusion. Level 3 consists of research that uses quasi-experimental designs, uncontrolled trials, observational studies, or descriptive studies. These research designs are less rigorous, mainly because they do not randomly assign participants to experimental and control groups. Level 4 includes anecdotal case reports; unsystematic clinical observations; descriptive reports; and single-case designs that do not include strict control of extraneous factors (for example, client maturation, the influence of other interventions). These studies do not include rigorous research designs but may offer practical information.

Level 5 consists of clinical opinions that are not based on research or consistently measured outcomes. Level 6 includes evidence of consistently poor outcomes for a particular population. It also includes research evidence concerning an intervention that is applied to the wrong population (a population other than that for which the intervention was intended). Level 7 includes what are known as emerging best practices, or promising practices, that is, interventions that have not been subject to rigorous research methods but that could be undergoing research review, have strong clinical utility, are liked by clients and families, and are deemed culturally appropriate.

Using this classification system, we can draw broad conclusions about what kinds of programs work for different kinds issues that struggling teens face. Evidence-based research on interventions for struggling teens falls into two general categories: program models and specific mental health and behavioral issues. We shall first take a bird's eye view of the body of research on what works with struggling teens. Then we will examine the literature on the effectiveness of different program models (for example, wilderness therapy, substance abuse treatment, drug court, and mentoring programs) and on the effectiveness of different interventions for specific behavioral and mental

health challenges (for example, posttraumatic stress disorder, depression, bipolar disorder, conduct disorder, anxiety disorders, substance abuse).

THE BROAD LANDSCAPE

The number of overlapping, intersecting intervention models, frameworks,
settings, and treatment strategies for struggling teens is staggering (Burns,
Hoagwood, and Mrazek 1999; Evans et al. 2005; Sells 2002; Straus 2007; Taffel
2005; Wolfe and Mash 2005). Although the intervention settings may vary
widely, from home based to community based to residential, many clinical interventions used in these settings are the same or similar. Hence, it
is difficult to differentiate precisely how some programs differ. Among the
better-known and widely used approaches for such clinical challenges as
depression, conduct disorder, anxiety, eating disorders, and bipolar disorder
are psychodynamic, insight-oriented therapy, cognitive-behavioral therapy,
multisystemic family therapy, coping skills training, parenting skills training,
dialectical behavior therapy, eye movement desensitization and reprocess-
ing therapy, biofeedback, hypnosis, group counseling, family counseling, and
psychotropic medication.

Several meta-analyses have examined the overall effectiveness of clinical
interventions with adolescents. For example, in an important meta-analysis
Weisz, Jensen-Doss, and Hawley (2006) compared the effectiveness of clinical interventions with youths that are based on empirical evidence (defined
by the authors as treatments that had been included in at least one list of
empirically validated treatments showing beneficial effects, such as cognitive-behavioral skills training, problem-solving training, anger management
training, parent management training, and assertiveness training) and clinical interventions that are not based on empirical evidence, or what the authors labeled "usual care" (defined by the authors as ordinary counseling or
case management provided as part of the regular services of providers, agencies, organizations, programs, or facilities for youth). The authors conducted
a comprehensive analysis of various outcome studies (studies that measure
the effectiveness of interventions) published between 1965 and 2004. All
the studies in the authors' sample included random assignment of youths
to intervention and treatment conditions, which is generally regarded as
the most sophisticated research methodology available to study intervention effectiveness. The authors found that interventions with youths that are
evidence based are significantly more effective than interventions that fall
within "usual care."

Also, Kazdin and Weisz (1998) conducted a meta-analysis of empirical
literature on clinical interventions with youths and found a host of promising

results. For example, the authors found strong evidence that cognitive-behavioral interventions in general can be quite effective for youths who struggle with anxiety. Cognitive-behavioral interventions typically begin with some form of psychoeducational therapy, relaxation, and self-soothing skills training. As part of the educational component, teens learn about the physical feelings in their bodies associated with anxiety (for example, tight stomach, dry mouth, sweaty palms, rapid heart beat, shallow breathing, nausea, dizziness). They may also learn specific skills to manage their discomfort, such as distracting themselves and reinterpreting their bodily sensations as benign. Cognitive-behavioral treatment also helps the teen to identify and change the unbidden thoughts that precede anxious feelings. Finally, a key element of all cognitive-behavioral interventions for adolescent anxiety is carefully guided exposure to the anxiety-producing stimulus. Therapists work with adolescents, and sometimes with their family members, to set up encounters with anxiety-arousing situations, starting with lesser and progressing to more anxiety-arousing stimuli (for example, moving from simply visualizing starting a conversation with a new acquaintance to actually starting a conversation with a new acquaintance). Frequently, exposure encounters—sometimes called "show that I can" tasks—take place first in treatment sessions that use imagination and role-playing before the youth actually grapples with his anxiety source in a real-life setting.

The authors also found strong evidence in the meta-analysis that coping skills training can help youths who have clinical depression. This training typically includes efforts to identify and modify patterns that contribute to depressed feelings and behaviors; coaching to improve social interactions (for example, how to start a conversation or make a friend), social problem solving (for example, how to resolve conflict without alienating others), and other competencies relevant to self-esteem (for example, setting performance goals and reaching them); training in progressive relaxation techniques to reduce muscular tension that can undermine enjoyment; scheduling pleasurable activities or activities that produce a sense of mastery; and keeping a written record of when the activities are performed, so the accomplishment is recognized and reinforced.

Kazdin and Weisz also found compelling evidence in their meta-analysis that certain interventions can be effective for adolescents who struggle with oppositional behavior, attention deficits and hyperactivity, aggressive and antisocial behavior, and delinquency (so-called externalizing problems; anxiety and depression are so-called internalizing problems). For example, the authors found that cognitive problem-solving skills training can be effective with teens who are oppositional and behave aggressively. The theory here is that their acting out is simply an inappropriate response to challenges to which they do not know how to respond in a constructive way. This training also helps them develop interpersonal problem-solving skills.

Although many variations of problem-solving training have been applied to adolescents with conduct problems, successful interventions tend to share several characteristics. First, the emphasis is on the thought processes that guide how the teens respond to interpersonal situations; they are taught to engage in a structured step-by-step thought process to address interpersonal conflicts. Second, prosocial behaviors, such as conflict resolution skills, are also taught, modeled, and rehearsed. Third, treatment uses structured tasks involving games, academic activities, and stories. During treatment the teen increasingly applies cognitive and behavioral problem-solving skills to real-life situations. Fourth, therapists usually play an active role in treatment. They model the cognitive processes by making verbal self-statements, applying the statements to particular problems, providing cues to prompt the teen's use of the skills, and delivering feedback and praise to develop the correct use of the skills. Finally, treatment usually combines several different procedures, including modeling and practice, role-playing, and reinforcement and mild punishment (loss of points or tokens). These procedures are deployed in systematic ways to develop increasingly complex response repertoires.

Another intervention for which Kazdin and Weisz found strong empirical support is parent management training for parents of teens who behave oppositionally or aggressively. Parent management training refers to procedures in which parents are trained to alter their child's behavior in the home. This approach is based on the general view that conduct problems are inadvertently developed and sustained in the home by maladaptive parent-child interactions (for example, directly attending to disruptive and deviant behavior, frequently and ineffectively using commands and harsh punishment, and failing to attend to appropriate behavior). Parent management training alters the pattern of interchanges between parent and child so that family members use prosocial, rather than coercive, behavior in their interactions. The variations of parent management training techniques have several characteristics in common. Treatment is conducted primarily with the parents, who implement procedures at home. The parents meet with a therapist who teaches them to use specific procedures to alter interactions with their child, to promote prosocial behavior, and to decrease deviant behavior. Parents are trained to identify, define, and observe problem behaviors in new ways. The treatment sessions provide concrete opportunities for parents to see how the techniques are implemented, to practice and refine their use of the techniques (for example, through extensive role-playing), and to review the behavior-change efforts used at home.

In addition, Kazdin and Weisz found evidence in their meta-analysis that multisystemic therapy for adolescents who engage in antisocial behavior can also be effective. Multisystemic therapy is a family-systems–based approach; it views children's clinical problems within the context of the family. The adolescent is embedded in multiple systems, including the family (immediate and extended), peers, school, and neighborhood. For example, within the context of the family a tacit alliance between one parent and child may contribute to parental disagreement and conflict about discipline. Treatment may be required to address the alliance and parental conflict in order to alter the child's behavior. Also, treatment may address the teen's relationships with peers at school. Finally, the systems approach focuses on the individual's behavior insofar as it affects others. Individual treatment of the child or parents may be a component. This simultaneous focus on multiple intersecting systems in which the teen and family exist illuminates multiple treatment possibilities, based on a comprehensive biopsychosocial assessment of each youth's situation. Thus multisystemic training can be viewed as a package of interventions used as needed and directed toward changes in the individual, family, and system.

With multisystemic training several therapy techniques, such as joining, reframing, enactment, paradox, and assigning specific tasks, are used to identify problems, increase communication, build family cohesion, and alter how family members interact (Kazdin and Weisz 1998). The goals of treatment are to help the parents respond effectively to the adolescent's behaviors, to overcome marital difficulties that impede the parents' ability to function as parents, to eliminate negative interactions between parent and adolescent, and to develop emotional connections and warmth among family members. Multisystemic training draws on many other techniques as needed to address problems at the individual, family, and outside-the-family levels. Different types of individual and marital therapy are used to influence interactions at home. In some cases treatment includes giving practical advice and guidance, such as suggesting that parents arrange for a tutor to monitor the youth's homework, thus freeing the parents and teen from conflictual interactions about that each evening. Although multisystemic training includes techniques from other approaches, it is not a mere amalgamation of them. The focus of treatment is on interrelated systems and how they affect each other. Multisystemic training identifies patterns of interaction that create and sustain difficulties, and seeks to change these patterns, thus resolving problems. The changes may be made by the parents, teen, teacher, school, court, neighbors, or others. Specific challenges, such as a parent's unemployment, may be addressed in treatment because they raise issues, such as parental stress, that play a role in the teen's functioning.

Several outcome studies have evaluated multisystemic training, primarily with delinquent youths with arrest and incarceration histories. Meta-analysis results show multisystemic training to be superior to "usual services," such as probation and court-ordered school attendance, individual counseling, and community-based eclectic treatment. Follow-up studies as much as two, four, and five years later with separate samples have shown that youths who received multisystemic training have lower arrest rates than youths who receive other services.

Meta-analysis research has also shown that multisystemic training affects critical processes that are thought to contribute to deviant behavior (Kazdin and Weisz 1998). Parents and teenagers who receive multisystemic training show a reduction in conflict and hostility and increases in mutual support and the quality of their verbal communication. Moreover, decreases in adolescent symptoms are correlated with increases in supportiveness and decreases in conflict between the mother and father.

In another major meta-analysis Weisz and colleagues (1995) examined 150 outcome studies of the effectiveness of psychotherapy on teens. They defined psychotherapy as any intervention intended to alleviate psychological distress, reduce maladaptive behavior, or enhance adaptive behavior through counseling, structured or unstructured interaction, a training program, or a predetermined treatment plan. Weisz and colleagues excluded treatments involving drugs, interventions involving only reading (known as bibliotherapy), teaching or tutoring intended only to increase knowledge of a specific subject, interventions involving only relocation (for example, moving children to a foster home), and exclusively preventive interventions intended to stop problems in youngsters considered to be at risk. This meta-analysis included psychotherapy conducted by fully trained professionals, as well as psychotherapy conducted by therapists in training (for example, clinical psychology and social work students and child psychiatry fellows) and by trained paraprofessionals (for example, teachers and parents). The authors' key finding is that research results across studies "reinforce previous evidence that psychotherapy with young people produces positive effects of respectable magnitude" (460). Weisz and colleagues found that behavioral methods—such as cognitive-behavioral therapy, social skills training, and parenting skills training—were associated with more substantial therapy effects than nonbehavioral methods (such as loosely structured one-on-one talking therapy, discussion groups). The pattern held up when the authors controlled for problem treated, therapist training, and child age and gender. In short, structured approaches in which problems, goals, interventions, and outcomes are stated in concrete, observable, measurable terms and that address the teen in the context of the school, neighborhood, peer group, and family show the best results. Loosely structured, nonspecific "talk" therapy that is not part of a coordinated package of interventions and that does not use cognitive-behavioral methods is less promising.

PROGRAM MODELS

Many different types of program models are used with struggling teens. Some rely on a carefully designed treatment or intervention protocol, such as intensive home-based services and wilderness therapy. Others, such as a drug court or truancy court, coordinate and refer youths to a range of services, such as counseling and tutoring, that are provided by other professionals and coordinated by a case manager.

Research evidence of the effectiveness of some types of programs is growing, although significant gaps exist. Researchers have paid particular attention to a number of widely used program models for struggling teens, including wilderness therapy, substance abuse treatment, drug court, and mentoring programs.[4] Assessing their effectiveness is challenging, as different programs that use the same name and follow the same general model can be quite different from one another. All wilderness therapy programs, for instance, are not entirely alike, although they may share some common elements. The same holds for drug courts, mentoring programs, and substance abuse treatment programs. Hence, conclusions culled from the literature are suggestive but not conclusive.

FAMILY-PRESERVATION SERVICES

Intensive, home-based family preservation services can provide significant help to the families of struggling teens (Bagdasaryan 2005; Berry, Cash, and Brook 2000; Blythe, Salley, and Jayaratne 1994; Dagenais et al. 2004; Fraser, Nelson, and Rivard 1997; Fraser, Pecora, and Haapala 1991; Kinney, Haapala, and Booth 1991; Kirk and Griffith 2004; McCroskey and Meezan 1997; Wells and Whittington 1993). In their comprehensive meta-analysis Fraser, Nelson, and Rivard (1997) reviewed published and unpublished studies of family preservation services since 1985. The goal of family preservation services is to keep children in their parents' home or to reunify families whose children are in out-of-home placements such as foster care, group homes, residential treatment, and juvenile correctional facilities. The meta-analysis focused on studies of intensive, in-home family preservation services in which workers have small caseloads and intervention lasts no more than twenty weeks. Excluded from the analysis were studies of family-centered casework, family therapy, and other family services for which contact with families averaged one hour or less per week and children were not viewed as at risk of out-of-home placement. Studies involving both maltreated and delinquent children were included in the sample because increasing numbers of oppositional, defiant children are referred to child welfare agencies and because important tests of family preservation have taken place in the juvenile justice system. The authors limited their meta-analysis to studies with control or comparison groups. Studies with weaker designs (for example, case overflow studies) were included only if experimental and control conditions were made equivalent before the intervention started through matching or were shown, through statistical comparison of experimental and control groups, to be equivalent before the intervention started.

Fraser, Nelson, and Rivard (1997) found that the most successful programs included a number of core elements. Although these elements are not present in every study, they appear to be the essential, cross-cutting components of family preservation programs with promising findings. They include

- In vivo focus—Services are focused and delivered in a home or community setting. They are action oriented, culturally sensitive, and address problems by working collaboratively with family members.
- Empowerment—Family members actively participate in setting service goals and are viewed as colleagues in defining a service plan.
- Crisis intervention—Supportive and backup services are available twenty-four hours a day.
- Skills building—Communication, problem-solving, parenting, household management, management of peer influences, use of medications, agency-level advocacy, and other skills are taught based on family members' needs.
- Marital and family intervention—Where needed, services are provided to deescalate parent-child or marital conflict.
- Collateral services—Workers make referrals to and coordinate community resources. They build partnerships with collateral services. For example, for a teen struggling with negative peer influences, the worker might help the school guidance counselor and a teacher involve the teen in an after-school program and might also help him enroll in weekend classes at the local recreation center.
- Concrete services—Workers help family members meet food, housing, clothing, financial assistance, transportation, health care, and other needs.

Fraser, Nelson, and Rivard found that family preservation services appear to be moderately effective in preventing placement outside the home of children who are in early adolescence and who are referred for truant, oppositional, or delinquent behavior. In the juvenile justice studies that the authors reviewed, findings suggest that arrests and incarcerations are reduced by risk-focused, multisystemic family intervention models. Moreover, with some exceptions, study results suggest that family preservation services may be effective in preventing placement into foster care, group homes, and residential treatment of youths referred for child behavior problems by the public child welfare system.

WILDERNESS THERAPY

There is considerable evidence that wilderness therapy (also known as outdoor behavioral health) can be an effective intervention with struggling teens. Two noteworthy meta-analyses of studies of wilderness therapy programs provide encouraging results (Hans 2000; Hattie et al. 1997). The results of the meta-analyses suggest that programs with therapeutic intentions, as opposed to a more recreational focus, can enhance teens' personal growth; personal sense of responsibility, competence, and control (known as locus of control and self-efficacy); and interpersonal and social skills.

Russell (2003) studied the results of seven wilderness therapy programs located in Arizona, Utah, Oregon, and Idaho. Adolescents participated in the programs for an average of forty-five days; they had been diagnosed primarily with substance abuse disorders, oppositional defiant disorder, and depression. Each program had a clinical supervisor, master's-level therapists, or counselors who periodically visited groups of teens in the field, and primary-care wilderness leaders and assistants with at least two years' experience who were with the teens continually in the wilderness settings.

Using a randomly selected sample of clients, Russell collected data on the youths' well-being and functioning at the time of admission and at discharge; he also collected data twelve months after discharge from the program. Youths' well-being and functioning were assessed using well-known standardized instruments: the Youth Outcome Questionnaire (completed by parents) and the Self-Report Youth Outcome Questionnaire (completed by the youths themselves). These instruments assess various clinical symptoms related to intrapersonal distress (anxiety, depression, fearfulness, hopelessness, and self-destructiveness); somatic complaints typical in psychiatric presentations (such as headaches, dizziness, stomachaches, nausea, and pain or weakness in joints); relationships with others (such as the teen's relationship with parents, other adults, and peers as well as the teen's attitude toward others, interaction with friends, aggressiveness, arguing, and defiance); social problems, including truancy, sexual problems, running away from home, destruction of property, and substance abuse; and behavioral dysfunction (the teen's ability to organize tasks, complete assignments, concentrate, and handle the kind of frustration that leads to inattention, hyperactivity, and impulsivity). The results indicated that at the time of admission the clients in the wilderness programs manifested clinical symptoms that were similar to those in teens admitted to inpatient settings; the symptoms for the teens in the wilderness programs were significantly reduced by the time of discharge, and the teens maintained their functioning twelve months later.

Although Russell's findings are encouraging, his study has some unfortunate, albeit unavoidable, limitations. As with most follow-up surveys, Russell's analysis was limited to those who chose to respond. People who choose to respond to surveys may be functioning better and have better news to report than those who do not respond, thus tilting the findings in a positive direction. Also, Russell was not in a position to randomly assign struggling teens to the wilderness therapy experience and to a control group or some other intervention; as a result Russell cannot conclude with certainty that wilderness therapy is more effective than no intervention or some alternative intervention. Nonetheless, Russell's findings suggest that wilderness therapy may hold considerable promise.

Several other studies also suggest that wilderness therapy programs can produce positive results:

■ Russell and Phillips-Miller (2002) examined the wilderness therapy process in order to better understand how the intervention affects change in problem behavior of adolescent clients. This study investigated four established wilderness therapy programs using a multisite case study approach and a variety of qualitative data-collection methods to carefully examine the wilderness therapy experience. Findings indicate that physical exercise and hiking, primitive wilderness living, peer feedback during group counseling sessions, and the relationships established with wilderness guides and therapists were key change agents, according to the adolescents in the sample. These factors helped adolescents come to terms with their behavior and want to change for the better.

■ Clark and colleagues (2004) empirically evaluated the effects of a twenty-one-day wilderness therapy program on the defense styles, perceived psychosocial stressors, dysfunctional personality patterns, clinical syndromes, and maladaptive behaviors of 109 struggling adolescents, as measured by the Defense Style Questionnaire–40, Millon Adolescent Clinical Inventory, and Youth Outcome Questionnaire–2.0. The study also sought to identify the types of mental health and clinical concerns for which wilderness therapy is most effective. Wilderness therapy resulted in statistically significant improvement on diverse clinical measures.

■ Russell (2005) evaluated youths' well-being twenty-four months after the conclusion of wilderness therapy and explored how youths make the transition to a variety of posttreatment settings. Transition from wilderness therapy often involves use of aftercare services, such as individual, group, or family therapy on an outpatient basis or residential services such as treatment in a psychiatric facility, therapeutic boarding schools, and others. The results suggest that 80 percent of parents and 95 percent of youths perceived wilderness therapy as effective, the majority of clients were doing well in school, and family communication had improved. Aftercare was used by 85 percent of the youths to facilitate the transition from an intensive wilderness experience to family, peer, and school environments. Results also indicated, however, that many program participants continued to use alcohol and/or drugs to varying degrees, had legal problems, and still had issues in forming friendships with peers. Parents and teens viewed wilderness therapy as a necessary, effective step in helping youths address, and eventually overcome, the emotional and psychological issues that drove the teens' destructive behavior before wilderness therapy.

■ Romi and Kohan (2004) studied the effect of a wilderness therapy program on a group of at-risk youths in Israel, comparing them with a group enrolled in an alternative therapy program (a six-day residential program) and a contrast group that did not participate in any intervention program. The research findings partially supported the authors' assumptions that self-esteem and locus of control for youths in the wilderness group would be improved in comparison with teens in the alternative therapy group and the contrast group.

In sum, there is evidence that wilderness therapy programs can be helpful to many teens who struggle with various issues. Which specific programs are helpful for which specific types of youths and which emotional and behavioral issues is less clear.

SUBSTANCE ABUSE TREATMENT

An impressive amount of research has been conducted on the effectiveness of treatment of adolescent substance abuse (Best 1997; Evans et al. 2005; Harrison and Asche 2001; Havivi 2006; Jainchill 2000; Mason 1996; Muck et al. 2001; Nissen 2006; Skiba, Monroe, and Wodarski 2004; Tourmbourou et al. 2007). Research evidence also indicates that early-intervention programs that use cognitive-behavioral components, in particular, life skills training and motivational interviewing, are most effective with adolescents (Borsari and Carey 2000; Botvin et al. 1990, 2001; Larimer and Cronce 2002; Monti et al. 2001; O'Hare 2005).

In their comprehensive and rigorous meta-analysis of fifteen controlled evaluations of substance abuse treatment of adolescents, Vaughn and Howard (2004) found that many treatments reduced adolescent substance abuse and increased abstinence rates; however, treatment gains often were not sustained. The strongest evidence of treatment effectiveness was associated with multidimensional family therapy and cognitive-behavioral group treatment. The empirical evidence for these interventions demonstrates clinically significant results achieved with rigorous research designs, including at least one year follow-up or replication. Fairly impressive results were also evident for treatment based on behavioral therapy, multisystemic therapy, combined cognitive-behavioral therapy and functional family therapy, family systems therapy, functional family therapy, life-skills training with supplemental social services, and psychoeducational therapy (see the glossary for more information about these and other processes). Although the results for these interventions were also clinically significant, the data come from following the teens for less than a year after discharge, and there was no replication of results.

A number of studies used relatively weak research designs and showed negligible or negative outcomes for several interventions: supportive group counseling, interactional group treatment, aftercare services, and residential treatment services. Finally, a number of studies that used relatively strong research designs showed negligible or negative outcomes for several interventions: individual counseling, family education, and adolescent group treatment.

The research results from widely cited controlled studies of substance abuse treatment programs designed for adolescents include these findings:

- Behavioral therapy was more effective than supportive group counseling in one study involving twenty-eight adolescents (Azrin et al. 1994).
- Family therapy and a parent group were comparably effective in the treatment of 135 adolescents (Friedman 1989).
- Life skills training was effective in the treatment of 201 court-adjudicated adolescents (Friedman, Terras, and Glassman 2002).
- Multisystemic therapy was significantly more effective than individual counseling and "usual" social services for 144 juvenile offenders (Henggeler et al. 1991, 2002; Henggeler, Pickrel, and Brondino 1999).
- Family systems therapy was particularly effective with eighty-nine adolescents, and adolescent group therapy and family drug education were also somewhat effective (Joanning et al. 1992).
- Cognitive-behavioral group treatment was particularly effective in two different samples ($N = 32$ and $N = 88$) of adolescents (Kaminer and Burleson 1999; Kaminer et al. 1998; and Kaminer, Burleson, and Goldberger 2002).

- Brief family therapy was particularly effective in the treatment of eighty-four adolescents (Lewis et al. 1990).
- Multidimensional family therapy was particularly effective in the treatment of ninety-seven adolescents (Liddle et al. 2001).
- Coping skills training was somewhat effective in the treatment of twenty-two adolescents (McGillicuddy et al. 2001).
- Brief strategic family therapy and general group treatment had a positive impact in the treatment of 126 adolescents (Santisteban et al. 2003).
- The combination of individual cognitive-behavioral therapy and functional family therapy was effective in the treatment of 114 adolescents (Waldron et al. 2001).
- A twelve-step program was effective in the treatment of 179 adolescents (Winters et al. 2000).
- Residential treatment produced only modest benefits that generally were not maintained posttreatment for 426 juvenile offenders (Sealock, Gottfredson, and Gallagher 1997).

In summary, substance abuse treatment can be helpful. While research findings are mixed, it appears that cognitive-behavioral methods, used in conjunction with multidimensional family therapy, show promise.

DRUG COURT

Juvenile drug courts began in the United States in the mid-1990s. Because of their recent origin, relatively little research on long-term outcomes has been conducted, although the number is increasing (Bryan, Hiller, and Leukefeld 2006; Butts and Roman 2004; Egbert, Church, and Byrnes 2006; Goldkamp, White, and Robinson 2001; Gottfredson, Najaka, and Kearley 2003; Green et al. 2007; Henggeler et al. 2006; Hepburn and Harvey 2007; Kalich and Evans 2006; Lindquist, Krebs, and Lattimore 2006; Marlowe et al. 2005; Office of Justice Programs 2006; Roll et al. 2005; Torgensen et al. 2004; Turner et al. 2002; Tyuse and Linhorst 2005). Research evidence summarized in a report released by the U.S. Office of Justice Programs (2006) indicates that drug courts can reduce recidivism and promote other positive outcomes. However, research has not determined which specific court processes affect which outcomes for which types of offenders. The magnitude of a court's impact may depend upon how consistently court resources match the needs of the offenders in the drug court program (Henggeler et al. 2006). The federal report also concludes that juveniles can be more difficult than adults to diagnose and treat. Many teens referred to drug court have no established pattern of substance abuse or physical addiction. Some have reached serious levels of criminal and drug involvement.

Drug court participants report that interactions with the judge are an important influence on their experience in the program. They respond to the judge's interpersonal skills and ability to resolve legal problems expeditiously and provide ready access to services. Evidence suggests that drug court participants who interact with a single drug court judge, rather than multiple judges, may be more likely to comply with program demands (Office of Justice Programs 2006).

An unusually in-depth evaluation of the Clark County (Las Vegas, Nevada) drug court found that fewer participants from 1993 through 1997 were rearrested (for any charge) than their counterparts in the comparison group (randomly selected from all felony drug cases that did not enter drug court): 53 percent versus 65 percent, respectively (Office of Justice Programs 2006). In another major study researchers examined drug courts in four communities: Bakersfield, California; Creek County, Oklahoma; Jackson County, Missouri; and St. Mary Parish, Louisiana (Office of Justice Programs 2006). They found that 17 percent of participants were arrested once and 16 percent were arrested two or more times during their participation in drug court. In addition, 76 percent of participants tested positive for drug use one or more times during their drug court involvement, and 61 percent tested positive two or more times. As expected, positive drug tests and in-program arrests are both negatively associated with program completion. Eighty-five percent of participants with in-program arrests and 50 percent of those with one or more positive drug tests were terminated from the program. In other words, participants who ultimately were terminated were two to three times more likely to test positive for drug use and four to five times more likely to be arrested during program participation than those who graduated.

Rearrest data for the 2,357 offenders in this study (Office of Justice Programs 2006) were obtained for the twelve months after their date of discharge from the drug court program. As a result researchers were able to examine the effects of compliance with program requirements on postprogram recidivism. Findings from this study confirm what other studies have found: Successful completion of the drug court program (graduation) is the variable most consistently associated with low postprogram recidivism. Forty-one percent of the participants who had been terminated and 9 percent of the graduates were rearrested. This means that, of the 722 participants in the postprogram follow-up who were rearrested, 90 percent had been expelled from their program. The rate of postprogram recidivism was considerably higher for terminated participants than for graduates at all four sites. This is not surprising, as drug court participants with more intractable alcohol or drug use are more likely to have difficulty maintaining sobriety. Moreover, terminated participants were rearrested faster—on average 4.5 months after leaving the program—than graduates, whose rearrest took about 6.6 months.

Other key findings from this multisite study were that

- Participants with low attendance at treatment sessions had a greater likelihood of being rearrested after being discharged from the program.
- Members of racial and ethnic minority groups were more likely than non-Hispanic whites to be rearrested.
- Participants with previous arrests at younger ages were more likely to be rearrested.
- Males were more likely than females to be rearrested.
- Participants with in-program arrests were twice as likely to have a postprogram arrest. Among the 1,581 participants with no in-program arrests, 23 percent were rearrested after being discharged from the program, whereas 48 percent of the 776 participants with in-program arrests were arrested again after discharge.

Several studies of drug courts designed for adolescents have produced valuable data. In a federal survey of drug courts that focused on juveniles (Office of Justice Programs 2006), 80 to 90 percent of the enrolled juveniles under review had been referred for alcohol or marijuana use. Researchers concluded that the programs they studied are not focusing treatment resources on those whom they are intended to serve—the adolescents least able to control their drug consumption and most at risk of prolonged and harmful substance abuse—and that too many courts are not yet clear about their purpose.

The evidence suggests that drug court personnel are most successful with younger adolescents when conversations are clear, open, and frank because many struggling teens have poor relationships with adults, limited life experience, little ability to deal with abstractions, and may learn best from direct experience. Researchers stress that the courtroom process should be short, easy to understand, and free of legal or medical jargon. Research results indicate that the first court appearance should occur soon after the precipitating offense because delayed consequences are less effective with adolescents (Henggeler et al. 2006; Office of Justice Programs 2006).

A compelling study evaluated the effectiveness of a juvenile drug court in Charleston, South Carolina, for 161 juvenile offenders meeting diagnostic criteria for substance abuse or dependence. The study sought to determine whether the integration of evidence-based practices enhanced the outcomes of juvenile drug court (Henggeler et al. 2006). The evaluators used a four-condition randomized design for their one-year study. They evaluated outcomes for a (1) family court that provided the usual community services, (2) drug court with the usual community services, (3) drug court that placed

young offenders in multisystemic therapy, and (4) drug court that used multisystemic therapy enhanced with contingency management (contingency
management assumes that if a desired behavior is reinforced or rewarded, it
is more likely to occur in the future). The study sought to determine outcome
patterns for youngsters referred for adolescent substance use, criminal behavior, and mental health symptoms, as well as the number of days they had
spent in out-of-home placement. In general, the study found that drug court
was more effective than family court services in decreasing rates of adolescent
substance use and criminal behavior. However, these relative reductions in
antisocial behavior did not translate to corresponding decreases in rearrest or
incarceration. This may be because youths involved in drug court are more
closely monitored by law enforcement officials and other professionals affiliated with the court and therefore are more likely to be caught if they engage
in misbehavior.

A key point noted by researchers is that most treatment models used by
drug courts are developed for adult clients with drug problems more severe
than what many youths have developed (Office of Justice Programs 2006).
Some approaches used in adult treatment programs may transfer well to
adolescent populations, particularly if the adolescents have drug addictions
involving substances such as heroin and cocaine, but others may not. More
research on the effectiveness of drug courts specifically designed for adolescents is needed.

One of the primary arguments for the establishment of juvenile drug courts
is that they are cost effective. A cost-benefit evaluation of Portland, Oregon's
Multnomah County Drug Court, the second oldest in the country, found that
the drug court cost taxpayers significantly less than traditional social services.
Total savings from drug court participation during the thirty-month study period—that is, costs for drug court participants subtracted from costs for the comparison group—were more than $5,000 per participant. With the court's aver-
age annual caseload of three hundred, that amounted to savings of more than
$1.5 million per year. The analysis examined three types of costs and benefits:

   Investment costs (actual costs of using public resources, such as a judge's time,
      an attorney's time, law enforcement time, drug tests)
   Benefits from avoided system costs (criminal justice costs that would have been
      incurred as a result of rearrest if the drug court participant had not received
      treatment)
   Avoided victimization costs (victims' lost days of work and medical expenses)

The total savings per drug court participant amounted to approximately
$1,400 in investment costs, $2,300 in avoided court and law enforcement

costs, and $1,300 in avoided victimization costs. These overall findings, while preliminary and not yet conclusive, tentatively suggest that use of drug courts for adolescents and juveniles may be promising and cost effective in some circumstances.

MENTORING PROGRAMS

Although mentoring programs have burgeoned and are used with large numbers of struggling teens in urban, rural, and suburban communities, relatively little formal, empirical research has been conducted on the model's effectiveness and to identify and test the core ingredients of effective mentoring. Most discussions of the model are conceptually oriented (Beam, Chen, and Greenberger 2002; Blinn-Pike 2007; Blue 2004; Britner et al. 2006; Broussard, Mosley-Howard, and Roychoudhury 2006; DuBois et al. 2006; DuBois and Karcher 2005; DuBois and Neville 1997; Hamilton et al. 2006; Hartley 2004; Karcher et al. 2006; Larson 2006; Philip and Hendry 2001; Rhodes 2002; Rhodes et al. 2006; Rose and Jones 2007; Spencer 2006; Zimmerman, Bingenheimer, and Notaro 2002).

Several studies of Big Brothers and Big Sisters, a nationally prominent mentoring program, have produced encouraging results. Grossman and Tierney's study (1998) found that the mentoring provided by Big Brothers and Big Sisters had a significant positive effect on the behavior of participating youth aged ten to sixteen. Data showed that these youths were less likely to start using drugs or alcohol, hit someone, or skip school. Students also reported feeling more confident about school performance and that their family relationships improved.

A more recent study of boys in Big Brothers programs found that mentored boys made significantly greater academic gains than did boys who were waitlisted for a mentor (Thompson and Kelly-Vance 2001). This study differed from previous research by administering individual achievement tests, rather than using grade-point average as an academic measure, and also by controlling for students' cognitive ability (Blue 2004).

Another study of Big Brothers and Big Sisters also produced encouraging results (Langhout, Rhodes, and Osborne 2004). The goal of this study was to empirically distinguish a range of mentor relationships and to evaluate their differential influence on adolescents. The study examined data that were collected as part of a national evaluation of Big Brothers/Big Sisters of America. The evaluation included 1,138 youth, ranging in age from ten through sixteen, who were assigned randomly to either a mentoring relationship or a control group and followed for eighteen months. A series of analyses, based on the matched youths' accounts of the mentoring relationships, suggested

four distinct types of relationships (i.e., moderate, unconditionally supportive, active, and low key). The four groups tended to distinguish themselves
from one another on the basis of perceived support, structure, and activity.
Compared with teens assigned to the control group, youth who characterized
their mentor relationships as providing moderate levels of both activity and
structure and conditional support derived the largest number of benefits from
the relationships. These included improvements in social, psychological, and
academic outcomes.

There is also evidence that mentoring can have a positive impact on teens'
sense of self-efficacy and their hopes for the future. Economically disadvantaged students in a formal mentoring program demonstrated improved educational and occupational aspirations if they were mentored for more than
one year (Lee and Cramond 1999); these youths had a lower probability of
dropping out of school. This study emphasized that to make a significant
difference, mentors needed to sustain a commitment to the child for at least
one year.

A valuable study conducted by Beier and colleagues (2000) suggests that
the use of mentors can reduce certain adolescent risk-taking behaviors among
suburban youths with mixed socioeconomic backgrounds. The authors found
that adolescents with mentors were significantly less likely to engage in several health-risk behaviors: carrying a weapon, using illicit drugs in the previous thirty days, smoking more than five cigarettes per day, and engaging in sex
with more than one partner in the previous six months. However, the study
found no significant difference in teens' alcohol use.

Keating and colleagues (2002) examined the effects of mentoring on youth
found to be at risk of juvenile delinquency or mental illness. Pre- and postint-
ervention surveys of parents, teachers, and youth showed significant positive
improvement in problem behaviors for the intervention group (Blue 2004). Keating and colleagues noted that such improvements could be affected as well
by other assistance, as many youth were also in family or school counseling.

Slicker and Palmer (1993) studied eighty-six tenth-grade students in a
large, suburban, racially and socioeconomically diverse Texas school district.
Using testing both before the study began and after six months of participation, Slicker and Palmer initially found no difference in dropout rates,
self-concept, or academic achievement between students mentored by adult
school personnel and the control group. However, a review of mentor logs
showed variations in the quality of mentoring that students received. Some
mentors met with students often, whereas others met infrequently. Slicker
and Palmer subdivided the data into two categories reflecting the quality of
mentoring: whether students were effectively or ineffectively mentored. The
post hoc analysis showed that effectively mentored students tended to have

lower dropout rates than ineffectively mentored students and that the grade-point averages of effectively mentored students were higher. No difference was found in students' self-concepts. Slicker and Palmer's study suggested that the quality of mentoring makes a difference and that academic achievement and dropout rates can be influenced by effective mentoring efforts. The study also suggested that other adult school personnel, in addition to school counselors, can be effective mentors.

Evidence also suggests that mentoring programs can help prevent negative outcomes for older teens who are aging out of foster care and preparing for independent living. Osterling and Hines (2006) used quantitative and qualitative data from an evaluation of the Advocates to Successful Transition to Independence program, a mentoring program designed to train mentors to help older adolescents in foster care acquire the skills and resources for successful transition into adulthood. The study's results suggest that a mentoring program for older adolescents in foster care can help prevent negative outcomes as youths move out of the foster care system and into independent young adulthood.

DuBois and colleagues (2002) provide considerable insight into the design and implementation of successful volunteer-based youth mentoring programs. Their meta-analysis of fifty-five empirical studies of youth mentoring programs indicates that mentoring can have an overall positive effect on struggling teens. However, youth mentoring is complex, and the authors note that the "average" youth will receive relatively modest benefits from mentoring programs. Of the mentoring programs studied by DuBois and colleagues (2002), the more successful programs were those that were directed toward youths experiencing environmental risk or disadvantage (that is, communities characterized by low socioeconomic status, high crime rates, poor quality housing), either alone or in combination with behavioral and emotional problems (for example, youths who struggle with posttraumatic stress disorder, depression, severe anxiety, attention-deficit/hyperactivity disorder, or substance abuse).

In the rigorous meta-analysis by DuBois and colleagues (2002), outcomes and elements of each of the fifty-five programs were evaluated along fourteen dimensions. Among the dimensions were the setting in which the mentoring took place, the existence of support groups for mentors, the role of parent support/involvement in the mentoring process, the youth's expected frequency of contact with the mentor, the youth's expected length of the mentoring relationship, and the average frequency of contact between mentor and youth. The analysis also considered whether the program had been evaluated by program staffers, the mentor had formal training in a helping profession, the program screened prospective mentors, mentors were carefully matched with youth, the program provided prematch training for the mentors, mentors received formal supervision, mentors received ongoing training, and whether the program provided structured activities for mentors and youth. Programs that included a majority of these components were associated with more positive outcomes than were programs that included few or none of them. Findings indicate that five dimensions were especially salient to positive outcomes: programs with a self-monitoring component, those that train mentors on an ongoing basis, and those that provide structured activities for mentor and mentee. Programs that encouraged parent support and involvement were shown to be very effective, as were programs that recruited mentors with a helping background (i.e., teachers, counselors).

Results also indicate that youth are more likely to benefit from mentoring that occurs in the home or community, as opposed to schools. This investigation also revealed that the success of a mentoring relationship is not dependent upon the type of mentoring program (that is, whether it stands alone or occurs in combination with other programs), nor is it dependent upon the program goal (that is, behavioral, psychosocial, academic, etc.) or model (so long as the five most effective dimensions are incorporated into the program). Additionally, programs targeting youth based solely upon their individual risk factors were shown to be effective if they also incorporated these fourteen dimensions in their guidelines. The gender, race, or ethnicity of the mentor correlated less with a successful mentoring relationship than did the mentor's having a background in a helping profession. This was especially the case for youth at risk for poor outcomes. The age, gender, race, and family structure of the youth were also found to be less important to the mentor-mentee match than were the mentor's attitudes and practices toward forming a close relationship with the youth. Some evidence indicates that mentoring relationships may do more harm than good for some vulnerable or at-risk youth if the mentor relationship terminates prematurely. DuBois and colleagues (2002) found that teens' frequency of contact with a mentor was not significant, but teens' *expectations* of that frequency were.

INTERVENTIONS FOR SPECIFIC CLINICAL CHALLENGES

In addition to evaluating the effectiveness of various intervention models, considerable research has focused on interventions for specific clinical and behavioral health challenges that are often found among struggling teens. Research has focused especially on the effectiveness of interventions for adolescent depression, bipolar disorder, anxiety, oppositional behavior, eating disorders, attention-deficit/hyperactivity disorder, and substance abuse and dependence.

ADOLESCENT DEPRESSION

Research evidence suggests that a number of cognitive-behavioral interventions for adolescents who are depressed can be effective, although some researchers caution against overstating the effects of treatment (Evans et al. 2005; McCarty and Weisz 2007; Weisz, McCarty, and Valeri 2006). According to O'Hare's 2005 comprehensive review of research evidence, cognitive-behavioral interventions can be particularly effective for moderately depressed adolescents but less so for severely depressed adolescents (Angold and Costello 1993; Asarnow, Scott, and Mintz 2002; Brent et al. 1997; Clarke, DeBar, and Lewinsohn 2003; Compton et al. 2002; Curry 2001; Glass 2004; Harrington 1995; Harrington, et al. 1998; Kahn et al. 1990; Klein, Dougherty, and Olino 2005; Lewisohn et al. 1990; Michael and Crowley 2002; Reinecke, Ryan, and DuBois 1998; Reynolds and Coats 1986; Stark et al. 1999; Weisz 2004). Based on their review of a decade's worth of research on the topic, Birmaher and colleagues (1996a, 1996b) concluded that cognitive-behavioral and behaviorally oriented family systems approaches were effective. These approaches might, for instance, educate the family about adolescent depression and help the family develop skills to cope with their adolescent's depression. Also, one-on-one interpersonal therapy may be helpful for some youths who are depressed, but this research evidence is less compelling (Curry 2001; Harrington 1995).

March and colleagues (2004) conducted a major study showing that treating depressed teenagers with a combination of antidepressants and psychotherapy is better than either treatment approach alone. The researchers compared the effectiveness of four different treatment approaches in 439 children and teens aged twelve to seventeen who had been diagnosed with major depression. The children were randomly assigned to receive a combination of Prozac and behavioral therapy, behavioral therapy alone, Prozac alone, or a placebo (sugar pill) for twelve weeks. The cognitive-behavioral therapy used in the study was a skills-oriented treatment based on changing negative thought patterns and increasing active, positive behaviors. The treatment consisted of fifteen sessions lasting fifty to sixty minutes each.

At the end of the treatment period researchers found that 71 percent of the teenagers had responded to the combination depression treatment, whereas 61 percent of those on Prozac alone, 43 percent of those who received behavioral therapy alone, and 35 percent of those on placebo had responded to the treatment. The results also suggest that combining antidepressant treatment with talk therapy may help alleviate some potentially harmful or suicidal behaviors that may be associated with antidepressant use. In short, results show that teenagers with major depression were more likely to get relief and were effectively treated for their condition with a combination of Prozac and cognitive-behavioral therapy than with antidepressants, psychotherapy, or placebo alone. The combination of Prozac and cognitive-behavioral therapy produced the greatest reduction in suicidal thinking.

BIPOLAR DISORDER

Most research on the effectiveness of interventions with people who struggle with bipolar disorder has been conducted on adults (Basco et al. 2007; Consoli et al. 2007; Evans et al. 2005; Fountoulakis et al. 2005; Geller and Luby 1997; Guttierez and Scott 2004; Huxley, Parikh, and Baldessarini 2000; Johnson and Leahy 2005; Keming and Calabrese 2005; Kemp et al. 2006; Landwehr 2005; Leahy 2007; Scott and Gutierrez 2004; Strober et al. 2006; Wilkinson, Taylor, and Holt, 2002; Zarate and Quiroz 2003). The emerging consensus among researchers is that the most effective interventions include a combination of psychotherapy, particularly cognitive-behavioral therapy, and mood-stabilizing medication (Basco et al. 2007; Bower 2007; Findling 2005; Greenspan and Glovinsky 2005; Kowatch et al. 2005; Pavuluri and Naylor 2005).

ANXIETY

As with the treatment of major depression and bipolar disorder among adolescents, the research literature provides considerable evidence that cognitive-behavioral interventions can be particularly effective in the treatment of adolescents who struggle with anxiety (Albano and Kendall 2002; Barrett 1998; Bernstein and Borchardt 1991; Cartwright-Hatton et al. 2004; Dadds et al. 1997; Evans et al. 2005; Flannery-Schroeder and Kendall 2000; In-Albon and Schneider 2007; Kohn and Golden 2001; Morris and March 2004; O'Hare 2005; Rome et al. 2003; Silverman and Treffers 2001). Much of the research literature regarding adolescents and anxiety has focused on the treatment of posttraumatic stress disorder (PTSD) and obsessive-compulsive disorder (OCD). Widely endorsed clinical interventions include cognitive restructuring (identifying thoughts that lead to anxious feelings, using alternative self-talk, and using written logs to keep track of self-talk, anxiety levels, and coping strategies), relaxation skills training, systematic desensitization (gradual exposure to a fearsome stimulus while using self-soothing techniques), problem-solving skills training, psychoeducational therapy, and contingency management methods such as collaborating with the family to provide positive reinforcement (Cartwright-Hatton et al. 2004; Compton et al. 2002;

Harrington 1995; Harrington, Whitaker, and Shoebridge 1998; Harrington, Wood, and Verduyn 1998; Kazdin 1994; Kendall 1992; King, Hamilton, and Ollendick 1988; Ollendick and King 1994).

OPPOSITIONAL BEHAVIOR

Substantial empirical evidence shows that several interventions can be very effective with teens whose behavior is oppositional. These effective interventions include teaching coping skills, social skills, behavioral self-control methods, parenting skills, cognitive restructuring, behavioral family therapy, and contingency management (using consequences to reward desired behaviors and decrease the frequency of undesired behaviors) (Kazdin et al. 1989; O'Hare 2005). Cognitive-behavioral treatment typically helps adolescents identify and label their feelings (self-awareness), use self-control messages, slow their responses, be less impulsive, and better differentiate hostile and nonhostile social cues (Kendall 1993; Springer 2004; Webster-Stratton and Herbert 1994).

Evidence shows that coping skills based on cognitive-behavioral principles can be particularly effective in the context of behavioral family therapy and multisystemic therapy (Alexander et al. 1988; Baily 1998; Christophersen and Finney 1999; Foster 1994; Geismar and Wood 1986; Gurman, Kniskern, and Pinsof 1986; Harnish, Tolan, and Guerra 1996; Henggeler and Sheidow 2003; Horne, Glaser, and Calhoun 1999; Kazdin 1997; Lebow and Gurman 1995; Northey et al. 2003; Springer 2004). The cognitive-behavioral approach with families helps parents to identify, relabel, and monitor adolescent behaviors and negotiate behavioral contracts with the teen. The model includes providing parents with psychoeducational therapy to enhance their understanding of normal adolescent development and develop effective parenting, problem-solving, and communication skills.

In a comprehensive review of extensive empirical evaluations of interventions with defiant, oppositional children and adolescents, Brestan and Eyberg (1998) conclude that only behaviorally oriented parent-training programs could be considered "established" treatments (O'Hare 2005). Similarly, comprehensive reviews by Farmer and colleagues (2002), Gacono and colleagues (2001), Palmer (1996), and Springer (2004) clearly suggest that cognitive-behavioral and family-oriented interventions, particularly multisystemic interventions, are most effective. Interventions with mixed outcomes include case management, job training, traditional counseling, and intensive probation and parole monitoring. Most important, Palmer's (1996) analysis of research results found that programs based on confrontation demonstrate minimal positive impact.

EATING DISORDERS

Controlled studies indicate that cognitive-behavioral therapy and interpersonal psychotherapy are effective interventions for adolescents who struggle with eating disorders, particularly bulimia nervosa and binge eating (Evans et al. 2005; Fairburn 1997; Schmidt 1998; Shekter-Wolfson, Woodside, and Lackstrom 1997; Smith, Marcus, and Eldredge 1994; Stein et al. 2001; Vitousek 2002; Wilson and Fairburn 1993, 1998). Interventions that draw primarily on family therapy based on communication models, psychodynamic theory, and feminist theory have not been shown to be effective or have produced mixed results (O'Hare 2005; Wilson, Grilo, and Vitousek 2007). Empirical results from several meta-analyses suggest that cognitive-behavioral interventions are effective for more than three-fourths of clients, with impressive long-term maintenance of gains; more than half of clients report successfully abstaining from bingeing and purging. Cognitive-behavioral interventions and interpersonal therapy have not been shown to be as effective with anorexia nervosa (O'Hare 2005).

Cognitive-behavioral interventions for eating disorders focus primarily on identifying and changing specific beliefs, attributions, expectations, values, and cognitive distortions that contribute to the eating disorder. Clinicians use cognitive and behavioral techniques to teach teens to be more aware of their thoughts, feelings, and behaviors and to learn how to identify and label their emotions and recurrent thinking patterns (Bowers, Evans, and van Cleve 1996). Possible explanations for the effectiveness of cognitive-behavioral interventions include cognitive changes about body shape and weight; reduction of dietary restraint, which subsequently reduces the tendency to binge eat; and increased self-efficacy, which results in improved ability to cope with precipitating stressors and enjoy normal eating (Fairburn 1993; O'Hare 2005).

Interpersonal therapy typically involves identifying and working on interpersonal problems (relationship problems) that affect eating disorders (Klerman and Weissman 1993; Weissman, Markowitz, and Klerman 2000). Interpersonal therapy focuses on interpersonal conflicts and related distress that may precipitate binge eating. Like cognitive-behavioral interventions, interpersonal therapy is typically a short-term treatment and goal oriented. Individual and/or group therapy formats exist for interpersonal therapy. Research shows that interpersonal therapy is as effective as cognitive-behavioral interventions in treating bulimia nervosa in the long term, although cognitive-behavioral interventions appears to have a faster effect (Fairburn 1997).

ATTENTION-DEFICIT/HYPERACTIVITY DISORDER

Extensive research evidence indicates that many adolescents who struggle with attention deficit hyperactivity disorder (ADHD) are best helped by a combination of psychostimulant medication and individual, family, and, when appropriate, classroom-based behavioral interventions (Anastopoulous 1998; Anastopoulous, Smith, and Wien 1998; Barkley 2002; Bernier and Siegel 1994; Braswell and Bloomquist 1991; Fabiano et al. 2007; Hinshaw, Klein, and Abikoff 1998; Kazdin 1994; Kendall 1993; O'Hare 2005; Pelham, Wheeler, and Chronis 1998; Rapport 1992; Root and Resnick 2003). Typical goals include using cognitive-behavioral interventions to help adolescents self-regulate (for example, organize their homework, stay on task, control disruptive behavior).

Farmer and colleagues (2002) reviewed more than 130 studies of intervention outcomes for youths diagnosed with ADHD. The strongest empirical support was for pharmacological treatments. Psychosocial treatments alone (such as cognitive-behavioral therapy, parent training, biofeedback training, and social skills training) demonstrated some positive results but smaller than those demonstrated for medication treatments. The effectiveness of combining psychosocial and pharmacological interventions is mixed. Some studies showed little or no benefit of adding psychosocial interventions to well-administered medication treatments, whereas others suggested that adding psychosocial interventions may make it possible to attain desired responses with lower doses of medication.

In recent years research on the effectiveness of diverse ways of intervening with, and helping, struggling teens has burgeoned. Although significant gaps in knowledge exist, we have learned a great deal about a range of constructive, ethical, positive, and nonabusive interventions. As we explore in the next chapter, these findings suggest a wide range of "best practices" that should be implemented in efforts to help struggling teens and their families.

5

A BLUEPRINT FOR REFORM

BEST PRACTICES FOR THE STRUGGLING-TEENS INDUSTRY

Since the advent of efforts in the 1800s to intervene with struggling teens and their families, we have learned a great deal about what to do—and what not to do—to be helpful and, especially, ethical. During the last half-century specialty schools and programs have proliferated, bringing with them a complex mix of both distressing scandals and inspiring successes. In recent decades we have learned much about the ways in which properly run schools and programs can have profoundly useful, meaningful, and lasting positive influences on struggling teens and their families. Sadly, we have also learned about the intense and disturbing harm that some schools and programs can cause.

We now have considerable accumulated wisdom about the wide range of different ways to help struggling teens and their families. This wisdom comes from rigorously conducted, formal research studies, professional experience, in-depth media reports, and compelling first-person accounts. Considered together, this rich fund of knowledge paints a picture of state-of-the art "best practices." These best practices are rooted in a collaborative, respectful focus on the basic human rights, strengths, and resilience of teens and their families. Our principal aim is to identify best practices to ensure quality programs and schools, effective regulation of the struggling-teens industry, and enhanced access so that all struggling teens can find high-quality programs and services.

THE STRENGTHS PERSPECTIVE

A distressing feature of some scandalous and abusive programs and schools is their inappropriate and destructive use of shame, blame, pejorative labels, and "tough love" tactics. These are programs whose practices reflect the view that "today's teens are so out-of-control and so morally compromised that only extreme harsh, perhaps even brutal tactics can keep them in line. A bit of cruelty is necessary, even kind—signifying good parenting, the opposite of abuse" (Szalavitz 2006:3). Fortunately, principled professionals in the field who pay careful attention to mainstream codes of ethics and empirically based knowledge have concluded that these tactics are shortsighted and harmful.[1] As participants in a state-of-the-science conference sponsored by the National Institutes of Health Consensus Development Program (2004) concluded, "The evidence indicates that 'scare tactics' don't work and there is some evidence that they may make the problem worse rather than simply not working." We now have an impressive body of research evidence that harsh, shaming, labeling, and pejorative responses to teens can have profoundly negative consequences (Sells 2002; Taffel 2005).[2]

Evidence suggests that the strengths perspective is a constructive approach to helping struggling teens and their families. Briefly, it focuses on what is "right" with people rather than on what is wrong. It identifies, builds upon, and amplifies people's strengths, resilience, and resources. While it recognizes and acknowledges people's problems (such as mental illness, physical disability, poverty, legal troubles), the strengths perspective views these as challenges and as needs to be addressed, not as deficits, pathologies, or character flaws. From a strengths perspective adolescence, like every developmental period throughout the life course, poses unique challenges that are opportunities for growth. Many of these challenges are predictable and need not be seen as pathology (Carter and McGoldrick 2005). This nonpunitive, nonblaming, nonshaming approach identifies and harnesses people's competence, resources, and capacities so they are better able to propel themselves toward positive goals. Substance abuse, mental health issues, school failure, and other challenges are opportunities for teens, families, schools, and communities to collaborate in pursuing a shared vision for the future.

A growing body of theoretical and research literature focuses on the usefulness of a strengths perspective with different populations that struggle with seemingly intractable challenges such as chronic and severe schizophrenia, homelessness, and substance abuse (Rapp and Goscha 2006; Saleebey 2006). A growing consensus in the helping professions is that a strengths perspective undergirds effective intervention. The strengths perspective does not condone or sanction misbehavior; rather, the strengths perspective recognizes misbehavior as an attempt to cope and solve problems, albeit perhaps a misguided one, and seeks to help the teen find more suitable behaviors and effective coping skills.

The strengths perspective is built on a series of core principles (Saleebey 2006):

1. *Every individual, group, family, and community has strengths.*

Practitioners who use the strengths perspective identify, mobilize, and respect the resources, assets, wisdom, and knowledge that every person, family, group, or community has. They view people as able to marshal these strengths to accomplish their goals.

2. *Trauma, abuse, illness, and struggle, while sources of difficulty and challenge, can also be sources of opportunity for growth and change.*

Negative experiences can yield knowledge, wisdom, insight, and compassion for others. This does not mean that scars and pain are not legitimate; of course they merit attention and validation. It does mean that humans who weather adversity are resilient, resourceful survivors who can cull meaning and skills from their travails. People who slog through suffering use their coping skills and can learn from their experience.

3. *Individual, group, and community goals matter.*

By aligning with the hopes, values, aspirations, and visions of teens and their families, professionals can help people enhance their promise and possibilities. Emphasizing people's limitations makes it difficult for them to identify and pursue goals. Labels ("He's paranoid," "She's an ADHD kid," "He's a schizophrenic," "She's an addict," "He's a quitter") can become verdicts or life sentences that impede people's self-perception and negatively shape others' beliefs about what is possible. Separating the person from the diagnosis acknowledges that illnesses and disabilities do not define the person—they are merely conditions the person has.

4. *Professionals serve people best by collaborating with them as colleagues on the intervention team.*

The professional who uses a strengths perspective may have specialized education, tools, and experience to offer but is also open to the wisdom, knowledge, and experience of the teen and her family. The professional works *with* the teen and family members rather than *on* their cases. The goals of the consumer, not the professional, are primary, and consumers' voices are heard and valued at all levels of intervention and in policy advocacy.

5. *Every environment is full of resources.*

Regardless of how poverty ridden or chaotic, every environment has individuals, families, informal groups, associations, and organizations that may be willing to provide help. Given the opportunity, they may contribute needed assets and resources. Once recognized and recruited, partnerships and strengths available in the community can be highly constructive.

6. *Caring, caretaking, and context are vitally important.*

Caring is essential to human well-being. Professionals can facilitate the processes by which families, groups, and communities provide care for each other.

In order to put these core principles to work, the professional must conduct a strengths-based assessment. Assessment is the process of collecting information from various sources in order to specify the concerns to be addressed in intervention, set goals, and choose intervention methods. A strengths-based assessment explores the following areas (Saleebey 2006):

What people have learned about themselves and others. People learn from the challenges they endure, their disappointments, failures, and accomplishments. Resiliency springs from the interplay of risk factors and the internal and environmental resources available to people.

Personal qualities, traits, and virtues. In coping with adversity, people may discover and develop such qualities in themselves as fortitude, patience, persistence, and moral fiber. They may develop new strengths and resources in order to meet life's challenges.

What people know about the world around them. Knowledge comes from different sources, including education, culture, and life experience. People develop skills and abilities through living. For instance, a teen might know much more than the professionals who work with him about how to survive without permanent shelter.

Talents people have. Frequently, professionals find that people have surprising talents. Many times people do not think to mention those talents, which seem irrelevant to what they are discussing with professionals. If professionals do not ask, they may miss opportunities to identify, support, and mobilize these attributes. Gathering information about people's strengths gives professionals a more accurate appreciation of the whole person and may open up a sense of possibilities and options for problem solving and personal development. For example, a teen may be good at whittling wood with a pen knife or making beautiful tile mosaics and thus able to earn money selling her creations.

Cultural and personal stories and lore. Narratives, myths, and cultural stories can enhance a person's sense of belonging and place in the world, as well as the person's identity, meaning, values, and inspiration for managing pain and suffering. For instance, a family's story about how its forebears emigrated to the United States may have been the genesis of its intergenerational emphasis on sticking together and providing each other with critically important support under difficult conditions.

Pride. When people overcome adversity, they develop a sense of pride and accomplishment. This pride becomes a strength and resource that facilitates coping with other challenges.

The community. Communities have assets that should be part of the assessment of teens and their families. Examples include informal social networks, religious institutions, bowling leagues, book groups, child-care co-ops, and volunteer opportunities. People can benefit from giving as well as receiving, since this enhances their sense of belonging and personal empowerment.

Spirituality. Spirituality can be a powerful source of strength. It can offer people a sense of perspective, purpose, meaning, beauty, and the connection to all living things. For many people spirituality provides hope and sustenance. Thus professionals should invite teens and their families to articulate their spiritual beliefs and practices, as cultivating these may help propel them toward their goals.

A key feature of the strengths perspective is that it acknowledges normal developmental trends and challenges in a teen's life. An especially important aspect of this developmental perspective is that it recognizes that the teenage brain is in the process of formation, so impulsive and irrational behavior, difficulty foreseeing consequences, decision-making gaffes and mishaps, and feelings of invulnerability are predictable, normal teenage phenomena. The human frontal lobe evolves on its own timetable and is implicated in problem solving, spontaneity, impulsivity, memory, initiative, judgment, and social and sexual behavior; significant brain maturation occurs from the teenage to the young adult years. Researchers have compared MRI scans of young adults aged 23 to 30 with those of teens aged 12 to 16 (Sowell et al. 1999, 2006). The researchers looked for signs of myelin, which would imply more mature, efficient connections within gray matter. The largest differences between young adults and teens occurred in areas of the frontal lobe. Increased myelination in the adult frontal cortex probably relates to the maturation of cognitive processing and other "executive functions" (Sowell et al. 1999, 2006). Thus teens need adults to help them stay physically and emotionally safe so their brains have time to mature. Harsh discipline, "tough love," and abusive words do not speed up this process. Instead, they can compromise the developmental process. Programs and schools for struggling teens should recognize that one of their functions is to keep struggling teens emotionally and physically safe in an incubator that is nurturing and challenging academically, socially, and emotionally. Verbal haranguing, shaming, and blaming cannot hasten physiological brain maturation. A quality program or school seeks to maintain this developmental perspective.

RESILIENCE

The concept of resilience is central to the strengths perspective (Goldstein and Brooks 2005; Ungar 2005). Resilience refers to the process of overcoming the negative effects of exposure to dangerous situations, coping successfully with traumatic experiences, and avoiding the negative trajectories associated with risks (Fergus and Zimmerman 2005). Resilience theory focuses on understanding how some people achieve healthy development even in the face of challenging circumstances.

Ideally, programs and schools for struggling teens enhance what Fergus and Zimmerman (2005) refer to as "promotive factors" to help teens avoid the negative effects of trauma and risky circumstances.[3] These promotive factors, sometimes also called protective factors, include both assets and resources. Assets are the internal positive factors that reside within the teen and family, such as competence, coping skills, and belief in one's efficacy. Resources are external positive factors that help teens and families overcome challenging and risky circumstances. For the teen these resources include parental love and financial support, adult mentors, counselors, teachers, schools, safe neighborhoods, and community organizations that promote positive youth development.

Researchers concerned about vulnerable teens have identified three distinct models of resilience—compensatory, protective, and challenge. Each model has important implications for designing effective services for struggling teens and their families (Garmezy, Masten, and Tellegen 1984; Masten 1999; Rutter 1985, 1987). A compensatory model involves the direct influence of a promotive factor on a risk factor (Zimmerman and Arunkumar 1994). Examples of promotive factors are mentoring or involvement in a religious organization. That is, adult mentoring or involvement in a religious community might help balance or offset the negative effects of a chaotic or abusive home environment that otherwise might lead to a teen's self-injury, delinquent activity, or substance abuse.

A second resilience model, the protective model, assumes that specific assets or resources moderate or reduce risks (Fergus and Zimmerman 2005). Examples of protective resources are stable housing, a close relationship with a teacher, or supervised after-school activities. These supports serve to protect otherwise vulnerable teens and minimize the negative impact of potentially toxic influences, such as living in an unsafe neighborhood or with a mental health issue such as depression.

A third resilience model, the challenge model, assumes that teens who are exposed to moderate, as opposed to unusually high or low, levels of challenging circumstances learn how to overcome it but are not exposed to so much of it that overcoming it is impossible (Garmezy, Masten, and Tellegen 1984; Luthar and Zelazo 2003). Under this model exposing teens to a modest level of challenge may be beneficial because doing so provides teens with a chance to develop and practice coping skills or use resources. For example, too little family conflict may not provide teens with an opportunity to learn how to cope with or solve interpersonal conflicts outside the home. However, too much conflict may be overwhelming and lead teens to feel hopeless and distressed. A moderate (typical) amount of family conflict may provide teens with enough exposure to learn how to manage and resolve conflict. Wilderness therapy programs put this concept to use when deliberately presenting teens with challenging, yet safe, situations that allow the teen to develop a sense of mastery, competence, pride, and self-confidence. This framework, based on three resilience models, can be used to guide interventions in programs and schools for struggling teens. Mobilizing community resources and putting teens and their families in contact with them can lead to the cultivation of the teen's resilience and compensatory and protective abilities.

The process of acquiring resilience may vary for different groups of adolescents (Fergus and Zimmerman 2005). Resilience for urban, suburban, and rural teens, for example, may differ as each environment offers different challenges and resources. Protective factors for teens in high and low socioeconomic groups, younger and older teens, teens of color and white teens, and males and females may differ. Also, different teens may respond differently to the same adverse events. Some teens may cope reasonably well with the death of a parent or their parents' divorce, while others may have a much more difficult time. Therefore individualized assessment and intervention are essential.

Research shows that many protective factors can prevent various high-risk adolescent behaviors, such as substance abuse, violent behavior, and certain sexual behaviors. Encouraging the following protective factors may prevent substance abuse:

- Academic achievement (Bryant and Zimmerman 2002; Bryant et al. 2003)
- Parental involvement with the teen's educational activities, for example, monitoring school performance, attending school events, staying in touch with school personnel (Fleming et al. 2002)
- Positive orientation toward school (Costa, Jessor, and Turbin 1999)
- Plans to attend college (Bryant et al. 2003)
- Constructive exercise of parental authority (Jackson 2002)
- Parental monitoring (Rai et al. 2003)
- Open communication with parents (Stanton et al. 2002)
- Parental support (Farrell and White 1998; Kim, Zane, and Hong 2002)
- Teens' sense of control over their life (Scheier, Botvin, and Miller 1999)
- Development of good self-esteem (Byerne and Mazanov 2001)

- Positive mood (Scheier, Botvin, and Miller 1999)
- Religious orientation (Wills, Yaeger, and Sandy 2003)
- Family connectedness (Fleming et al. 2002; Lloyd-Richardson et al., 2002)
- Participation in extracurricular and community activities (Crosnoe 2002; Elder et al. 2000; Feldman 1992)
- Acquisition of decision-making skills (Botvin et al. 1998)

Research evidence suggests that promoting the following protective factors can prevent violent behavior among adolescents:

- Prosocial beliefs (Huang et al. 2001)
- Religious orientation (Barkin, Kreiter, and Durant 2001)
- Anger-control skills (Griffin et al. 1999)
- Paternal support (Howard, Qiu, and Boekeloo 2003; Zimmerman, Steinman, and Rowe 1998)
- Parental monitoring (Griffin et al. 1999; Howard, Qiu, and Boekeloo 2003; Zimmerman, Steinman, and Rowe 1998)
- Parental presence (Borowsky, Ireland, and Resnick 2002)
- Parent-child attachment (Borowsky, Ireland, and Resnick 2002)
- Academic performance (Borowsky, Ireland, and Resnick 2002)
- School connectedness (Borowsky, Ireland, and Resnick 2002)

Finally, research evidence suggests that these protective factors can prevent risky sexual behavior:

- Self-esteem (Paul et al. 2000)
- Participation in extracurricular activities (Anteghini et al. 2001)
- School achievement (Kumpfer and Alvarado 2003; Magnani et al. 2002; Paul et al. 2000; Santelli et al. 2004)
- Connection to the school environment (Kumpfer and Alvarado 2003; Magnani et al. 2002; Paul et al. 2000; Santelli et al. 2004)
- Teacher support (Anteghini et al. 2001)
- Religious orientation (Lammers et al. 2000; Magnani et al. 2002)
- Knowledge of HIV and reproductive health (Magnani et al. 2002)
- Positive attitudes toward condoms (Malow et al. 2001)
- Intentions to engage in safer sex (Malow et al. 2001)
- Seeing sex as risky behavior (Santelli et al. 2004)
- Parental monitoring (Rai et al. 2003)
- Open parental communication (Stanton et al. 2002)

In short, identifying and amplifying specific protective factors can be a promising strategy for building strengths and resilience to help a struggling teen. Many strengths-based, resilience-building programs and services exist. However, often they are hard to locate or afford.

ACCESSING SERVICES

Typically, parents seek help for their struggling teen by going to mental health professionals, school personnel, child welfare agencies, court officials, and clergy in their community. Often professionals who are concerned about struggling teens and their families are not entirely familiar with the full range of available options, both locally and, when necessary, outside the local community. Ideally, professionals who have contact with struggling teens and their families would have a thorough knowledge of available services and ways to access them (Reamer and Siegel 2006).

When local services have been exhausted or have not been fruitful, parents may need to consider out-of-home resources, such as wilderness therapy programs, emotional growth boarding schools, therapeutic boarding schools, and residential treatment centers. Naturally, most parents have little knowledge of these programs or how to find and screen them. Hence, some may turn to an educational consultant for help with that task. The job of an educational consultant is to help parents locate programs, services, and schools that meet their child's needs. For a fee educational consultants assess each teen's unique strengths and needs and help the parents find the most appropriate services, schools, or programs.[4] Many educational consultants monitor students' progress in the new program or school and, when necessary, advocate for the teen with that program or school when challenging issues arise.

Educational consulting is a relatively young and largely unregulated industry and, as a result, suffers from a lack of quality control. Many educational consultants are impressively credentialed, experienced, and competent; others, however, lack the expertise to provide high-quality services. Some educational consultants enter the field primarily as a result of their own experiences parenting a struggling teen and do not have the rich academic or professional foundation that educational consulting requires. There is no educational consultant license, so consumers have no assurance that their educational consultant has formal training in the fields of education, learning disabilities, adolescent development, counseling, and mental and behavioral health, even though advance knowledge in all these areas is essential to adequately assess a teen's needs and match them with appropriate programs and services. Some educational consultants do have a license in a related field, such as social work, counseling, or psychology. Others have a graduate degree in a relevant discipline, such as education. But these allied licenses and degrees may or may not indicate that an educational consultant's training and experience pass muster for the role of educational consultant.

The Independent Educational Consultants Association (IECA) has done much to professionalize and advance the quality of its members. However, one need not belong to IECA in order to hold oneself out as an educational consultant. To gain professional membership in IECA and advertise one's affiliation with that organization as an educational consultant for struggling teens and their families, a candidate must have

A master's degree or higher from an accredited institution. Alternatively, an applicant may demonstrate comparable educational training or appropriate professional experience.

Three years of experience in counseling or admissions, with a minimum of one year of independent practice.

Advised at least fifty students while the candidate was employed in an institutional setting or working in private practice.

Conducted at least twenty-five "evaluative campus visits" to "troubled teen programs."

Professional references from at least two college or independent school admissions officers or psychologists/counselors with whom the candidate has worked in the admission process. The organization requires a third reference from an IECA member, another educational professional, or a client family.

To its credit IECA requires its members to adhere to a set of ethical standards contained in the association's "Principles of Good Practice" (IECA 2006).[5] Its standards and membership criteria constitute a valuable effort to enhance the quality of educational consulting. But they are only a first step. For one thing, membership in IECA is voluntary, unlike legally enforceable licensing requirements that exist in professions. Also, the IECA membership criteria are not nearly as rigorous, clearly defined, or specific as the typical licensing regulations for the prominent allied helping professions, such as social work, psychology, marriage and family therapy, and counseling. For example, although IECA requires members to have a master's degree or higher, the membership criteria do not require specific coursework in areas relevant to educational consulting for struggling teens. Thus, for instance, someone with a Ph.D. whose education focused on geriatric psychology might be eligible for IECA membership as a specialist in finding programs and schools for struggling teens. Further, although IECA requires that members have advised at least fifty students while employed in an institutional setting or working in private practice, the association does not specify the nature of the advising or ensure that it was in-depth and comprehensive as opposed to superficial or unrelated to struggling teens' issues. In addition, although IECA requires that members have conducted at least twenty-five "evaluative campus visits" to "troubled teen programs," the association does not publicize criteria for what constitutes in-depth and comprehensive visits.

To enhance the likelihood of high-quality educational consulting and protect teens and their families, IECA and state regulatory bodies must establish more rigorous quality-control standards with regard to educational qualifications and experience. These quality-control criteria and regulatory standards, including continuing education requirements and disciplinary protocols, can be modeled on widely accepted licensing standards for the established professions.[6] In the absence of adequate credentialing and licensing of educational consultants, parents and teens cannot be assured that the educational consultant from whom they seek help is adequately informed or skilled.

PROGRAM DESIGN AND IMPLEMENTATION

While many community-based programs and residential schools and programs for struggling teens are of high quality, many also engage in ineffective or harmful practices. Chapter 3 provides examples of a disturbing number of abusive and unethical schools and programs.

An adequate program or school for struggling teens must have several crucial features. Educational consultants, school and program administrators, and accrediting and regulatory bodies that oversee the schools and programs should implement these critically important programmatic features:

ASSESSMENT OF TEENS' NEEDS

At intake or during the first meeting educational consultants, programs, and schools should always conduct a comprehensive biopsychosocial assessment based on widely accepted protocols in the human services in order to meet a teen's needs (Hess and Howard 1981; Jordan and Franklin 2003; Karls and Wandrei 1994; Meyer 1993; O'Hare 2005). The assessment provides a picture of each teen's unique strengths, challenges, and needs so services can be appropriately tailored to that particular youth. Although many programs and schools conduct competent and thorough assessments and explore the fit between what the program has to offer and what the teen needs, too many do not. Some programs accept just about any teen who is willing to attend and whose family has the means to pay; these programs run on the belief that their model and approach are right for nearly everyone. Some programs "flex," or adjust, their intake criteria when their census is low and the program needs to generate revenue.[7] These practices put teens at risk of placement in programs that cannot meet their needs.

An adequate, comprehensive assessment should include information about the teen's biological, social, and psychological history to help identify strengths, needs, and issues that merit support and intervention. Such an assessment should include the circumstances of the teen's birth—noteworthy events during the pregnancy that may have affected the teen, such as premature birth, prenatal drug exposure, or trauma during pregnancy or delivery. Was the teen adopted or placed in foster care at birth? Noteworthy developmental milestones include when the teen reached typical developmental milestones (for example, those related to speech, social skills, and fine and gross motor skills).

The assessment also should consider the teen's strengths and supports and the teen's successes: Who are the teen's supports, such as caring and involved family members, friends, teachers, youth advisers, coaches, clergy, or other members of the community? What experiences has the teen had where he or she was successful? What made these successes possible? When did these occur and what were the circumstances?

Ethnic heritage and religious heritage and considerations also are an important part of the assessment. What is the teen's ethnic heritage and how comfortable with and proud of this heritage is the teen? What kinds of racism and discrimination has the teen experienced? How sensitive to the teen's ethnicity must the new school or program be? What is the teen's religious heritage? How comfortable is the teen with this heritage? What kind of religious discrimination has the teen experienced? What kind of religious programs and supports does the teen need in the new school or program?

The consultant also will want to take the teen's temperament and social relationships into consideration in recommending a placement. To what extent has the teen, faced with everyday challenges, behaved in predictable ways that have led to problems? Has the teen been consistently defiant, explosive, and irritable? Impatient and impulsive? Passive and indifferent? Has the teen had difficulty with transitions from school to school or community to community? Also, how well has the teen made and kept friends? What are the friendships like? How many friends does the teen typically have? How long do these relationships last? How well does the teen get along with friends?

The consultant also will need to take into account the teen's history with respect to moods, thoughts and perceptions, and cognitive functioning. What, if any, mental health issues has the teen been diagnosed with? For example, does the teen have anxiety, depression, obsessive-compulsive disorder, posttraumatic stress disorder, bipolar disorder, oppositional defiant disorder, Asperger's syndrome, a pervasive developmental disorder, sensory integration dysfunction, or adjustment reactions?

Also, what are the stressors in the teen's life (such as illness or disability in the family, divorce, poverty, unsafe housing or neighborhood, frequent moves and changes in school, loss of loved ones, family violence, learning disability, or sexual abuse)? And what have been the most significant problems in the teen's life (for example, emotional, behavioral, educational, medical, social)? What are the symptoms? How severe have the problems been? How long has the teen struggled with the problems? When have these problems not been present or been less severe?

Also significant to the teen's history are past efforts to address problems, including the mental health, educational, and other social services the teen has received (such as psychiatric hospitalization, outpatient counseling, tutoring, and substance abuse treatment). In what ways have these services and programs been helpful or unhelpful?

The consultant should look closely as the teen's education history—what have been the teen's successes in school? What challenges has the teen faced in school? Has the teen been formally evaluated for learning disabilities? What is the teen's learning style (visual, auditory, kinesthetic/tactile)? What accommodations and compensatory strategies help the teen learn best? Does the teen have a 504 plan or an IEP (an individualized education program)? If so, what are the plan's components? What changes in the plan do the teen, parents, or school personnel think are needed?

The teen's employment/vocational history also should be part of the assessment. What paid or volunteer jobs has the teen held? How successful were these experiences? What kinds of structures or supports enhance the teen's likelihood of success on the job?

The consultant will want to determine what illegal behaviors the teen has engaged in (for example, driving under the influence, reckless driving, drug possession, truancy, and shoplifting). Is the teen facing any legal charges? Has the teen been placed on probation or incarcerated?

No less important is a thorough understanding of the teenager's awareness of his or her current circumstances. How does the teen define the problem(s)? To what does the teen attribute the problem(s)? What are the teen's ideas about solutions? To what extent does the teen take responsibility for her or his choices and behavior? How much insight does the teen have? How motivated does the teen appear to be to address his or her challenges? What kind of help does the teen want?

Finally, the consultant must attempt to gain a thorough family history as well as a good picture of how the teen's family regards the teen's current circumstances. What is the teen's current family situation? Who lives in the home with the teen? With what family members does the teen have positive or conflictual relationships? How do family members get along with one another? What kinship resources are available to the teen? If the teen is in foster care or adopted, what is the teen's relationship with the biological parents and other biological family members? How are foster care and adoption issues discussed in the teen's current household? What feelings and thoughts does the teen have about foster care and adoption?

Further, what family members has the teen lost as a result of divorce, separation, foster care, adoption, or death? What family members have been added to the family as a result of remarriage or adoption? How has the family addressed these losses and additions?

The family history of mental health issues, substance abuse, and medical problems will also have a direct bearing on the placement the consultant recommends. What mental health diagnoses appear on the family tree? What illnesses, medical conditions, or physical disabilities in the family have affected the teen?

The family's financial history is germane as well, and not just its ability to pay for the teen's services or room and board in a residential program. How adequate has the family's income been? To what extent have poverty and unemployment been part of the family's history?

The consultant also needs a good idea of how parents and other key family members understand the teen's current circumstances. How do the teen's parents and other important people in his or her life understand the teen's current challenges? What do they think has led to the teen's current situation? What strengths, skills, and resources does the teen's family have that have helped it cope with the challenges of a struggling teen? What patterns of family interaction have emerged around the teen's struggles? How ready do the teen's parents, and other important people in her or his life, feel to address the issues and be part of interventions, services, and treatments? What do they think would be most helpful to them and the teen?

ENSURING QUALITY IN PROGRAMS AND SERVICES

The review of the literature in chapter 4 highlights research evidence of factors that are important for ensuring that programs and schools are of high quality. Professionals in the struggling-teens industry who are concerned about ineffective, abusive, and negligent practices should keep these factors in mind as they assess and monitor programs and schools.

These factors also are important for parents to consider as they screen programs and schools in their search for help for their teen. Parents often enroll their struggling teen in a program or school during a crisis, when the adults are desperate for a solution to complex challenges. This is understandable. But, as the adage goes, haste makes waste. It is vitally important for parents and their advisers to thoroughly examine schools and programs before deciding which is most appropriate. Educational consultants and parents should not select a school or program based on word of mouth, glossy brochures, sweeping claims of success, glitzy promotional videos, or eye-catching Web sites. They need to look deep beneath the surface and probe for detailed information from multiple, informed sources. Impulsive choices can backfire with explosive force and lead to more disruption and distress for the entire family; a teen who is mismanaged by a program or school, and who needs to leave precipitously, is likely to leave with more issues than when she or he first arrived. Professionals working with parents must avoid being seduced by the most readily available placement, if at all possible; they need to slow down and proceed with caution, looking as carefully as possible for the most suitable placement.[8]

In choosing a program or school, parents *and* professionals should carefully assess the extent to which the placement meets standards derived from the literature on what works. The research evidence reviewed in chapter 4 is a good place to start. When we examine the literature on the strengths perspective, resilience, adolescent brain development, the critical role of relationship in the professional helping process, program models, adolescent education, and mental health diagnoses and interventions, several core guiding principles emerge. These principles should underpin any efforts to help struggling teens and their families along every point in the continuum of care, including initial assessment, crisis intervention, home-based services, community-based counseling, alternative community-based education, mentoring, drug and truancy courts, wilderness therapy programs, emotional growth boarding schools, therapeutic boarding schools, and residential psychiatric treatment.

Principle 1. Above all else, do no harm. The struggling-teens industry must adopt this core principle of the Hippocratic Oath. Noble intentions do not always produce good outcomes. Verbal, emotional, and physical abuse are unacceptable; the ends never justify these means.

Principle 2. Schools and programs should focus on strengths, resilience, and a developmental perspective. These points of view are compatible with, and can be incorporated into, multiple educational and therapeutic modalities. They help professionals avoid destructive and harmful interventions.

Schools and programs should use the language and concepts of strengths, resilience, and developmental perspectives in their written descriptions of their program, policies, procedures, and day-to-day practices. This translates into daily staff-teen interactions that hold great helping potential. When the teen makes unwise choices, is noncompliant, withdraws, misbehaves, breaks rules, or is otherwise unresponsive to direction, these mishaps are viewed and addressed as learning opportunities, not as character flaws. Staffers recognize that obnoxious behaviors that appear to be willful disobedience could perhaps simply reflect a teen's slowly maturing brain or mental health issues stemming from insufficient brain development. While willful disobedience most certainly does occur, it is best to apply firm, consistent consequences and manipulate, in a nonpunitive manner, the conditions that lead to misbehavior. Administrators and staffers take the stance of, "She needed to behave that way at this time. Our job is to clearly state the rules and consequences, have high expectations and standards, believe in her ability to grow and mature over time, and provide constructive discipline, structure, and compassion as she moves through adolescence in her unique way and at her own pace. We trust that when the time is right, she will come along." This nonjudgmental, firm stance is deeply rooted in the strengths, resilience, and developmental perspectives.

Principle 3. Avoid coercion. Coercion can be traumatic and cause more harm than good. It is easily misused, with lasting consequences.

At times a teen may need to be restrained or transported against his or her will. A suicidal teen must be prevented from killing herself or himself. A violent teen must not be allowed to hurt others. A relentlessly defiant teen who repeatedly disappears to use harmful drugs, commit crimes, and engage in risky sex, and who refuses to accept help and treatment, may need to be escorted to a program equipped to help him deal with these behaviors and the reasons for them. In these extreme circumstances only ethical, skilled, and properly trained escort services should be used.

When an escort service, program, or school needs to apply physical restraint, staffers must adhere to written policies and protocols that comply with widely accepted national standards.[9] Physical coercion and restraint lie on a slippery slope; while they may be needed in extreme circumstances to prevent harm, they must be used in ways that do no harm, emotionally or physically.

Principle 4. Disciplinary methods should use logical, natural consequences that are safe and fair. Teens must be provided with unambiguously written rules and information about which behaviors will earn the teen more independence and privileges. The consequences of rule violations must be spelled out in advance and administered consistently and fairly. These disciplinary practices are fully supported by the behavior modification literature (Kazdin 1997, 2000). "Discipline" that blindsides the teen, and consequences that come out of nowhere for transgressions the teen did not know about, are forms of emotional ambush that corrode mental health, contradict research evidence on "what works," and violate key principles of the strengths, resilience, and developmental perspectives.

Principle 5. Complete and comprehensive licensing, regulation, and accreditation by all relevant organizations are crucial. A school or program that serves struggling teens, whether publicly or privately funded, should be fully credentialed by all relevant and reputable educational, behavioral health, health-care, child welfare, and residential care organizations. One must be aware that some components of a program, for example, the educational curriculum, may be accredited by an educational organization, while other components may not be, such as the program's dormitory program or counseling services. A program or school may cleverly camouflage its shortcomings by obtaining licenses and credentials selectively. The end result is that professionals and parents may be given a false sense of assurance that the overall program meets minimum standards. Some programs are in the no-man's land left by the erratic patchwork of accreditation, regulatory, and licensing organizations. For example, a privately owned "character education" boarding school that mistreats students may not be subject to investigation by state child abuse investigators because the school falls outside the agency's legislatively mandated purview. No single entity—private or governmental—has overarching authority to monitor, investigate, and prosecute negligent and abusive programs and schools in the struggling-teens industry. Oversight is fragmented and piecemeal. Different regulatory functions are performed by different oversight agencies. For example, a health-care complaint might be directed to the state health department. Complaints about educational curriculum might be addressed by regional organizations that accredit schools. Accusations of criminal misconduct might be investigated by the state or county prosecutor. But where would a teen or parent go with crucial concerns about such issues as verbal abuse, enforced sleep deprivation, untrained dormitory staff, forced exercise to the brink of exhaustion, using male students to physically restrain sexually abused female students, and so forth? It is in these interstices that many abuses flourish.

Accreditation agencies typically require schools and programs to undergo a thorough review that includes periodic site visits, interviews with teenagers and staff, and examination of school and program policies, programs, documents, and records. The goal of the accreditation process is to ensure that programs and schools meet standards regarding admission procedures, services provided, staffing, health and safety practices, facilities, governance and administration, and finances. Accreditation does not guarantee that programs and schools are of high quality, but it does demonstrate that programs and schools are willing to undergo outside review and scrutiny and attempt to meet standards. Unfortunately, even an accredited program may be of questionable quality. A program or school may have high-quality written policies that are not followed in actual practice (Reamer 2001, 2006b). It may put on a good face during an accreditation site visit, only to return to negligent, unethical, and abusive practices once site visitors depart. Program and school administrators may handpick the students, clients, patients, parents, alumni, and staff members for interviews with site visitors and keep disgruntled individuals out of sight. So parents cannot rely on accreditation alone for quality assurance.

Various organizations accredit programs and schools for struggling teens.[10] Parents and professionals need to determine which accrediting bodies are relevant to a program or school and get written verification that the program or school is properly accredited by all relevant bodies. Prominent accreditation organizations include the Commission on Accreditation of Rehabilitation Facilities, which accredits alcohol and substance abuse treatment programs; child and youth service programs; mental health and behavioral health programs; and supported living programs. Also, the Joint Commission on Accreditation of Healthcare Organizations accredits a wide range of healthcare organizations, including behavioral health programs that serve struggling teens; and the Council on Accreditation accredits organizations that provide community-based and residential services such as alcohol and chemical dependency counseling; case management; supported and independent living; individual and family counseling; and day treatment.

In the United States regional, rather than national, organizations accredit educational institutions—including boarding schools that serve struggling teens. The major and most prominent regional organizations are the Independent Schools Association of the Central States; Independent Schools Association of the Southwest; Middle States Association of Colleges and Schools; New England Association of Schools and Colleges; North Central Association of Colleges and Schools; Pacific Northwest Association of Independent Schools; Southern Association of Colleges and Schools; and the Western Association of Schools and Colleges.

Principle 6. Words matter. Staffers' and administrators' choice of words, tones of voice, facial expressions, and nonverbal cues shape the teen's experiences in a school or program. "It's not just what you say, but also how you say it" is the pertinent adage. For example, suppose a teen is suspected of stealing an expensive pen from a staffer's office desk. Adults might be tempted to bellow, "I'm sick of not being able to trust you! I'm sick of *you*! You're a chronic liar and a thief. Get out, get out, get out!" While this verbal outburst is fully understandable, it may be preferable for the adult to say, "I need to be able to trust kids in my office. It angers me when my stuff is missing. When my pen is returned to me and we've discussed what happened, you might be allowed back in here. Until then, you and I will have to meet in the lounge instead." Treating teens with respect, even when their behavior is outrageous, models for them constructive ways of dealing with intense emotion, interpersonal conflict, and other problems. This modeling can be a feature of a coordinated plan for helping teens change their behavior.

Principle 7. Relationship matters. In fact, relationship is the essential vehicle for much of adolescent development. As the bumper sticker says, "Love and learning go hand in hand." Brutal, disempowering, countercontrolling, coercive adult behaviors in programs and schools for struggling teens parallel, replicate, and model in a negative way the problematic behaviors of many struggling teens and therefore are unhelpful responses. That kind of response can exacerbate the problems that the struggling teen needs to address. Quality programs and schools recognize this dysfunctional dynamic. A teen's manipulative, provocative, defiant, and noncompliant behaviors tend to provoke in many adults a perfectly understandable inner response of "How dare you! I cannot let you get away with that." While certain, clear, firm, and fair consequences delivered in a timely manner are absolutely necessary, they must be administered in a way that cultivates a positive, warm, affirming, nurturing adult-teen relationship. When staff behaviors toward the teen are manipulative, dishonest, controlling, and disrespectful, a healthy adult-teen bond is eroded. The program or school milieu becomes countertherapeutic.

Positive treatment of teens by staffers is possible only when colleagues, administrators, and supervisors offer warm, nurturing, and supportive affirmations to front-line staffers. Working with struggling teens is demanding, challenging, and often difficult. At times the patience of staffers will wear thin. Teens' struggles inevitably will trigger a staffer's personal issues. Emotions may flare. Staffers need to know that before they have "had it," they have an emotional and logistical escape hatch. A program or school should never be short-staffed; caregivers who are at their wits' end should have access to respite and be able to cool off. This is a wise abuse-prevention measure.

Nurturing the staff means that employees too are treated according to the strengths, resilience, and developmental perspectives. Newer staffers may need more frequent, attentive support and supervision than veterans. All staffers need to know that their reasonable mistakes will be handled as learning opportunities, not character flaws. Similarly, as with the teens, administrators will enunciate clear, firm, certain, and fair consequences for staff misbehavior and positive reinforcement for desired behavior.

Principle 8. Size matters. Smaller schools and programs generally can provide more personalized, individualized attention and close supervision and monitoring.[11] Regardless of staff-to-teen ratio, a program with forty teens obviously is in a better position to pay individual attention than one with

180 teens, where a teen can more easily blend into the woodwork. For-profit programs and schools may have a compelling financial incentive to accept larger numbers of teens in order to enhance revenue by capitalizing on economies of scale. In smaller programs the staff is more likely to be able to control the "contagion effect," whereby peers negatively influence one another (see principle 18).

Some larger programs (such as conscientiously run wilderness therapy programs) only use small groups for the teen's entire stay. The teen is never with more than six to ten teens at a time. Hence, the total number of teenagers in a program may not be as important as the amount and quality of attention the teenager receives from consistent caregivers who spend time with the teen and truly know, understand, and have a positive working relationship with the youngster.

Principle 9. Optimum challenge is important. The literature on resilience notes that an optimum level of challenge—not too much and not too little—pushes and provides opportunity for growth but does not overwhelm. Hence, programs and schools that seek to break the teen's will in order to build the teen back up are not supported by the literature. Nor are programs and schools that have unnecessarily low expectations. A program's or school's expectations must be realistically calibrated to the individual teen's intellectual, academic, social, emotional, and physical abilities. A one-size-fits-all level of challenge most certainly cannot fit every teen's unique constellation of needs.

Principle 10. Interventions should be based primarily on multisystemic and cognitive-behavioral protocols. Given the compelling research support for the effectiveness of multisystemic therapy, a program or school should address the whole teen in her or his family, peer, neighborhood, medical, mental health, spiritual, cultural, and educational context. Similarly, cognitive-behavioral forms of intervention should be used, if appropriate, as part of the multisystemic package of services because of the extensive body of research indicating their effectiveness (see chapter 4).

Principle 11. Schools and programs should address teens' unique clinical, spiritual, cultural, and sexual orientation needs. Some schools and programs wisely offer specialized services—counseling, special education, behavior management—tailored to each teenager's needs. However, other schools and programs use a single model with every youth. These programs—for example, some "character education" boarding schools—may assume a doctrinaire approach based on a firm belief that its model is best for everyone.

Staffers in these programs discourage criticism or critical questions from parents or others about the goodness-of-fit between the program's approach and their teen's specific needs. If the model is not working, staffers claim that it is because of the "bad attitude" of the teen or parents or lack of cooperation.

Programs and schools also need to support teens' cultural and spiritual practices. Some teens who are members of ethnic, cultural, or religious minority groups may not feel comfortable in programs and schools where there are no or few other teens like them. Further, programs and schools need to be sensitive to and support teens' sexual orientation and gender identity. Teenagers who feel out of place may not benefit fully from the services available because of the extra burden of isolation and differentness. Staffers may be actively, purposefully, passively, or unintentionally unresponsive to a teen's religious, ethnic, cultural, or sexual orientation and gender identity needs.

Principle 12. Schools and programs should treat parents and guardians as equal members of the collaborative team. Parents and guardians have a great deal to contribute to the assessment of teens' needs and interventions; they can be crucial colleagues on the intervention team. Program and school staffers should contact parents and guardians routinely and when promised, respond to telephone and e-mail messages (within reason), keep parents and guardians regularly informed about teens' progress, and treat parents and guardians with respect. Some parents may feel so alienated, hurt, angry, or disempowered that they withdraw from their child and need to be nurtured back into more active involvement. Others may be enmeshed or overinvolved with their child and need affirmation and support in their efforts to give the teen more space. Either way, parents tend to know the child and the family history well and are invaluable resources.

Principle 13. Schools and programs should handle teens' mental health needs professionally. Staffers should recognize that teenagers' emotional and behavioral struggles sometimes are a result of their mental health challenges rather than simply willful choices. Before admission and upon intake, staffers should ask parents to provide detailed written information from mental health professionals who have had contact with the teen. That information should be taken into account in designing an individualized package of services for the teen. It should also inform how staffers respond to challenges and crises that arise in the teen's life.

Also, staffers should be willing to administer psychotropic medication at the times recommended by the teenager's physician, rather than when it is most convenient for the program or school staff. Some programs and schools will not tailor their medication schedules to meet teenagers' unique needs and a physician's instructions. As a result of this medication mismanagement, teenagers may have difficulty complying with instructions and expectations; the resulting noncompliant or inappropriate behaviors are treated as disciplinary issues instead of signs of medical neglect.

Principle 14. Schools and programs should handle teens' special education needs professionally.
Staffers should recognize that teenagers' academic struggles sometimes are a result of their special education challenges rather than simply willful choices. Before admissions and upon intake, staffers should ask parents to also provide detailed written information from education professionals who have had contact with the teen. That information should be taken into account in designing an individualized package of educational services for the teen. It should also inform how staffers respond to academic challenges and crises that arise in the teen's life. For example, a teen who has a verbal learning disability or attention-deficit/hyperactivity disorder may need more time to complete assignments. The teen who has ADHD may not intentionally forget to bring his textbook to class; rather than punishment, he may need strategies for remembering what materials to bring.

Principle 15. Staffers should have appropriate education, training, and credentials. Parents should assess the extent to which the teaching, clinical, health-care, dormitory, and recreational staffers have appropriate education, training, credentials, and experience. Some schools and programs lack strict hiring criteria for teachers and other staff. This, as we have seen, may have been a factor in abuses and scandals documented in chapter 3. For example, unprofessional and unscrupulous schools and programs may hire for teaching positions college graduates who have no training in how to teach or expertise in the subject matter they are teaching. These schools may assign staffers who lack graduate degrees in a mental health profession to supervise "seminars" that mimic group therapy. These group sessions can be destructively confrontational, emotionally abusive, and model dysfunctional communication styles and poor problem-solving skills.

Principle 16. Schools and programs should not have unusually high attrition rates. Administrators should be candid about the attrition rate for their program or school and the reasons for it. Given the nature of the struggling teen population, some attrition is to be expected. But some programs and schools have a pattern of relatively high attrition. Often this is a red flag. High teen turnover or a low graduation rate year after year may be a sign of program turmoil and instability, weak preadmission screening to ensure a good teen-program match, or a punitive, hostile, non-nurturing environment that pushes teens to "melt down." Parents who are unhappy or disenchanted with a program are more likely to withdraw their child, leading to high attrition. While all programs and schools have some disgruntled parents, some have a disproportionate number. Accurate attrition and graduation rates should be readily available in writing when parents and educational consultants ask for that information.

Principle 17. Residential schools and programs should not have unusually high runaway rates. Residential programs or schools must have constructive methods for helping teens develop the ability to comply with rules and expectations. High runaway rates may be evidence that the methods of the program or school are ineffective or of a poor match between the needs of the teen and the ability of the program or school to meet those needs.

Principle 18. Schools and programs should seek to minimize "contagion." Programs and schools must try to minimize the opportunities for teens to influence each other negatively. Struggling, impressionable teens in such programs regularly associate with one another day after day (and night after night); these peer interactions can exacerbate negative behavior. Dishion and Dodge refer to this as the risk of "deviant peer contagion": "Inadvertent negative effects associated with intervention programs that aggregate peers in the delivery of a therapeutic protocol, educational service, or community program" (2006:14). Programs and schools should be aware of factors that, according to research, can increase the likelihood of negative peer contagion: teens' personality and temperament, severity of teens' behavioral and emotional challenges, age, individual susceptibility, skills of program and school staffers, and extent of program or school structure (Dishion and Andrews 1995; Dishion and Dodge 2005; Dishion, Andrews, and Crosby 1995; Dishion, Bullock, and Granic 2002; Dishion et al. 2004; Dishion, McCord, and Poulin 1999; Dishion, Poulin, and Burraston 2001; Dodge and Sherrill 2006; Eddy and Chamberlain 2000; Fraser, Nelson, and Rivard 1997; Jones and Jones 2000; Weiss et al. 2005). A prominent commission that examined negative peer influences in programs and schools for struggling teens concluded that risks of contagion increase for younger teens and those who have experimented with serious mischief—such as vandalism, illegal drug use, and shoplifting—but have not yet committed themselves to a deviant lifestyle, are exposed to peers who are slightly more deviant than they are, and interact with struggling peers in unstructured, unsupervised settings. The risk of negative peer influences is greatest for behaviors that are usually acquired through social interactions, for example, delinquency, substance abuse, and violence (Dishion, Dodge, and Lansford

2006). Hence, programs and schools for struggling teens generally should limit opportunities for younger and older teens, and less deviant and more deviant, to mix on a regular basis. Unstructured, unsupervised time should be limited, particularly when younger and older teens, and less and more deviant teens, are together. Limiting the contagion effect is another reason why smaller programs and schools are generally preferable to larger settings, as staffers can keep a closer eye on peer interactions.

Principle 19. Aftercare is critical. In keeping with the multisystemic approach, a quality program or school creates an aftercare plan for each teen. Follow-up for program or school alumni is essential. Important relationships between adults and teens during the period of enrollment are not severed forever. Instead, because of the importance of such relationships, the program or school formulates a carefully designed weaning period of planned, occasional contacts—perhaps the program or school staffers send the teen a postcard, e-mail message, or holiday greeting card. The teen might be permitted to have a planned visit six months (or so) after the teen's departure; this gives the teen an opportunity to forge ahead but with assurance that the staffers to whom the teen has said goodbye still care.

Ideally, programs, schools, educational consultants, and other professionals are thoughtful about the most appropriate next step. Some teens leave a program or school without an appropriate "next step" in place. This is a recipe for disaster. For example, teens who have made considerable progress in a wilderness therapy program may need a transition school—such as an emotional growth boarding school—for a year or two before returning home in order to sustain the growth. And before returning home from the emotional growth boarding school, the teens may need a carefully graduated process of gaining freedom and privileges in the community surrounding the boarding school so they can practice making wise and safe community-based choices before going home. Teens who have spent a year in a residential treatment center may need a therapeutic boarding school as part of the "step-down," or transition, process. That is, most struggling teens need a gradual descent that entails increasing degrees of independence. Abrupt changes that lack coherence, coordination, sufficient supportive services, and a gradual lessening of structure and supervision should be avoided at all cost. Abrupt transitions may overwhelm any teen's coping capacities and be a setup for regression. Even with careful aftercare planning and services, some regression is common; it should be anticipated and planned for. Otherwise, the regression can blindside both teens and parents.

Principle 20. Program evaluation is a must. A program or school should regularly survey participants, alumni, parents, and educational consultants to assess consumer satisfaction, gauge well-being, and solicit feedback about program and school strengths and areas for improvement. This is ethically imperative (Reamer 2006a).

Parents and professionals should view with suspicion broad, emphatic claims about the "success rate" of a program or school. Some tout "survey results" that indicate that, for example, "94 percent of our students' parents would recommend this school to others" or "98 percent of our graduates are accepted by a college." One should always probe and ask hard questions about the research methodology to ensure that the claims are valid. How recent are the data? How were the survey questions worded? Did they avoid any bias or pressure to respond positively? Did the program or school survey *all* students, alumni, and parents who enrolled in the program or school or only those who did not withdraw or get expelled? If the survey was based only on those who completed the program or school "successfully," the data are clearly biased toward positive results. If the program or school claims superior results compared with other options, are the claims based on controlled, methodologically rigorous research protocols? When the program or school claims that eventually every student "gets into college," is that in part because staffers demand that every student submit multiple applications, regardless of whether the teen intends to go to college right after graduation? Too often, programs and schools make unsubstantiated, exaggerated claims that are neither valid nor supported by solid research. A competent and assertive educational consultant can help parents pose these questions and assess the quality of the responses.

REGULATING PROGRAMS AND SCHOOLS: CONSTRUCTIVE OVERSIGHT

Without question, one of the greatest challenges facing the struggling-teens industry is the lack of conscientious, constructive, sustained oversight at regular intervals by external organizations. We are not interested in establishing a controlling, intrusive bureaucracy that stifles creativity and vision, drains staff attention from direct care and relationship building with teens, and merely produces tomes of meaningless paperwork. However, oversight may help prevent the horrifying scandals and abuses that have occurred, and continue to occur, in some programs and schools.

In this sense the struggling-teens industry is like the adolescent who wants to be able to enjoy considerable freedom and resents hovering parents. Yet we know that laissez-faire parenting does not work; adolescents require constructive supervision and structure. Without it the likelihood of serious problems increases exponentially.

So too with the struggling-teens industry. Unfortunately, the current oversight apparatus is far too anemic, even nonexistent, particularly with respect to residential programs and schools. For example, two prominent and valuable organizations in the industry—the National Association of Therapeutic Schools and Programs and the Outdoor Behavioral Healthcare Industry Council —promulgate ethical standards and principles of good practice but have little enforcement authority.[12] Similarly, the Independent Educational Consultants Association promulgates principles of good practice, but membership in the organization is voluntary. Educational consultants who choose not to meet IECA standards are free to eschew them without penalty. Accreditation agencies—such as the Commission on Accreditation of Rehabilitation Facilities, the Council on Accreditation, the Joint Commission on Accreditation of Healthcare Organizations, and regional accreditation agencies for independent schools—do, to some extent, assess and monitor the quality of some programs for struggling teens through their ability to grant, suspend, and revoke accreditation. However, an open question is whether these organizations perform this task adequately, because their explicit mission is not to accredit programs and schools for struggling teens. Some programs that these organizations accredit do serve some struggling teens. For example, the Joint Commission on Accreditation of Healthcare Organizations may accredit a psychiatric hospital that serves struggling teens but not an emotional growth boarding school. A regional accreditation body for independent schools, such as the New England Association of Schools and Colleges, may be in a good position to assess an emotional growth boarding school's academic program but is not necessarily prepared to assess the adequacy of the school's mental health care. The bottom line is that no centralized organization exists whose primary mission is formal accreditation or oversight of programs for struggling teens.

The most ambitious attempt to address oversight and regulation issues comes from the Alliance for the Safe, Therapeutic, and Appropriate Use of Residential Treatment (ASTART) under the auspices of the University of South Florida (USF) and the Bazelon Center for Mental Health Law (Friedman et al. 2006). As we discussed in chapter 3, ASTART was established in 2004 to address growing concern about abusive residential programs for struggling teens. In 2005 the organization, along with USF's Department of Child and Family Studies and the Bazelon Center, sponsored a press briefing in Washington, D.C., about the urgent need for regulation of private residential treatment facilities. The allied organizations were seeking an investigation into these facilities by the Government Accountability Office.[13] Among the diverse statements made at the briefing (ASTART 2005) were these:

> I have become increasingly alarmed by the reports of youth being transported hundreds, if not thousands of miles away from their home, often after being

awakened in the middle of the night by hired "escorts," to be taken to unlicensed and non-accredited residential programs that have somehow persuaded their desperate parents that they offer the best hope for helping their children. . . . I have heard from young adults who were in some of these programs as adolescents, from parents who sent their children to these programs, from former staff members of these programs, and from numerous journalists who have investigated these programs. . . . The stories of mistreatment, abuse, and even death within these programs have been so compelling that I could not turn away from trying to learn more. . . .

Many programs . . . are neither licensed by their state, nor accredited by independent national accreditation organizations, and . . . some of these programs are exploiting the desperation of parents, and mistreating the youth that they serve. The issue is that we don't even know how many youngsters are living in these programs, or how many have died in them. . . .

We must ensure that programs that present themselves as serving children with special challenges are licensed by the state in which they are located, and accredited by independent national accrediting organizations. We recognize that even with oversight there will be tragedies but we view such oversight as one part of a multi-faceted effort to protect the safety and well-being of our young people.

—Robert Friedman, professor/chair, Department of Child and Family Studies,
University of South Florida

Think of what youth must experience in programs where they are expected to live by standards common in the prisons for the worst offenders, or in the former Soviet gulag. Think of the impact when youth are subject to unskilled or abusive interventions for normative behaviors that violate rules that are supportive of healthy adolescent development. Think of the impact on those youth who have been beaten, raped, or physically harmed in programs where staff, who may not have the barest training or moral qualities to make them fit for working with youth, are out of control. Think of the impact on families when a troubled youth sent to such a program is returned in a coffin. Such is the situation in many so-called special schools and residential programs for troubled youth in this country.

It is our hope that we can see such terrible facilities closed down when examined and found lacking reasonable standards of care for troubled youth.

—Charles Huffine, M.D., child and adolescent psychiatrist

I am here today, not as just another concerned mental health professional, but as one who has worked within unregulated residential treatment facilities and experienced first-hand compelling concern for the inadequate and harmful care of youth in such facilities. . . .

I was sickened as I witnessed counseling staff at the 6 week wilderness intervention program be told that every child about to complete it should and must be referred to the 2-year programs at one of the 3 boarding schools, regardless of the clinical improvements they were supposed to have made during their . . . brief stay. I watched tearful mothers lament that they wanted to bring their child home to try to "repair" their relationship and rebuild—only to have program staff manipulate them by threatening that their child might end up in jail or dead if they didn't send them to a boarding school.

Each day at this job brought new discomfort. Scared and confused, I called several governing organizations from a campus phone and whispered hushed concerns to agency representatives only to be told that emotional growth boarding schools in Idaho were not regulated at that time by their mental health or education agencies and that they could do nothing about my concerns.

—Nicki Bush, former program staff member

I am here today to share my experience and express my concerns as someone who received inadequate care and suffered greatly at the hands of under-qualified staff in an unregulated residential program for youth in Montana. . . .

The "interventions" vary across programs—some use forced confessions, labor and exercise like the program I attended, some force kids to lie on the ground or lock them in small rooms by themselves for days, weeks and months at a time, some twist kids' arms and legs, some tell kids their parents don't love them, some make them do disgusting things. What we all have in common is that we've been intimidated, humiliated, and taught to question our own reality. We haven't received the kind of professional care that we deserved and that our families worked hard to pay for. We are outraged by this type of treatment under the guise of care.

—Kathryn Whitehead, former program participant

My son attended unregulated residential programs from August, 2000 until December, 2001, when he was 15–1/2 to almost 17 years old. I am here to share with you our family's experience, to illustrate some of the issues and hardships that families face when they seek support through unregulated programs. . . .

Other parents say over and over that what they believed they were investing in—education and credentialed help—turned out not to be true. Some of the parents liquidated their assets and sold their homes to get help for their children, and then their children were mistreated. NONE of the parents wanted their kids to be abused. These kids are coming home traumatized, and it is a hard thing to admit . . . what we may have done as parents by sending our kids to these programs. All of the programs in the Teen Help industry need to be regulated.

—Cristine Gomez, parent of former program participant

Two actions . . . should be taken to address the lack of accountability—passage of the End Institutional Abuse of Children Act and a congressional request for a Government Accountability (GAO) study of unregulated and unlicensed RTFs [residential treatment facilities]. . . . We need to know how many of these facilities are operating, in this country and overseas, without any oversight. We also need to know who is responsible for the children in these RTFs—what are their credentials, what is the staff-child ratio? What kinds of so-called treatment are being practiced? Are practices abusive? Dangerous? Are these facilities following federal requirements for providing educational services while the children and young people are away from their regular schools? What kinds of complaints or lawsuits are being brought against RTFs, and what entities (if any) are making this information available to parents?

—Tammy Seltzer, senior staff attorney, Bazelon Center for Mental Health Law

The Child Welfare League of America (CWLA) and our 900 member child-caring, public and private agencies nationwide . . . believe that Congress needs to take action to ensure the safety of the children participating in these [unlicensed residential] programs by requesting that the U.S. Government Accountability Office conduct an investigation. . . .

These programs are often unregulated. . . . Allegations of neglect and abuse . . . include the inappropriate use of medications, the employment of vigorous physical means of restraint, or individual seclusion or isolation. . . . These unlicensed programs use aggressive marketing techniques that target the parents of troubled youth who have problems with substance abuse or behavior disorders, promising cures at a high cost to the families. While research has demonstrated that consistent family involvement is a major element in producing positive outcomes for children and families, many of these programs limit or restrict family involvement for long periods of time, sometimes for the entire length of time a child is in the program. . . .

Licensing and monitoring should be required for all programs, not just those receiving government funds. This requirement is necessary to ensure the safety and health of our children and youth.

—Shay Bilchik, president and chief executive officer, Child Welfare League of America

In 2005 U.S. Representative George Miller, D-California, introduced a bill that would strengthen regulation of residential programs for teens, the End Institutionalized Abuse Against Children Act of 2005. The law would have authorized investigation of alleged abuse, neglect, and human rights violations in residential treatment facilities and, where warranted, imposed civil and criminal penalties. Unfortunately, the bill did not pass.

In 2005 one state, Utah, passed a law that expands state licensing requirements to all residential treatment programs, including "therapeutic schools."[14]

The Utah law requires the state Department of Human Services, Office of Licensing, to establish health and safety standards for residential treatment programs and schools related to client safety and protection, staff qualifications and training, and the administration of medical procedures and standards. The new law also empowers the licensing office to revoke licenses if covered residential programs fail to meet the law's standards or engage in conduct that poses a substantial risk of harm to any person. Any facility that continues to operate in violation of the law is guilty of a misdemeanor, if the violation endangers the welfare of clients. The law also requires the licensing office to designate local government officials as residential treatment facility inspectors and charges them with conducting compliance assessments. The extent to which this law adequately regulates the struggling-teens industry in Utah is not clear. But one state legislature's decision to require monitoring of abuse and neglect in residential programs and schools is a step in the right direction.

Recently, the American Bar Association (ABA) has confronted this issue. In August 2004 the ABA approved Standards for the Custody, Placement and Care; Legal Representation; and Adjudication of Unaccompanied Alien Children in the United States. The standards state that unaccompanied children who are in residential facilities must always be treated with dignity, respect, and special concern for their particular vulnerability. The ABA asserted that these children are entitled to a reasonable right of privacy, including the ability to talk to parents and guardians privately on the phone without automatic monitoring; to receive and send uncensored mail; and to meet privately with attorneys and other visitors. The standards also state that children must be protected from all forms of physical, sexual, or mental violence, injury, or abuse, as well as neglect, abandonment, maltreatment, and exploitation while in residential care. In 2007 the American Bar Association issued a formal resolution strongly recommending strict regulation of privately operated residential treatment facilities.[15] According to the ABA report that accompanied the resolution:

> Well-meaning parents send an estimated 10,000 to 14,000 at-risk children each year to unregulated private residential treatment facilities, which . . . promise to modify troublesome behaviors and make bad kids good. The facilities that compose this booming, billion-dollar business are generally not regulated, licensed, or monitored by state or federal governments; too many aspects of this alternative care system for youth are rife with mistreatment, including physical, sexual, and mental abuse by facility staff. This American Bar Association policy resolution urges state, territorial, and tribal legislatures to pass laws that require the licensing, regulating, and monitoring of residential treatment facilities that

are not funded by public or government systems but offer treatment to at-risk children and youth for emotional, behavioral, educational, or other problems or issues.

The ABA resolutions carry no legislative or regulatory authority; they are simply aspirational statements. What they demonstrate, however, is emerging and compelling consensus that the struggling-teens industry needs greatly enhanced oversight and regulation. The daunting challenge is simultaneously to create effective oversight and regulatory mechanisms that ensure safety and quality while not stifling schools' and programs' creativity or impeding quality care through meaningless, burdensome, and redundant bureaucratic requirements. Striking this balance is essential. Absorbing staff time with paperwork and meetings that merely create the illusion of quality assurance would be unfortunate indeed.

The distressing lack of progress in efforts to oversee and monitor the struggling-teens industry is the result of diverse factors. There is no consensus among professionals in the field that oversight and regulation are necessary. Some professionals—including some educational consultants, administrators, and staffers in programs and schools, and mental health practitioners—agree that the time has come for oversight and monitoring, but others are indifferent or actively oppose such initiatives (Behar et al. 2007). As with any reform efforts, competing interests among stakeholders can slow down or derail ambitious proposals. Some professionals in the struggling-teens industry fear that the introduction of monitoring and regulatory mechanisms will be intrusive, disruptive, and burdensome, ultimately interfering with the autonomy that schools and programs have enjoyed for decades and stifling their creativity. Others recognize that the credibility of programs and schools serving struggling teens is at risk if the industry does not monitor and regulate itself or agree to competent and fair outside scrutiny; hold programs and schools to high standards; and assure the public that quality-control mechanisms are in place. Fragmentation and disagreements within the struggling-teens industry have paralyzed several earnest efforts to introduce much-needed reforms. As Behar and colleagues (2007) note:

> Depending on the state, failure to provide state oversight of residential programs for minors may occur because these programs (1) do not accept public funds; (2) are affiliated with religious organizations; or (3) describe themselves (inappropriately) as outdoor programs, boarding schools, or other types of nontreatment programs. In some cases, strong lobbying efforts by interested parties have contributed to creating and maintaining these exclusions. An additional problem in some states is that, although regulations exist, there is ineffective monitoring

of programs for compliance; this may be an issue of insufficient resources being assigned to monitoring, which ultimately is an issue of insufficient priority.

(401–402)

CONFRONTING SOCIAL DISPARITIES

One of the most troubling realities of the struggling-teens industry is that many of the youths with the greatest needs have the least access to high-quality services. The hard, cold fact is that low-income teens are overrepresented in many, although not all, risk areas. For example, we know from the National Longitudinal Study of Adolescent Health, based on data from a nationally representative sample of more than ten thousand teens, that lower-income teens are significantly more likely to be victims of weapons-related violence and to engage in sexual intercourse at earlier ages (Blum et al. 2000). According to the Annie E. Casey Foundation (2006), lower-income teens and teens of color are significantly overrepresented among "disconnected youths" and teens in the child welfare and juvenile justice systems. The teens who are enrolled in expensive, private-sector schools and programs, however, are overwhelmingly white, from families with sufficient financial resources or loans to pay for costly care. Although some specialty programs and schools offer scholarships to low-income teens, the slots are few. Such disparities permeate children's and teen's mental health services and behavioral health care across the United States. As a senior official with the Bazelon Center for Mental Health Law notes,

> The nation has a long way to go to eliminate disparities in access to appropriate services. The rate of unmet needs is higher for minorities—88% of Latino children do not receive needed mental health care. And although Latino youths have the highest rate of suicide, they are also less likely than others to be identified by a primary care physician as having a mental disorder. Similarly, African American youths are more likely to be sent to the juvenile justice system for behavioral problems than placed in psychiatric care.   (ASTART 2005:15)

Addressing poverty, discrimination, and their correlates must be critical elements in any serious, earnest attempt to help struggling teens. According to the U.S. Census Bureau, approximately one in five children lives in poverty (U.S. Census Bureau 2006). Efforts designed to prevent poverty among teens, and the problems that we know flow from it (such as delinquency, violence, substance abuse, and pregnancy), require substantial and sustained investment of national resources. We should do so not only because we owe this to our nation's youth but because such investment is also cost effective. Underwriting the cost of high-quality community-based services for families, after-school programs, mentors, crisis intervention and counseling services, and, when necessary, wilderness therapy programs, emotional growth boarding schools, therapeutic boarding schools, and residential treatment, is likely to prevent more costly expenses as teens grow older. The costs associated with community-based, preventive services for teens pale in comparison with the long-term costs of teenage pregnancy, dropping out of school, addiction, and incarceration. The math is not complicated. Investment in social capital for teens and their families makes raw economic sense and pays off in dollars saved and suffering avoided (Curtis, Alexander, and Lunghofer 2001; Dagenais et al. 2004; Dembo and Walters 2003; Liddle 1998; Nissen 2006; Schiraldi, Hollman, and Beatty 2000; Weisz 2004).

However, despite the best, most skilled prevention efforts, some teens will struggle. For a variety of reasons—including the impact of poverty, genetics, biochemistry, and family dysfunction—some teens are going to face a variety of behavioral and emotional challenges. Sadly, relatively few families of struggling teens can afford the staggering costs associated with the best care available. Families without adequate health insurance and mental health coverage have difficulty paying the per-hour fee for community-based counseling. Families with modest incomes and assets find it nearly impossible to pay for wilderness therapy programs and specialty boarding schools. The annual costs associated with residential schools and programs are at least as expensive as the cost of an elite private college education. Many programs and schools, especially those with built-in therapeutic services, cost far more than that. For too many parents the idea of financing the services, programs, and schools that their child needs seems as realistic as arranging a trip to the moon.

Teens of low- and moderate-income families need the same access to high-quality, regulated services and programs as teens in more affluent households. The needs of lower-income teens are no less compelling. Ideally, public funds, insurance, and support from philanthropic foundations would make this possible. Realistically, some form of public financing is necessary to reduce access disparities. The current state of affairs amply demonstrates that the private sector cannot generate enough money to provide services to all the teens and families with need. Our strong belief is that, at the very least, public child welfare agencies and school districts and departments must increase their commitment to struggling teens who require specialty services. In communities across the United States parents of teens with special needs fight for access to school district resources for their children who need care from specialty schools and programs. Many of these parents have to hire lawyers to advocate, and sometimes litigate, on their behalf. These adversarial confrontations waste vital resources. Federal, state, and local governments must do their part, through public financing, to ensure that vulnerable teens' needs are met.

In addition, public child welfare and school officials need to learn about the full range of programs and schools available to help struggling teens. Too often we encounter public officials who have incomplete, outdated, and inaccurate information about specialty programs and schools. They need to think much more creatively and flexibly about the impressive array of options. Limiting one's thinking to the least expensive options is shortsighted. It takes persistent, earnest effort to view teens' needs through different and newer lenses. Professionals must use a different template, one that incorporates creative options that are supported by solid research evidence. Governmental and insurance funding for an effectively regulated, comprehensive continuum of care for all teens and families who struggle is essential for the nation's economic and social well-being. A chaotic, disconnected patchwork that favors families of means is unacceptable.

The struggling-teens industry is coming of age. Like many coming-of-age stories, this one is filled with a complicated mix of inspiring tales of maturation and disconcerting and disturbing episodes.

There is no question that many specialty programs and schools are administered by principled, skilled, and dedicated professionals who get up each morning to change teens' lives for the better, and they do it well. Regrettably, the industry is also fraught with too many incompetent, abusive, unenlightened, and arrogant administrators and staff who either do not know about or refuse to abide by widely accepted standards in the field, evidence-based practice principles, and ethical guidelines. The pages of this book are filled with a distressing number of such stories and outcomes.

The contemporary struggling-teens industry is now about a half-century old. It has gone from fairly primitive, naive beginnings—starting with Mel Wasserman's CEDU program in the 1960s—to a remarkably diverse collection of community-based and largely unregulated residential programs. With the benefit of the kind of insight and hindsight that only extensive experience can provide, today's professionals know a great deal about evidence-based, ethical practices and interventions that work, either reasonably or very well, and about frighteningly risky practices that should be avoided at all cost. The last half-century's track record, with all its good and bad news, is remarkably instructive.

Going forward, our task is clear. The struggling-teens industry needs further study of what works, with whom, and under what conditions. All programs and schools must empirically assess the extent to which the teens and families they serve feel helped and move toward intervention goals. A carefully articulated, adequately funded national policy creating a coherent continuum of care is critical. The struggling-teens industry must be adequately monitored by effective regulatory and accreditation agencies. Verbal, emotional, and physical abuse of teens in programs and schools must end. A respectful, humane perspective that focuses on teens' strengths, resilience, and developmental stage should permeate relevant policies and practices. Quality community-based and residential services must be financially accessible to all families with struggling teens. A two-tiered, bifurcated scenario that provides more care for the haves and less care for the have-not's is unacceptable. Pursuing these tasks requires continual, passionate public education and advocacy.

The reality is that some teens will struggle. It is a fact of life. Fortunately, an impressive array of helpful professionals and resources exists that can make a difference. We need to be steadfast, compassionate, and purposeful as we guide these teens to adulthood.

AFTERCARE SERVICES. Services provided to adolescents and other family members following a residential placement or other intensive treatment. Typical aftercare services include crisis counseling, emergency services, individual and family counseling, home-based family services, and self-help or support groups.

BEHAVIORAL THERAPY. Focuses on changing unwanted behaviors by changing the antecedent conditions that set the stage for those unwanted behaviors to occur, or by changing the consequences that reinforce unwanted behaviors. Often involves the cooperation of others, especially family and close friends, to reinforce a desired behavior.

COGNITIVE-BEHAVIORAL THERAPY. Helps the client modify thoughts, with the aim of positively influencing emotions and behaviors. Widely accepted as an evidence-based, cost-effective psychotherapy for many disorders, its techniques vary according to the client or issue but commonly include keeping a diary of significant events and associated thoughts, feelings, and behaviors; questioning and testing assumptions or habits of thought that might be unhelpful and unrealistic; gradually engaging in activities that the client may have avoided; and trying out new ways of thinking and behaving. Often also includes relaxation and distraction techniques. When used with groups of people, it is known as *cognitive-behavioral group treatment* (Heimberg and Becker 2002). The techniques are also commonly presented in self-help manuals that are accompanied by self-help software packages.

EXPOSURE THERAPY. A form of behavioral treatment for anxiety that involves teaching relaxation skills, then exposing the client to an anxiety-arousing stimulus, usually slowly, while the client is in a relaxed state. Can be very effective.

FAMILY EDUCATION. Provides information about mental health and substance abuse challenges in order to improve family members' coping skills and their ability to help a struggling adolescent. Like psychoeducation, the goals are instructional and supportive.

FAMILY SYSTEMS THERAPY. Identifies and seeks to change patterns of family interaction. This approach regards the family as a complex system made up of constantly interacting and dynamic components. The therapist views the problems and concerns of the family members as by-products of the family's dynamics and interaction patterns. Several family members often attend therapy sessions together so the therapist can observe their patterns of interaction. This perspective focuses on understanding the family unit as a whole, not its individual members, to change patterns of family interaction rather than any one family member.

504 ACCOMMODATION PLAN. Usually called a "504 plan" after section 504 of the Rehabilitation Act of 1973, a civil rights law guaranteeing equal opportunity for Americans with disabilities. It is designed to accommodate the unique needs of an individual with a disability, as required by the Americans with Disabilities Act. Teens who have disabilities that do not interfere with their ability to progress in general education, and who are not eligible for special education services, may be entitled to a 504 plan. A school district may be required to provide specialized instruction, modifications to the curriculum, accommodations in nonacademic and extracurricular activities, adaptive equipment or assistive technology devices, an aide, assistance with health-related needs, school transportation, or other related services and accommodations.

FUNCTIONAL FAMILY THERAPY. A family-based intervention program for acting-out adolescents and their families (Sexton and Alexander 1999). A major goal is to improve family communication and supportiveness while decreasing the intense negative interactions and conflict often found in families with teens whose behavior is oppositional, noncompliant, or defiant. Other goals include helping family members adopt positive solutions to family problems and developing positive behavior change and parenting strategies. Conducted by a family therapist in a clinical setting, which is standard for most family therapy programs; more recent programs with multiproblem families involve in-home treatment.

In individual sessions the therapist and adolescent work on such important skills as decision making, communicating thoughts and feelings verbally and clearly, problem-solving strategies to deal with life stressors, and job skills. Parallel to these individual sessions with the adolescent is work with the parents (Liddle 1998). Although originally designed to treat middle-class families with delinquent and pre-delinquent youth, the program has recently included poor, multiethnic, multicultural populations with such problems as conduct disorder, adolescent drug abuse, and violence.

INDIVIDUALIZED EDUCATION PROGRAM (IEP). Required under the federal Individuals with Disabilities Education Act to provide specialized instruction and services to support the education of students with disabilities. The program, to be developed by a team that includes the student, parents, and school personnel, should provide detailed information, which then is to be used to make appropriate decisions about a student's educational placement and supportive services. The IEP must list the special education and related services to be provided to the teen or on behalf of the teen, including supplementary aids and services, as well as modifications to the program or support provided to school personnel—such as training or professional development—in order to assist the teen. Unfortunately, the design and implementation of IEPs sometimes fall short of this protocol. Some parents find it necessary to work with educational advocates to ensure that schools comply with the law.

INTERACTIONAL GROUP TREATMENT. Involves the use and application of psychotherapy in small groups. The social interaction within these groups is used to help individuals attain personal goals and confront issues. Emphasis is on creating an environment in which members feel comfortable about discussing personal problems. Through active participation in the group process, members become more aware of themselves, identifying thoughts and feelings triggered in a variety of interactions with different people. The group also provides a safe forum to discover how individual members experience one another and the extent to which members have accurate perceptions of others' reactions to them.

INTERPERSONAL THERAPY. Typically involves identifying and working on relationship problems that affect eating disorders, specifically, the interpersonal conflicts and related distress that may precipitate binge eating. Like cognitive behavioral therapy, it is typically goal oriented and short term. Individual and/or group therapy formats for interpersonal therapy exist (Fairburn 1997).

LIFE-SKILLS TRAINING. Highly interactive, skills-based program designed to promote positive health and personal development for high school youth (Botvin 2004). Helps students achieve competency in skills found to reduce and prevent substance use and violence. Focuses on personal self-management skills (strategies for decision making, managing stress, and anger), general social skills (strategies to strengthen teens' communication skills and build healthy relationships), and drug resistance skills (strategies to help students understand the consequences of substance use and risk taking and the influences of the media).

META-ANALYSIS. The statistical synthesis of data from a set of comparable studies of a problem leading to a quantitative summary of the pooled results. Includes aggregating the data and results of a set of studies, preferably as many as possible using the same or similar methods and procedures; and reanalyzing the data from the combined studies to generate larger numbers and more stable rates and proportions for statistical analysis and significance testing than can be achieved by any single study. This statistics-based analysis uses data only from previously published peer-reviewed studies of a particular problem. Because the original studies investigated different independent variables on different scales (for example, depression scores, arrest rates, suicide attempts, frequency of drug use), the dependent (or outcome) variable in a meta-analysis is some standardized measure of what is known as *effect size*. The usual effect size indicator is the standardized mean difference, which is the standard score equivalent to the difference between means, or an odds ratio if the outcome of the experiments is a dichotomous variable (success versus failure). A meta-analysis can be performed on studies that describe their findings in correlation coefficients, as, for example, studies of the correlation between childhood trauma history and clinical depression. In these cases the correlation itself is the indicator of the effect size (Lipsey and Wilson 2001).

MULTIDIMENSIONAL FAMILY THERAPY. Focuses on the adolescent's development in multiple aspects of her life. The therapy is organized into phases and relies on success in one phase before moving to the next. This approach understands adolescent drug use, for example, in terms of a network of influences (i.e., individual, family, peer, community). It suggests that reductions in target symptoms and increases in prosocial target behaviors occur along multiple pathways, in differing contexts, and through different mechanisms. Thus it includes sessions with various family members and people important to the family. Sessions are held in the clinic, in the home, or with family members at the family court, school, or other relevant community locations. Change for the adolescents and parents is intrapersonal and interpersonal, with neither more important than the other.

MULTISYSTEMIC THERAPY. Targets those factors in the adolescent's social network that contribute to his problematic behavior (Swenson et al. 2004). Typically aims to improve caregiver discipline practices, enhance family relationships and interactions, decrease the teen's association with peers who are involved in troubling behaviors, increase the teen's association with prosocial peers, improve the teen's school or vocational performance, engage the teen in prosocial recreational outlets, and develop an indigenous support network of extended family, neighbors, and friends who help the teen to achieve and maintain such changes. Specific treatment techniques draw from those therapies that have the most empirical support, including cognitive, behavioral, and family therapies focused on specific behavioral goals.

The treatment plan is designed in collaboration with family members and therefore is family driven rather than therapist driven. The ultimate goal is to empower families to build an environment by harnessing child, family, and community resources that promote positive functioning. Therapy typically lasts about four months, with multiple therapist-family contacts each week.

PSYCHOEDUCATIONAL THERAPY. Designed to teach people about their problem, how to treat it, and how to recognize signs of relapse so that they can get treatment before their difficulty worsens or recurs. Family psychoeducation includes teaching coping strategies and problem-solving skills to families, friends, and/or caregivers to help them deal more effectively with the individual.

SUPPORTIVE GROUP COUNSELING. Provides adolescents with an opportunity to meet together, discuss challenges in their lives, and gain support from one another. Supportive group counseling usually is facilitated by a mental health professional.

1. THE INVENTION OF "TROUBLED TEENS"

1. Educational consultants come from diverse professional and personal backgrounds and bring remarkably different types of education and expertise to their task. Like programs and schools for struggling teens, the educational consultant industry is largely unregulated. There are no licensing requirements to become an educational consultant, although some educational consultants have a license in another profession, such as psychology, social work, or counseling. Membership in the field's national organization, the Independent Educational Consultants Association (IECA), is voluntary. See chapter 5 for more information about IECA.

    Perhaps the best-known directory of specialty schools and programs is *Woodbury Reports* and its companion Web site, www.strugglingteens.com. Created by an educational consultant, Lon Woodbury, these resources provide detailed information about specialty schools and programs for struggling teens, reports on schools and programs prepared by educational consultants with whom Woodbury collaborates, a newsletter, articles on struggling teens, current events and "breaking news," book reviews, and Internet links to paid advertisers (educational consultants, schools, and programs). Woodbury's *Parent Empowerment Handbook*, available in print and electronically, has become an industry standard. The handbook includes summaries and overviews of specialty schools and programs written by educational consultants who have visited them. Readers should recognize that the summaries and overviews reflect the opinions of the educational consultants who wrote them and the results of the publisher's annual surveys of independent consultants nationwide.

2. Portions of this discussion are drawn from Shireman and Reamer (1986).

3. Boys Town is now a major component of the struggling-teens industry, offering programs in fifteen states in the United States.

4. The human potential movement featured a mix of relatively benign programs that sponsored self-help, mutual-aid groups of people seeking personal growth, and much more controversial programs, such as Synanon in California. Synanon, a rehabilitation program that gained notoriety in the 1960s, is a key example of a

human potential program that was known for cultlike, confrontational qualities that eventually were adopted by some programs for struggling teens. Synanon, founded by Charles "Chuck" Dederich Sr., closed in the 1990s awash in controversy about its methods, bankruptcy, and legal problems with the Internal Revenue Service (Janzen 2001).

2. THE STRUGGLING-TEENS INDUSTRY

1. An example of a nontraditional option offered by local school districts in several states is the Diploma Plus program of the Commonwealth Corporation, which collaborates with local school districts, charter schools, and community organizations. The Diploma Plus program "serves youth who have overcome a variety of obstacles in order to re-engage with school and prepare themselves for post-secondary education. Many Diploma Plus students have had difficult and frustrating experiences in a traditional high school setting." According to the Commonwealth Corporation, most Diplomas Plus students have "reported that they had struggled academically in their prior school, with some citing poor grades and low skills as reasons they were not successful. Students also experienced personal issues that made attendance and success in school difficult, including unstable living situations, involvement with the criminal justice system, mental health and substance abuse problems, and learning disabilities" (www.commcorp.org/diplomaplus/students.html; February 21, 2008). The Diploma Plus program is based on a structured curriculum and uses a competency-based, mastery approach to education, allowing students to progress at their own pace. Students build a portfolio that includes work that they have had the opportunity to revise and polish until it meets standards for graduation. Promotion and graduation are based on the students' ability to demonstrate their competency and knowledge.

2. The connotations of the term emotional growth boarding school have changed over time. During the earliest years of the struggling-teens industry, the term was associated with schools led by charismatic figures who sometimes used controversial, confrontational, and emotionally abusive methods. More recently, the term has been used to refer to schools that accept struggling teens who are not in crisis, have done some hard therapeutic work—often in a therapeutic boarding school or wilderness therapy program that explicitly includes mental health treatment as part of the program—and are handling life much better than they once did. Students who enroll in emotional growth boarding schools are ready for a residential school that is sensitive to the adolescent's emotional and behavioral struggles and employs trained staff members who are prepared to respond constructively to the struggling teen's challenges. Typically, these schools do not include a formal psychiatric or mental health component on site. Many students in emotional growth boarding schools receive counseling from an independent therapist who is not employed by the school and who, with appropriate informed consent, collaborates and consults with school staff.

3. Some defiant teens refuse to go voluntarily to a wilderness therapy program, therapeutic boarding school, or residential treatment program. In these cases parents may need to hire specially trained professionals who transport the teen to his or her destination. Teen transport professionals are trained in nonviolent crisis

intervention techniques, crisis deescalation, anger management, suicide awareness and prevention, and conflict resolution. They accompany the teen to the program or school to ensure the child's safety and compliance during the travel. Parents need to screen transport agencies carefully to ensure that they are reputable, professional, and ethical.

3. A LEGACY OF SCANDALS

1. In some publications and media reports the World Wide Association of Specialty Schools and Programs is referred to as WWASP.
2   Szalavitz (2006) argues that the tough love philosophy "can be summed up as the notion that love and freedom must be made contingent on good behavior" (6). Further, tough love is "a way of breaking people down with attack therapy, isolation, and rigid restrictions, and gradually restoring limited freedom and positive affirmation to those who complied" (7). This tough love stance does not acknowledge that many struggling teens are unable to respond to the tough love model and methods because of their learning disabilities, physical disabilities, mental health struggles, and frontal lobe immaturity. For these teens this approach is equivalent to telling a person who is without legs or prostheses that he should run a long-distance marathon.
3   See www.sembler.com/company.php?id=1 (June 25, 2007).
4. Marc Polonsky shared this story with the authors. Details are reported here with Polonsky's permission.
5. For discussion of the Hyde Schools, see Traub (2005), a thoughtful, balanced, carefully considered analysis in Education Next, a publication of the Hoover Institution, the conservative think tank headquartered at Stanford University. Traub concludes that Hyde, which markets a unique brand of what it describes as "character education," "feels almost like a cult" (2005:31). Traub explores the profound, controversial influence that the school's founder, Joe Gauld, has had on Hyde. According to Traub, "The board forced Gauld out of his own school in 1980"; Malcolm Gauld, Joe's son, stayed on as a Hyde administrator and "was able to engineer his father's return five years later" (28). Traub's discussion suggests that Gauld's influence in many ways resembles that of charismatic and divisive leaders such as Mel Wasserman (CEDU), Robert Lichfield (WWASPS), Ken Kay (WWASPS), Mel Sembler (Straight), and Miller Newton (Straight), whose programs and organizations, like Hyde's, have enthusiastic proponents and harsh critics.

4. HELPING STRUGGLING TEENS

1. This discussion is based on V. Vandiver, "Evidence-Based Mental Health Practice: Overview," n.d., Graduate School of Social Work, Portland State University, www.ssw.pdx.edu/focus/ebp/ (July 13, 2007).
2. We recognize and acknowledge the importance of qualitative research on programs and interventions for struggling teens. Findings from qualitative inquiries provide rich data and a valuable supplement to knowledge gained from quantitatively oriented, controlled studies. Here we focus especially on quantitatively oriented meta-analyses of large numbers of individual studies because of their

ability to aggregate findings and identify important patterns and trends that can help professionals determine "best practices" in the field.

3. The Cochrane Library is a subscriber service, but copies are available in most medical libraries. Summaries are available on line at www.cochrane.org/index.htm.

4. For a number of years therapeutic foster care—where teens who cannot live at home are placed in homes with foster parents who have been trained to provide a structured environment that addresses teens' unique social and emotional needs—has been an appealing alternative to group homes, traditional foster homes, and residential treatment. Unfortunately, there is relatively little empirical research evaluating or documenting the effectiveness of this model (Curtis, Alexander, and Lunghofer 2001; Hahn et al. 2004).

5. A BLUEPRINT FOR REFORM

1. See codes of ethics ratified by the National Association of Social Workers, American Psychological Association, American Counseling Association, American Psychiatric Association, the American Association for Marriage and Family Therapy, and the National Education Association.

2. The behavior modification literature carefully documents that punishment can produce avoidance, escape, and aggression. While punishment may be associated with reduction in target behaviors, it may be most effective when it is part of a collaborative, strengths-based approach and coupled with positive reinforcement and cognitive-behavioral skills training (Kazdin 2000).

3. This discussion draws on the pioneering work of Fergus and Zimmerman (2005).

4. Many parents do not have the money to purchase services from an educational consultant, which can be quite costly. Assistance might be available through public or private child welfare, family service, and mental health agencies.

5. It is unethical for educational consultants to accept referral fees from schools and programs to which they refer teens. Educational consultants should refer a teen to only a program or school that truly fits the teen's unique needs. Parents and professionals who consider working with an educational consultant should ask whether the consultant receives a referral fee or maintains any kind of a financial relationship with programs and schools to which the consultant refers. There is a human inclination to refer to programs and schools that pay for referrals. This could lead an educational consultant to favor, perhaps unwittingly, programs and schools that pay referral fees. Clearly, accepting a referral fee would constitute a conflict of interest. IECA recognizes the potential for conflicts of interest and addresses the phenomenon, at least in broad form, if not explicitly with regard to referral fees, in its "Principles of Good Practice": "Members are expected to avoid multiple relationships that could reasonably and foreseeably give rise to actual or perceived conflicts of interest, interfere with the ability of the consultant to provide objective service, embarrass the student or family, or compromise the confidence or trust basic to the client-consultant relationship" (IECA 2006).

6. Licensing standards for professions such as social work, psychology, and counseling can be found in state statutes and regulations. Centralized sources for state licensing laws and regulations include the Association of Social Work Boards

(www.aswb.org/), the Association of State and Provincial Psychology Boards (www.asppb.org/), and the American Association of State Counseling Boards (www.aascb.org/).

7. Parents should be aware that some schools and programs are owned by for-profit corporations. These schools and programs have a financial incentive to admit teens who may not be a good fit. The profit motive may entice schools and programs to admit teens without taking the time to assess their needs.

8. In cases of suicide risk or risk of other serious self-injury, and threats of serious harm to others, immediate psychiatric hospitalization is medically, ethically, and legally required.

9. See, for example, the guidelines developed by the National Association of State Mental Health Program Directors. According to this organization's policies, "seclusion and restraint . . . are safety interventions of last resort and are not treatment interventions. Seclusion and restraint should never be used for the purposes of discipline, coercion, or staff convenience, or as a replacement for adequate levels of staff or active treatment. The use of seclusion and restraint creates significant risks for people. . . . These risks include serious injury or death, retraumatization of people who have a history of trauma, and loss of dignity and other psychological harm. In light of these potential serious consequences, seclusion and restraint should be used only when there exists an imminent risk of danger to the individual or others and no other safe and effective intervention is possible" (www.nasmhpd.org/general_files/position_statement/posses1.htm [August 19, 2007]).

10. The Child Welfare League of America publishes influential guidelines, Standards of Excellence for Residential Services, www.cwla.org/programs/standards/cwsstandardsgroupcare.htm (February 18, 2008). These "best practice" guidelines address issues related to state licensing and monitoring; types of services; staff qualifications, orientation, training, and supervision; staff-to-child ratios; appropriate and prohibited behavior support and interventions; and use of medications.

11. For an overview of research on the impact of school and classroom size, see American Educational Research Association (2003) and Darling-Hammond (1997).

12. Members of the national association include therapeutic schools, residential treatment programs, wilderness therapy programs, outdoor therapeutic programs, young adult programs, and home-based residential programs. Outdoor council members include wilderness therapy programs for struggling teens.

13. Cosponsors of the briefing included the American Psychological Association, American Association of Community Psychiatrists, American Orthopsychiatric Association, Child Welfare League of America, Federation of Families for Children's Mental Health, National Alliance for the Mentally Ill, and the National Mental Health Association. For the press release announcing the briefing, see Bazelon Center for Mental Health Law (2005).

14. Licensure of Programs and Facilities, S.B. 107, 55th Leg., 2005 sess. (Utah 2005). This effort is particularly important because a large number of programs and schools for struggling teens are located in Utah.

15. The text of "American Bar Association Policy Requiring Licensure, Regulation, and Monitoring of Privately Operated Residential Treatment Facilities for At-Risk Children and Youth" and accompanying February 2007 report may be found

at http://209.85.135.104/search?q=cache:T82qo1tpsbsJ:www.abanet.org/leader-
ship/2007/midyear/docs/SUMMARYOFRECOMMENDATIONS/hundredfour-
teen.doc+end+institutional+abuse+against+children+act+miller&hl=en&ct=cl
nk&cd=10&gl=us&client=firefox-a (July 18, 2007).

REFERENCES

Adams, J. S. 2005. "Spring Creek's Short Leash: Montana's Behavior Modification Programs Watch Their Troubled Charges Like Hawks." *Missoula News*, June 16. www.missoulanews.com/index.cfm?do=article.details&id=C3D32183-2BF4-55D0-F1F03ECE24E119C0 (July 1, 2007).

Albano, A. and P. Kendall. 2002. "Cognitive Behavioural Therapy for Children and Adolescents with Anxiety Disorders: Clinical Research Advances." *International Review of Psychiatry* 14:129–34.

Alexander, J., H. Waldron, A. Newberry, and N. Liddle. 1988. *Family Approaches to Treating Delinquents*. Newbury Park, Calif.: Sage.

"American Bar Association Policy Requiring Licensure, Regulation, and Monitoring of Privately Operated Residential Treatment Facilities for At-Risk Children and Youth." 2007. *Family Court Review* 45:414–20.

American Educational Research Association. 2003. "Class Size: Counting Students Can Count." *Research Points* 1:1–4.

American Psychiatric Association. 2000. *Diagnostic and Statistical Manual of Mental Disorders: DSM-IV-TR*. 4th ed. Washington, D.C.: American Psychiatric Association.

Ammerman, R., M. Hersen, and C. Last, eds. 1999. *Handbook of Prescriptive Treatments for Children and Adolescents*. 2d ed. Boston: Allyn and Bacon.

Anastopoulous, A. 1998. "A Training Program for Parents of Children with Attention-Deficit/Hyperactivity Disorder." In J. Briesmeister and C. Schaefer, eds., *Handbook of Parent Training: Parents as Co-therapists for Children's Behavior Problems*, 27–60. New York: Wiley.

Anastopoulous, A., J. Smith, and E. Wien. 1998. "Counseling and Training Parents." In R. Barkley, ed., *Attention-Deficit Hyperactivity Disorder: A Handbook for Diagnosis and Treatment*, 373–93. New York: Guilford.

Angold, A. and E. Costello. 1993. "Depressive Comorbidity in Children and Adolescents: Empirical, Theoretical, and Methodological Issues." *American Journal of Psychiatry* 150:1779–91.

Annie E. Casey Foundation. 2006. *Race Matters: How to Talk about Race*. Baltimore: Annie E. Casey Foundation.

——. 2007. *2007 KIDS COUNT Data Book: State Profiles of Child Well-being*, www. aecf.org/KnowledgeCenter/Publications.aspx?pubguid={4592AE36-DB63-4D5E-B858-E05BFFCD24BF} (March 10, 2008).

Anteghini, M., H. Fonseca, M. Ireland, and R. Blum. 2001. "Health Risk Behaviors and Associated Risk and Protective Factors among Brazilian Adolescents in Santos, Brazil." *Journal of Adolescent Health* 28:295–302.

Asarnow, J., C. Scott, and J. Mintz. 2002. "A Combined Cognitive-Behavioral Family Education Intervention for Depression in Children: A Treatment Development Study." *Cognitive Therapy and Research* 26:221–29.

ASTART (Alliance for the Safe, Therapeutic, and Appropriate Use of Residential Treatment). n.d. Fact Sheet. http://astart.fmhi.usf.edu/AStartDocs/factsheet.pdf (June 23, 2007).

——. 2005. "A Press Briefing on Exploitation of Youth and Families: Perspectives on Unregulated Private Residential Treatment Facilities." Press release. Department of Child and Family Studies, University of South Florida, Tampa.

Azrin, N., B. Donohue, V. Besalel, E. Kogan, and R. Acierno. 1994. "Youth Drug Abuse Treatment: A Controlled Outcome Study." *Journal of Child and Adolescent Substance Abuse* 3:1–16.

Bacon, B. 2007. "Testimony of Bob Bacon, father of Aaron Bacon," October 10, U.S. House Committee on Education and Labor. 110th Cong., 1st sess. http://edlabor. house.gov/testimony/101007BobBaconTestimony.pdf (March 2, 2008).

Bagdasaryan, S. 2005. "Evaluating Family Preservation Services: Reframing the Question of Effectiveness." *Children and Youth Services Review* 27:615–35 .

Baily, V. 1998. "Conduct Disorders in Young Children." In Graham, *Cognitive-Behaviour Therapy for Children and Families*, 95–109.

Barkin, S., S. Kreiter, and R Durant. 2001. "Exposure to Violence and Intentions to Engage in Moralistic Violence during Early Adolescence." *Journal of Adolescence* 24:777–89.

Barkley, R. 2002. "Psychosocial Treatments for Attention Deficit/Hyperactivity Disorder in Children." *Journal of Clinical Psychiatry* 63:36–43.

Barrett, P. 1998. "Evaluation of Cognitive-Behavioural Group Treatments for Childhood Anxiety Disorders." *Journal of Clinical Child Psychology* 27:459–68.

Barstow, D. 1991. "State Takes a Hard Look at Straight." *St. Petersburg Times*, July 31.

Basco, M., G. Ladd, D. Myers, and D. Tyler. 2007. "Combining Medication Treatment and Cognitive-Behavior Therapy for Bipolar Disorder." *Journal of Cognitive Psychotherapy* 21:7–15.

Bazelon Center for Mental Health Law. 2005. "Press Briefing on Unregulated Private Residential Treatment Facilities," October 13, www.bazelon.org/newsroom/ archive/2005/10-13-05PressBriefingforOct18.htm (February 19, 2008).

Beam, M., C. Chen, and E. Greenberger. 2002. "The Nature of Adolescents' Relationships with Their 'Very Important' Nonparental Adults." *American Journal of Community Psychology* 30:305–25.

Behar, L., R. Friedman, A. Pinto, J, Katz-Leavy, and W. Jones. 2007. "Protecting Youth Placed in Unlicensed, Unregulated Residential 'Treatment' Facilities." *Family Court Review* 45: 399–413.

Beier, S., W. Rosenfeld, K. Spitalny, S. Zansky, and A. Bontempo. 2000. "The Potential Role of an Adult Mentor in Influencing High-Risk Behaviors in Adolescents." *Archives of Pediatric Adolescent Medicine* 154:327–31.

Bentham, J. [1789] 1973. "An Introduction to the Principles of Morals and Legislation." In *The Utilitarians*, 7–398. New York: Anchor.

Berman, S. 1959. "Antisocial Character Disorder: Its Etiology and Relationship to Delinquency." *American Journal of Orthopsychiatry* 29:612–21.

Bernier, J. and D. Siegel. 1994. "Attention Deficit Hyperactivity Disorder: An Ecological and Family Systems Perspective." *Families in Society* 75:142–51.

Bernstein, G. and C. Borchardt. 1991. "Anxiety Disorders of Childhood and Adolescence: A Critical Review." *Journal of the American Academy of Child and Adolescent Psychiatry* 30:519–32.

Berry, M., S. Cash, and J. Brook. 2000. "Intensive Family Preservation Services: An Examination of Critical Service Components." *Child and Family Social Work* 5:191–203.

Best, D. 1997. "Adolescent Substance Abuse: Assessment, Prevention and Treatment." *Addiction Research* 4:393–94.

Billman, J. 2003. "SAFE (or Else)." *Orlando Weekly*, January 16. www.orlandoweekly. com/util/printready.asp?id=2947 (June 30, 2007).

Birmaher, B., N. Ryan, D. Williamson, D. Brent, J. Kaufman, and R. Dahl. 1996a. "Childhood and Adolescent Depression: A Review of the Past Ten Years." Part 1. *Journal of the American Academy of Child and Adolescent Psychiatry* 35:1427–39.

Birmaher, B., N. Ryan, D. Williamson, D. Brent, and J. Kaufman. 1996b. "Childhood and Adolescent Depression: A Review of the Past Ten Years." Part 2. *Journal of the American Academy of Child and Adolescent Psychiatry* 35:1575–83.

Blinn-Pike, L. 2007. "Benefits Associated with Youth Mentoring Relationships." In T. Allen and L. Eby, eds., *The Blackwell Handbook of Mentoring: A Multiple Perspectives Approach*, 165–87. Malden, Mass.: Blackwell.

Bloch, H. and A. Niederhoffer. 1958. *The Gang: A Study in Adolescent Behavior*. New York: Philosophical Library.

Blue, D. 2004. "Adolescent Mentoring." *Study of High School Restructuring* 1:1–5.

Blum, R., T. Beuhring, M. Shew, L. Bearinger, R. Sieving, and M. Resnick. 2000. "The Effects of Race/Ethnicity, Income, and Family Structure on Adolescent Risk Behaviors." *American Journal of Public Health* 90:1879–84.

Blythe, B., M. Salley, and S. Jayaratne. 1994. "A Review of Intensive Family Services Research." *Social Work Research* 18:213–24.

Bolton, A. 2007. "Lawsuits Hit a Romney Money Man." *Hill*, June 20. http://thehill. com/leading-the-news/lawsuits-hit-a-romney-money-man-2007-06-20.html (July 1, 2007).

Borowsky, I., M. Ireland, and M. Resnick. 2002. "Violence Risk and Protective Factors among Youth Held Back in School." *Ambulatory Pediatrics* 2:475–84.

Borsari, B. and K. Carey 2000. "Effects of Brief Motivational Intervention with College Student Drinkers." *Journal of Consulting and Clinical Psychology* 68:728–33.

Botvin, G. 2004. "Advancing Prevention Science and Practices: Challenges, Critical Issues and Future Directions." *Prevention Science* 5:69–72.

Botvin, G., E. Baker, L. Dusenbury, L. Tortu, and E. Botvin. 1990. "Preventing Adolescent Drug Abuse through a Multimodal Cognitive-Behavioral Approach: Results of a Three-year Study." *Journal of Consulting and Clinical Psychology* 58:437–46.

Botvin, G., K. Griffin, T. Diaz, and M. Ifill-Williams. 2001. "Preventing Binge

Drinking during Early Adolescence: One- and Two-Year Follow-up of a School-Based Prevention Intervention." *Psychology of Addictive Behaviors* 15:360–65.

Botvin, G., R. Malgady, K. Griffin, L. Scheier, and J. Epstein. 1998. "Alcohol and Marijuana Use among Rural Youth: Interaction of Social and Intrapersonal Influences." *Addictive Behaviors* 23:379–87.

Bower, B. 2007. "Psychotherapy Aids Bipolar Treatment." *Science News* 171:253.

Bowers, W., K. Evans, and L. van Cleve. 1996. "Treatment of Adolescent Eating Disorders." In Reinecke, Dattilio, and Freeman, *Cognitive Therapy with Children and Adolescents*, 227–50.

Braswell, L. and M. Bloomquist. 1991. *Cognitive-Behavioural Therapy with ADHD Children: Child, Family, and School Interventions.* New York: Guilford.

Brent, D., D. Holder, D., Kolko, B. Birmaher, M. Baugher, and C. Roth. 1997. "A Clinical Psychotherapy Trial for Adolescent Depression Comparing Cognitive, Family, and Supportive Therapy." *Archives of General Psychiatry* 54:877–85.

Brestan, E. and S. Eyberg. 1998. "Effective Psychosocial Treatments of Conduct-Disordered Children and Adolescents: Twenty-nine Years, 82 Studies, 5,272 Kids." *Journal of Clinical Child Psychology* 27:180–89.

Britner, P., F. Balcazar, E. Blechman, L. Blinn-Pike, and S. Larose. 2006. "Mentoring Special Youth Populations." *Journal of Community Psychology* 34:747–63.

Broussard, A., S. Mosley-Howard, and A. Roychoudhury. 2006. "Using Youth Advocates for Mentoring At-Risk Students in Urban Settings." *Children and Schools* 28:122–27.

Bryan, V., M. Hiller, and C. Leukefeld. 2006. "A Qualitative Examination of the Juvenile Drug Court Treatment Process." *Journal of Social Work Practice in the Addictions* 6:91–114.

Bryant, A. and M. Zimmerman. 2002. "Examining the Effects of Academic Beliefs and Behaviors on Changes in Substance Use among Urban Adolescents." *Journal of Educational Psychology* 94:621–37.

Bryant, A., J. Schulenberg, P. O'Malley, J. Bachman, and L. Johnston. 2003. "How Academic Achievement, Attitudes, and Behaviors Related to the Course of Substance Use during Adolescence: A Six-Year, Multiwave National Longitudinal Study." *Journal of Research on Adolescence* 13:361–97.

Bryson, A. J. 2004. "N.Y. Probing Utah-based Youth Programs." *Deseret (Salt Lake City) News*, April 9, http://deseretnews.com/dn/view/0,1249,595054928,00.html (July 1, 2007).

——. 2005. Utah-Based Group under Fire." *Deseret (Salt Lake City) Morning News*, April 21, http://deseretnews.com/dn/print/1,1442,600128053,00.html (July 1, 2007).

Burgess, J. 1983. "Held at Drug Center against His Will, Fairfax Man Says." *Washington Post*, May 10.

Burns, B., K. Hoagwood, and P. Mrazek. 1999. "Treatment for Mental Disorders in Children and Adolescents." *Clinical Child and Family Psychology Review* 2:199–254.

Bustamante, E. 2000. *Treating the Disruptive Adolescent: Finding the Real Self behind Oppositional Defiant Disorders.* New York: Jason Aronson.

Butts, J. and J. Roman, eds. 2004. *Juvenile Drug Courts and Teen Substance Abuse.* Washington, D.C.: Urban Institute Press.

Carter, B. and M. McGoldrick, eds. 2005. *The Expanded Family Life Cycle: Individual, Family, and Social Perspectives.* 3d ed. Boston: Allyn and Bacon.

Cartwright-Hatton, S., C. Roberts, P. Chitsabesan, C. Fothergill, and R. Harrington. 2004. "Systematic Reviews of the Efficacy of Cognitive Behaviour Therapies for Childhood and Adolescent Anxiety Disorders." *British Journal of Clinical Psychology* 43:421–36.

Christophersen, E. and J. Finney. 1999. "Oppositional Defiant Disorder." In Ammerman, Hersen, and Last, *Handbook of Prescriptive Treatments*, 102–13.

Clark, J., L. Marmol, R. Cooley, and K. Gathercoal. 2004. "The Effects of Wilderness Therapy on the Clinical Concerns (on Axes I, II, and IV) of Troubled Adolescents." *Journal of Experimental Education* 27:213–32.

Clarke, G. N., L. DeBar, and P. Lewinsohn. 2003. "Cognitive-Behavioral Group Treatment for Adolescent Depression." In A. Kazdin, ed., *Evidenced-Based Psychotherapies for Children and Adolescents*, 120–34. New York: Guilford.

Cloward, R. and L. Ohlin. 1960. *Delinquency and Opportunity*. New York: Free Press.

Cohen, A. 1955. *Delinquent Boys: The Culture of the Gang*. Glencoe, Ill.: Free Press.

Compton, S., B. Burns, H. Egger, and E. Robertson. 2002. "Review of the Evidence Base for Treatment of Childhood Psychopathology: Internalizing Disorders." *Journal of Consulting and Clinical Psychology* 70:1240–66.

Consoli, A., E. Deniau, C. Huynh, D. Purper, and D. Cohen. 2007. "Treatments in Child and Adolescent Bipolar Disorders." *European Child and Adolescent Psychiatry* 16:187–98.

Corcoran, K. and V. Vandiver. 2004. "Implementing Best Practice and Expert Consensus Procedures." In Roberts and Yeager, *Evidence-Based Practice Manual*, 15–19.

Costa, F., R. Jessor, and M. Turbin. 1999. "Transition into Adolescent Problem Drinking: The Role of Psychosocial Risk and Protective Factors." *Journal of Studies on Alcohol* 60:480–90.

Crosnoe, R. 2002. "Academic and Health-related Trajectories in Adolescence: The Intersection of Gender and Athletics." *Journal of Health and Social Behavior* 43:317–35.

Curry, J. 2001. "Specific Psychotherapies for Childhood and Adolescent Depression." *Biological Psychiatry* 49:1091–1100.

Curtis, P., G. Alexander, and L. Lunghofer. 2001. "A Literature Review Comparing the Outcomes of Residential Group Care and Therapeutic Foster Care." *Child and Adolescent Social Work Journal* 18:377–92.

Dadds, M., S. Spence, D. Holland, P. Barrett, and K. Laurens. 1997. "Prevention and Early Intervention for Anxiety Disorders: A Controlled Trial." *Journal of Consulting and Clinical Psychology* 65:627–35.

Dagenais, C., J. Begin, C. Bouchard, and D. Fortin. 2004. "Impact of Intensive Family Support Programs: A Synthesis of Evaluation Studies." *Children and Youth Services Review* 26:249–63.

Darling-Hammond, L. 1997. *The Right to Learn: A Blueprint for Creating Schools That Work*. San Francisco: Jossey-Bass.

Dembo, R. and W. Walters. 2003. "Innovative Approaches to Identifying and Responding to the Needs of High Risk Youth." *Substance Use and Misuse* 38:1713–38.

Derloshon, G. 1982. *The Success Merchants: A Guide to Major Influences and People in the Human Potential Movement*. Englewood Cliffs, N.J.: Prentice-Hall.

Dishion, T. J. and D. W. Andrews. 1995. "Preventing Escalation in Problem Behaviors with High-Risk Young Adolescents: Immediate and One-Year Outcomes." *Journal of Consulting and Clinical Psychology* 63:538–48.

Dishion, T. J. and K. A. Dodge. 2005. "Peer Contagion in Interventions for Children and Adolescents: Moving towards an Understanding of the Ecology and Dynamics of Change." *Journal of Abnormal Child Psychology* 33:395–400.

——. 2006. "Deviant Peer Contagion in Interventions and Programs." In Dodge, Dishion, and Lansford, *Deviant Peer Influences in Programs for Youth*, 14–43.

Dishion, T. J., D. W. Andrews, and L. Crosby. 1995. "Antisocial Boys and Their Friends in Early Adolescence: Relationship Characteristics, Quality and Interactional Process." *Child Development* 66:139–51.

Dishion, T. J., B. M. Bullock, and I. Granic. 2002. "Pragmatism in Modeling Peer Influence: Dynamics, Outcomes, and Change Processes." *Development and Psychopathology* 14:969–81.

Dishion, T. J., K. Dodge, and J. Lansford. 2006. "Findings and Recommendations: A Blueprint to Minimize Deviant Peer Influence in Youth Interventions and Programs." In Dodge, Dishion, and Lansford, *Deviant Peer Influences in Programs for Youth*, 366–94.

Dishion, T. J., J. McCord, and F. Poulin. 1999. "When Interventions Harm: Peer Groups and Problem Behavior." *American Psychologist* 54:755–64.

Dishion, T. J., S. N. Nelson, C. Winter, and B. M. Bullock. 2004. "Premature Adolescent Autonomy: Parent Disengagement and Peer Process in the Amplification of Problem Behavior." *Journal of Adolescence* 27:515–30.

Dishion, T. J., F. Poulin, and B. Burraston. 2001. "Peer Group Dynamics Associated with Iatrogenic Effects in Group Interventions with High-Risk Young Adolescents." *New Directions for Child and Adolescent Development* 91:79–92.

Dodge, K. and M. Sherrill. 2006. "Deviant Peer Group Effects in Youth Mental Health Interventions." In Dodge, Dishion, and Lansford, *Deviant Peer Influences in Programs for Youth*, 97–121.

Dodge, K., T. Dishion, and J. Lansford, eds. 2006. *Deviant Peer Influences in Programs for Youth: Problems and Solutions.* New York: Guilford.

DuBois, D. and M. Karcher, eds. 2005. *Handbook of Youth Mentoring.* Thousand Oaks, Calif.: Sage.

DuBois, D. and H. Neville. 1997. "Youth Mentoring: Investigation of Relationship Characteristics and Perceived Benefits." *Journal of Community Psychology* 25:227–234.

DuBois, D., F. Doolittle, B. Yates, N. Silverthorn, and J. Tebes. 2006. "Research Methodology and Youth Mentoring." *Journal of Community Psychology* 34:657–76.

DuBois, D., B. Holloway, J. Valentine, and C. Harris. 2002. "Effectiveness of Mentoring Programs for Youth: A Meta-Analytic Review." *American Journal of Community Psychology*, 30:157–97.

Eddy, J. M. and P. Chamberlain. 2000. "Family Management and Deviant Peer Association as Mediators of the Impact of Treatment Condition on Youth Antisocial Behavior." *Journal of Consulting and Clinical Psychology* 68:857–63.

Egbert, S., W. Church II, and E. Byrnes. 2006. "Justice and Treatment Collaboration: A Process Evaluation of a Drug Court." *Best Practice in Mental Health: An International Journal* 2:74–91.

Elder, C., D. Leaver-Dunn, M. Q. Wang, S. Nagy, and L. Green. 2000. "Organized Group Activity as a Protective Factor against Adolescent Substance Use." *American Journal of Health Behavior* 24:108–13.

Evans, D., E. Foa, R. Gur, H. Hendin, C. O'Brien, M. Seligman, and T. Walsh, eds. 2005. *Treating and Preventing Adolescent Mental Health Disorders: What We Know and What We Don't Know.* New York: Oxford University Press.

Fabiano, G., W. Pelham Jr., E. Gnagy, L. Burrows-MacLean, E. Coles, A. Chacko, B. Wymbs, et al. 2007. "The Single and Combined Effects of Multiple Intensities of Behavior Modification and Methylphenidate for Children with Attention Deficit Hyperactivity Disorder in a Classroom Setting." *School Psychology Review* 36:195–216.

Fairburn, C. 1993. "Interpersonal Psychotherapy for Bulimia Nervosa." In Klerman and Weissman, *New Applications of Interpersonal Psychotherapy,* 353–78.

——. 1997. "Towards Evidence-Based and Cost-Effective Treatment for Bulimia Nervosa." *European Eating Disorders Review* 5:145–48.

Farmer, E., S. Compton, B. Burns, and E. Robertson. 2002. "Review of the Evidence Base for Treatment of Childhood Psychopathology Externalizing Disorders." *Journal of Consulting and Clinical Psychology* 70:1267–1302.

Farrell, A. and K. White. 1998. "Peer Influences and Drug Use among Urban Adolescents: Family Structure and Parent-Adolescent Relationship as Protective Factors." *Journal of Consulting and Clinical Psychology* 66:248–58.

Feldman, R. A. 1992. "The St. Louis Experiment: Effective Treatment of Antisocial Youths in Prosocial Peer Groups." In J. McCord and R. E. Tremblay, eds., *Preventing Antisocial Behavior: Interventions from Birth to Adolescence,* 233–52. New York: Guilford.

Fergus, S. and M. Zimmerman. 2005. "Adolescent Resilience: A Framework for Understanding Healthy Development in the Face of Risk." *Annual Review of Public Health* 26:399–419.

Findling, R. 2005. "Update on the Treatment of Bipolar Disorder in Children and Adolescents." *European Psychiatry* 20:87–91.

Finkel, D. 1987. "Going Straight." *St. Petersburg Times,* May 3.

Flannery-Schroeder, E. and P. Kendall. 2000. "Group and Individual Cognitive-Behavioral Treatments for Youth with Anxiety Disorders: A Randomized Clinical Trial." *Cognitive Therapy and Research* 24:251–78.

Fleming, C., H. Kim, T. Harachi, and R. Catalano. 2002. "Family Processes for Children in Early Elementary School as Predictors of Smoking Initiation." *Journal of Adolescent Health* 30:184–89.

Foster, S. 1994. "Assessing and Treating Parent-Adolescent Conflict." In M. Hersen, R. Eisler, and P. Miller, eds., *Progress in Behavior Modification,* 29:53–72. New York: Academic Press.

Fountoulakis, K., E. Vieta, J. Sanchez-Moreno, S. Kaprinis, J. Goikolea, and G. Kaprinis. 2005. "Treatment Guidelines for Bipolar Disorder: A Critical Review." *Journal of Affective Disorders* 86:1–10.

Fraser, M., K. Nelson, and J. Rivard. 1997. "Effectiveness of Family Preservation Services." *Social Work Research* 21:138–53.

Fraser, M., P. Pecora, and D. Haapala. 1991. *Families in Crisis: The Impact of Intensive Family Preservation Services.* Hawthorne, N.Y.: de Gruyter.

Friedman, A. 1989. "Family Therapy vs. Parent Groups: Effects on Adolescent Drug Abusers." *American Journal of Family Therapy* 17:335–47.

Friedman, A., A. Terras, and K. Glassman. 2002. "Multimodel Substance Use Intervention Program for Male Delinquents." *Journal of Child and Adolescent Substance Abuse* 11:43–65.

Friedman, R. M., A. Pinto, L. Behar, N. Bush, A. Chirolla, M. Epstein, A. Green, et al. 2006. "Unlicensed Residential Programs: The Next Challenge in Protecting Youth." *American Journal of Orthopsychiatry* 76:295–303.

Gacono, C., R. Nieberding, A. Owen, J. Rubel, and R. Bodholdt. 2001. "Treating Conduct Disorder, Antisocial, and Psychopathic Personalities." In J. Ashford, B. Sales, and W. Reid, eds., *Treating Adult and Juvenile Offenders with Special Needs*, 99–129. Washington, D.C.: American Psychological Association.

Garmezy, N., A. Masten, and A. Tellegen. 1984. "The Study of Stress and Competence in Children: A Building Block for Developmental Psychopathology." *Child Development* 55:97–111.

Geismar, L. and K. Wood. 1986. *"Family and Delinquency: Resocializing the Young Offender.* New York: Human Sciences Press.

Geller, B. and J. Luby. 1997. "Child and Adolescent Bipolar Disorder: A Review of the Past Ten Years." *Journal of the American Academy of Child and Adolescent Psychiatry* 36: 1168–76.

Glass, R. 2004. "Treatment of Adolescents with Major Depression." *Journal of the American Medical Association* 292:861–63.

Goldkamp, J., M. White, and J. Robinson. 2001. "Do Drug Courts Work? Getting inside the Drug Court Black Box." *Journal of Drug Issues* 31:27–72.

Goldstein, S. and R. Brooks, eds. 2005. *Handbook of Resilience in Children.* New York: Kluwer Academic/Plenum.

Gordon, G. 2000. "Deadly Discipline? Some Say Unregulated Wilderness Schools Are a Threat to Troubled Teens' Lives." *Oregonian*, February 12, www.caica.org/NEWS%20Deaths%20Oregonian.htm (March 2, 2008).

Gorenfeld, John. 2006. "Drop and Give Me $20: The Man behind Scooter Libby's Defense Fund." *Mother Jones*, May–June, www.motherjones.com/news/outfront/2006/05/drop_and_give_20.html (June 25, 2007).

Gottfredson, D., S. Najaka, and B. Kearley. 2003. "Effectiveness of Drug Treatment Courts: Evidence from a Randomized Trial." *Criminology and Public Policy* 2:171–96.

Graham, P., ed. 1998. *Cognitive-Behaviour Therapy for Children and Families.* New York: Cambridge University Press.

Green, B., C. Furrer, S. Worcel, S. Burrus, and M. Finigan. 2007. "How Effective Are Family Treatment Drug Courts? Outcomes from a Four-Site National Study." *Child Maltreatment* 12:43–59.

Greenspan, S. and I. Glovinsky. 2005. "Bipolar Patterns in Children: New Perspectives on Development, Prevention and Treatment." *Brown University Child and Adolescent Behavior Letter* 21:1–6.

Griffin, K., L. Scheier, G. Botvin, T. Diaz, and N. Miller. 1999. "Interpersonal Aggression in Urban Minority Youth: Mediators of Perceived Neighborhood, Peer, and Parental Influences." *Journal of Community Psychology* 27:281–98.

Grossman, J. B. and J. P. Tierney. 1998. "Does Mentoring Work? An Impact Study of the Big Brothers/Big Sisters Program." *Evaluation Review* 22:403–26.

Gurman, A., D. Kniskern, and W. Pinsof. 1986. "Research on Marital and Family Therapies." In S. Garfield and A. Bergin, eds., *Handbook of Psychotherapy and Behavior Change*, 565–626. 3d ed. New York: Wiley.

Guttierez, M. and J. Scott 2004. "Psychological Treatment for Bipolar Disorders: A Review of Randomized Controlled Trials." *European Archives of Psychiatry and Clinical Neuroscience* 254:92–98.

Hahn, R., J. Lowy, O. Bilukha, S. Snyder, P. Briss, A. Crosby, M. Fullilove, et al. 2004. "Therapeutic Foster Care for the Prevention of Violence: A Report on Recommendations of the Task Force on Community Preventive Services." *Morbidity and Mortality Weekly Report* 53:1–8.

Hamilton, S., M. Hamilton, B. Hirsch, J. Hughes, J. King, and K. Maton. 2006. "Community Contexts for Mentoring." *Journal of Community Psychology* 34: 727–46.

Hans, T. 2000. "A Meta-Analysis of the Effects of Adventure Programming on Locus of Control." *Journal of Contemporary Psychotherapy* 30:33–60.

Harnish, L., P. Tolan, and N. Guerra. 1996. "Treatment of Oppositional Defiant Disorder." In Reinecke, Dattilio, and Freeman, *Cognitive Therapy with Children and Adolescents*, 62–78.

Harrington, R. 1995. *Depressive Disorder in Childhood and Adolescence*. New York: Wiley.

Harrington, R., F. Campbell, P. Shoebridge, and J. Whittaker. 1998. "Meta-Analysis of CBT for Depression in Adolescents." *Journal of the American Academy of Child and Adolescent Psychiatry* 37:1005–1006.

Harrington, R., J. Whittaker, and P. Shoebridge. 1998. "Psychosocial Treatment of Depression in Children and Adolescents: A Review of Treatment Research." *British Journal of Psychiatry* 173:291–98.

Harrington, R., A. Wood, and C. Verduyn. 1998. "Clinically Depressed Adolescents." In Graham, *Cognitive Behaviour Therapy for Children and Families*, 156–93.

Harrison, P. and S. Asche. 2001. "Adolescent Treatment for Substance Use Disorders: Outcomes and Outcome Predictors." *Journal of Child and Adolescent Substance Abuse* 11:1–17.

Hartley, R. 2004. "Young People and Mentoring." *Family Matters* 68:22–27.

Hattie, J., H. Marsh, J. Neill, and G. Richards. 1997. "Adventure Education and Outward Bound: Out-of-Class Experiences That Make a Lasting Difference." *Review of Educational Research* 67:43–87.

Havivi, A. 2006. "Substance Abuse in Teens: A Clinical Approach to Assessment and Treatment." *Adolescent Psychiatry* 29:33–53.

Heimberg, R. and R Becker. 2002. *Cognitive-Behavioral Group Therapy for Social Phobia: Basic Mechanisms and Clinical Strategies*. New York: Guilford.

Henggler, S. and A. Sheidow. 2003. "Conduct Disorder and Delinquency." *Journal of Marital and Family Therapy* 29:505–22.

Henggeler, S., C. Borduin, G. Melton, B. Mann, L. Smith, J. Hall, L. Cone, and B. Fucci. 1991. "Effects of Multisystemic Therapy on Drug Use and Abuse in Serious Juvenile Offenders: A Progress Report from Two Outcome Studies." *Family Dynamics of Addiction Quarterly* 1:40–51.

Henggeler, S., G. Clingempeel, M. Brondino, and S. Pickrel. 2002. "Four-Year Follow-up of Multisystemic Therapy with Substance-Abusing and Substance-Dependent Juvenile Offenders." *Journal of the American Academy of Child and Adolescent Psychiatry* 41:868–74.

Henggeler, S., C. Halliday-Boykins, P. Cunningham, Phillippe, J. Randall, S. Shapiro, and J. Chapman. 2006. "Juvenile Drug Court: Enhancing Outcomes by Integrating Evidence-Based Treatments." *Journal of Consulting and Clinical Psychology* 74:42–54.

Henggeler, S., S. Pickrel, and M. Brondino. 1999. "Multisystemic Treatment of Substance-Abusing and Dependent Delinquents: Outcomes, Treatment Fidelity, and Transportability." *Mental Health Services Research* 1:171–84.

Hepburn, J. and A. Harvey. 2007. "The Effect of the Threat of Legal Sanction on Program Retention and Completion: Is That Why They Stay in Drug Court?" *Crime and Delinquency* 53:255–80.

Hess, P. and T. Howard. 1981. "An Ecological Model for Assessing Psychosocial Difficulties in Children." *Child Welfare* 60:499–518.

Hinshaw, S., R. Klein, and H. Abikoff. 1998. "Childhood Attention Deficit Hyperactivity Disorder: Nonpharmacological and Combination Treatments." In Nathan and J. Gorman, *A Guide to Treatments That Work*, 26–41.

Horne, A., B. Glaser, and G. Calhoun. 1999. "Conduct Disorders." In Ammerman, Hersen, and Last, *Handbook of Prescriptive Treatments*, 84–101.

Howard, D., Y. Qiu, and B. Boekeloo. 2003. "Personal and Social Contextual Correlates of Adolescent Dating Violence." *Journal of Adolescent Health* 33:9–17.

Huang, B., R. Kosterman, R. Catalano, J. Hawkins, and R. Abbott. 2001. "Modeling Mediation in the Etiology of Violent Behavior and Adolescence: A Test of the Social Developmental Model." *Criminology* 39:75–107.

Hurley, T. 1907. *Origin of the Illinois Juvenile Court Law*. Chicago: Visitation and Aid Society.

Hurst, J. 1990. "Drug Program's Tough Tactics Draw Fire." *Los Angeles Times*, March 24.

Huxley, N., S. Parikh, and R. Baldessarini. 2000. "Effectiveness of Psychosocial Treatments in Bipolar Disorder: State of the Evidence." *Harvard Review of Psychiatry* 8:126–40.

IECA (Independent Educational Consultants Association). 2006. "Principles of Good Practice," December. www.educationalconsulting.org/pdf/IECA_Principles_of_Good_Practice.pdf (July 20, 2007).

In-Albon T. and S. Schneider. 2007. "Psychotherapy of Childhood Anxiety Disorders: A Meta-Analysis." *Psychotherapy and Psychosomatics* 76:15–24.

Individual Rights and the Federal Role in Behavior Modification: A Study Prepared by the Staff of the Subcommittee on Constitutional Rights of the Committee on the Judiciary. 1974. 93d Cong., 2d sess. Washington, D.C.: U.S. Government Printing Office.

"Investigation Shows Troubled School May Be Buying Interest with Lawmakers." 2004. *Daily (Provo, Utah) Herald*, September 20, http://old.heraldextra.com/modules.php?op=modload&name=News&file= article&sid=34937 (July 1, 2007).

Ivey, J. 2000. *Boys Town: The Constant Spirit*. Chicago: Arcadia.

Jackson, C. 2002. "Perceived Legitimacy of Parental Authority and Tobacco and Alcohol use during Early Adolescence." *Journal of Adolescent Health* 31:425–32.

Jainchill, N. 2000. "Substance Dependency Treatment for Adolescents: Practice and Research." *Substance Use and Misuse* 35:2031–60.

Janzen, R. 2001. *The Rise and Fall of Synanon: A California Utopia*. Baltimore: Johns Hopkins University Press.

Joanning, H., W. Quinn, R. Thomas, and R. Mullen. 1992. "Treating Adolescent Drug Abuse: A Comparison of Family Systems Therapy, Group Therapy, and Family Drug Education." *Journal of Marital and Family Therapy* 18:345–56.

Johnson, S. and R. Leahy, eds. 2005. *Psychological Treatment of Bipolar Disorder.* New York: Guilford.

Johnston, L. D., P. M. O'Malley, J. G. Bachman, and J. E. Schulenberg 2007. *Monitoring the Future: National Results on Adolescent Drug Use—Overview of Key Findings, 2006.* Bethesda, Md.: National Institute on Drug Abuse, U.S. Department of Health and Human Services.

Jones, M. B. and D. R. Jones. 2000. "The Contagious Nature of Antisocial Behavior." *Criminology* 38:25–46.

Jordan, C. and C. Franklin, eds. 2003. *Clinical Assessment for Social Workers: Quantitative and Qualitative Methods.* 2d ed. Chicago: Lyceum.

Kahn, J., T. Kehle, W. Jenson, and E. Clark. 1990. "Comparison of Cognitive-Behavioral, Relaxation and Self-modeling Interventions for Depression among Middle School Students." *School Psychology Review* 19:196–211.

Kalich, D. and R. Evans. 2006. "Drug Court: An Effective Alternative to Incarceration." *Deviant Behavior* 27:569–90.

Kaminer, Y. and J. Burleson. 1999. "Psychotherapies for Adolescent Substance Abusers: Fifteen-Month Follow-up of a Pilot Study." *American Journal on Addictions,* 8:114–19.

Kaminer, Y., J. Burleson, and R. Goldberger. 2002. "Cognitive-Behavioral Coping Skills and Psychoeducation Therapies for Adolescent Substance Abuse." *Journal of Nervous and Mental Disease* 190:737–45.

Kaminer, Y., J. Burleson, C. Blitz, J. Sussman, and B. Rounsaville. 1998. "Psychotherapies for Adolescent Substance Abusers: A Pilot Study." *Journal of Nervous and Mental Disorders* 186:684–90.

Karcher, M., G. Kuperminc, S. Portwood, C. Sipe, and A. Taylor. 2006. "Mentoring Programs: A Framework to Inform Program Development, Research, and Evaluation." *Journal of Community Psychology* 34:709–25.

Karls, J. and K. Wandrei, eds. 1994. *The PIE Classification System for Social Functioning Problems.* Washington, D.C.: NASW Press.

Kazdin, A. 1994. "Psychotherapy for Children and Adolescents." In A. Bergin and S. Garfield, eds., *The Handbook of Psychotherapy and Behavior Change,* 543–94. 4th ed. New York: Wiley.

——. 1997. "Practitioner Review: Psychosocial Treatments for Conduct Disorder in Children." *Journal of Child Psychology and Psychiatry* 38:161–78.

——. 2000. *Behavior Modification in Applied Settings.* Belmont, Calif.: Wadsworth.

Kazdin A. and J. Weisz. 1998. "Identifying and Developing Empirically Supported Child and Adolescent Treatments." *Journal of Consulting and Clinical Psychology* 66:19–36.

Kazdin, A., D. Bass, T. Siegel, and C. Thomas. 1989. "Cognitive-Behavioral Therapy and Relationship Therapy in the Treatment of Children Referred for Antisocial Behavior." *Journal of Consulting and Clinical Psychology* 57:522–35.

Keating, L., M. Tomishima, S. Foster, and M. Alessandri. 2002. "The Effects of a Mentoring Program on At-Risk Youth." *Adolescence* 37:717–34.

Keming, G. and J. Calabrese. 2005. "Newer Treatment Studies for Bipolar Depression." *Bipolar Disorders* 7:13–23.

Kemp, D., G. Keming, D. Muzina, and J. Calabrese. 2006. "Progress in the Treatment of Bipolar Depression: Advances and Challenges." *Psychiatric Times* 23:39–44.

Kendall, P. 1992. *Anxiety Disorders in Youth: Cognitive Behavioral Interventions.* Boston: Allyn and Bacon.

——. 1993. "Cognitive-Behavioral Therapies with Youth: Guiding Theory, Current Status, and Emerging Developments." *Journal of Consulting and Clinical Psychology* 61:235–47.

Kim, I., N. Zane, and S. Hong. 2002. "Protective Factors against Substance Abuse Use among Asian American Youth: A Test of the Peer Cluster Theory." *Journal of Community Psychology* 30:565–84.

King, N., D. Hamilton, and T. Ollendick. 1988. *Children's Phobias: A Behavioural Perspective.* Chichester, U.K.: Wiley.

Kinney, J., D. Haapala, and C. Booth. 1991. *Keeping Families Together: The Homebuilders Model.* Hawthorne, N.Y.: de Gruyter.

Kirk, R. and D. Griffith. 2004. "Intensive Family Preservation Services: Demonstrating Placement Prevention Using Event History Analysis." *Social Work Research* 28:5–16.

Klein, D., L. Dougherty, and T. Olino 2005. "Toward Guidelines for Evidence-Based Assessment of Depression in Children and Adolescents." *Journal of Clinical Child and Adolescent Psychology* 34:412–32.

Klerman, G. and M. Weissman, eds. 1993. *New Applications of Interpersonal Psychotherapy.* Washington, D.C.: American Psychiatric Association.

Kohn, M. and N. Golden. 2001. "Eating Disorders in Children and Adolescence: Epidemiology, Diagnosis, and Treatment." *Pediatric Drugs* 3:91–99.

Kowatch, R., M. Fristad, B. Birmaher, K. Wagner, R. Findling, and M. Hellander. 2005. "Treatment Guidelines for Children and Adolescents with Bipolar Disorder." *Journal of the American Academy of Child and Adolescent Psychiatry* 44:213–35.

Krakauer, J. 1995. "Loving Them to Death." *Outside*, October, http://outside.away.com/magazine/1095/10f_deth.html (June 30, 2007).

Kumpfer, K. and R. Alvarado. 2003. "Family-Strengthening Approaches for the Prevention of Youth Problem Behaviors." *American Psychologist* 58:457–65.

Lammers, C., M. Ireland, M. Resnick, and R. Blum. 2000. "Influences on Adolescents' Decision to Postpone Onset of Sexual Intercourse: A Survival Analysis of Virginity among Youths Aged Thirteen to Eighteen Years." *Journal of Adolescent Health* 26:42–48.

Landwehr, K. 2005. "Psychological Treatment of Bipolar Disorder." *Psychiatric Rehabilitation Journal* 28:415–16.

Langhout, R, J. Rhodes, and L. Osborne. 2004. "An Exploratory Study of Youth Mentoring in an Urban Context: Adolescents' Perceptions of Relationship Styles." *Journal of Youth and Adolescence* 33:293–306.

LaPeter, L. 2006. "Dirt and the Diplomat." *St. Petersburg Times*, November 11, www.sptimes.com/2006/11/11/Tampabay/Dirt__the_diplomat.shtml (June 29, 2007).

Larimer, M. and J. Cronce. 2002. "Identification, Prevention, and Treatment: A Review of Individual-Focused Strategies to Reduce Problematic Alcohol Consumption by College Students." *Journal of Studies on Alcohol* 63:148–63.

Larson, R. 2006. "Positive Youth Development, Willful Adolescents, and Mentoring." *Journal of Community Psychology* 34:677–89.

Latimer, L. 1984. "False Imprisonment Ruling Upheld: Drug Program Ordered to Pay Virginia Man $220,000." *Washington Post*, November 27.

Leahy, R. 2007. "Bipolar Disorder: Causes, Contexts, and Treatments." *Journal of Clinical Psychology* 63:417–24.

Leahy, R. and S. Johnson, eds. 2003. *Psychological Treatment of Bipolar Disorder.* New York: Guilford.

Lebow, J. and A. Gurman. 1995. "Research Assessing Couple and Family Therapy." *Annual Review of Psychology* 46:27–57.

Lee, J. and B. Cramond. 1999. "The Positive Effects of Mentoring Economically Disadvantaged Students." *Professional School Counseling* 2:172–78.

Leichtman, M. 2006. "Residential Treatment of Children and Adolescents: Past, Present, and Future." *American Journal of Orthopsychiatry* 76:285–94.

Lewis, R., F. Piercy, D. Sprenkle, and T. Trepper. 1990. "Family-Based Interventions for Helping Drug-Abusing Adolescents." *Journal of Adolescent Research* 50:82–95.

Lewisohn, P., G. Clarke, H. Hops, and J. Andrews. 1990. "Cognitive-Behavioral Treatment for Depressed Adolescents." *Behavior Therapy* 21:385–401.

Liddle, H. 1998. *Multidimensional Family Therapy Treatment Manual.* Miami: Center for Treatment Research on Adolescent Drug Abuse, University of Miami School of Medicine.

Liddle, H., G. Dakof, K. Parker, S. Diamond, K. Barrett, and M. Tejeda. 2001. "Multidimensional Family Therapy for Adolescent Drug Abuse: Results of a Randomized Clinical Trial." *American Journal of Drug and Alcohol Abuse* 27: 651–88.

Lindquist, C., C. Krebs, and P. Lattimore. 2006. "Sanctions and Rewards in Drug Court Programs: Implementation, Perceived Efficacy, and Decision Making." *Journal of Drug Issues* 36:119–46.

Lipsey, M. and D. Wilson. 2001. *Practical Meta-Analysis.* Thousand Oaks, Calif.: Sage.

Lloyd-Richardson, E., G. Papandonatos, A. Kazura, C. Stanton, and R. Niaura. 2002. "Differentiating Stages of Smoking Intensity among Adolescents: Stage-Specific Psychological and Social Influences." *Journal of Consulting and Clinical Psychology* 70:998–1009.

Luthar, S. and L. Zelazo. 2003. "Research on Resilience: An Integrative Review." In S. Luthar, ed., *Resilience and Vulnerability: Adaptation in the Context of Childhood Adversities,* 510–50. New York: Cambridge University Press.

Magnani, R., A. Karim, L. Weiss, K. Bond, M. Lemba, and G. Morgan. 2002. "Reproductive Health Risk and Protective Factors among Youth in Lusaka, Zambia." *Journal of Adolescent Health* 30:76–86.

Malow, R., J. Devieux, T. Jennings, B. Lucenko, and S. Kalichman. 2001. "Substance-Abusing Adolescents at Varying Levels of HIV Risk: Psychosocial Characteristics, Drug Use, and Sexual Behavior." *Journal of Substance Abuse* 13:103–17.

March, J., S. Silva, S. Petrycki, J. Curry, K. Wells, J. Fairbank, B. Burns, et al. 2004. "Fluoxetine, Cognitive-Behavioral Therapy, and Their Combination for Adolescents with Depression; Treatment for Adolescents with Depression Study (TADS) Randomized Controlled Trial." *Journal of the American Medical Association* 292:807–20.

Marcus, D. 2005. *What It Takes to Pull Me Through: Why Teenagers Get in Trouble and How Four of Them Got Out.* Boston: Houghton Mifflin.

Marlowe, D., D. Festinger, C. Foltz, P. Lee, and N. Patapis. 2005. "Perceived Deterrence and Outcomes in Drug Court." *Behavioral Sciences and the Law* 23:183–98.

Mason, M. 1996. "A Comprehensive Review and Critical Examination of Interdisciplinary Approaches towards Adolescent Substance Abuse Treatment." *Journal of Ministry in Addiction and Recovery* 3:43–66.

Masten, A. 1999. "Resilience Comes of Age: Reflections on the Past and Outlook for the Next Generation." In M. Glantz and J. Johnson, eds., *Resilience and Development: Positive Life Adaptations*, 281–96. New York: Kluwer Academic/ Plenum.

McCarty, C. and J. Weisz. 2007. "Effects of Psychotherapy for Depression in Children and Adolescents: What We Can (and Can't) Learn from Meta-Analysis and Component Profiling." *Journal of the American Academy of Child and Adolescent Psychiatry* 46:879–86.

McCroskey, J. and W. Meezan. 1997. *Family Preservation and Family Functioning.* Washington, D.C.: Child Welfare League of America Press.

McGillicuddy, N., R. Rychtarik, J. Duquette, and E. Morsheimer. 2001. "Development of a Skill-Training Program for Parents of Substance-Abusing Adolescents." *Journal of Substance Abuse Treatment*, 20:59–68.

McKinley, C. 2005. "Tough-Love Schools Are Both Loved and Hated." Fox News, June 11, www.foxnews.com/story/0,2933,159276,00.html (July 1, 2007).

McWhirter, J., B. McWhirter, E. McWhirter, and R. McWhirter. 2007. *At-Risk Youth: A Comprehensive Response.* 4th ed. Belmont, Calif.: Thomson.

Meyer, C. 1993. *Assessment in Social Work Practice.* New York: Columbia University Press.

Michael, K. and S. Crowley. 2002. "How Effective Are Treatments for Child and Adolescent Depression? A Meta-Analytic Review." *Clinical Psychology Review* 22:247–69.

Mill, J. [1859] 1943. "On Liberty." In *The Utilitarians*, 474–600. New York: Anchor.

Monti, P., N. Barnett, T. O'Leary, and S. Colby. 2001. "Motivational Enhancement for Alcohol-Involved Adolescents." In P. Monti, S. Colby, and T. O'Leary, eds., *Adolescents, Alcohol and Substance Abuse: Reaching Teens through Brief Interventions*, 145–82. New York: Guilford.

Moore, M. 1982. "'Straight' to Open Area Chapter." *Washington Post*, July 28.

Morgenstern, J. 1995. "A Death in the Desert." *Los Angeles Times Magazine*, January 15.

Morris, T. and J. March, eds. 2004. *Anxiety Disorders in Children and Adolescence.* 2d ed. New York: Guilford.

Muck, R., K. Zempolich, J. Titus, and M. Fishman. 2001. "An Overview of the Effectiveness of Adolescent Substance Abuse Treatment Models." *Youth and Society* 33:143–68.

Nathan, P. and J. Gorman, eds. 1998. *A Guide to Treatments That Work.* New York: Oxford University Press.

National Institute of Mental Health. 1999. "Brief Notes on the Mental Health of Children and Adolescents." November, www.medhelp.org/NIHlib/GF-233.html (June 26, 2007).

——. 2006. *Going to Extremes, Bipolar Disorder*, www.mental-health-matters.com/ articles/article.php?artID=226 (March 3, 2008).

National Institutes of Health Consensus Development Program. 2004. "Preventing Violence and Related Health-Risking Social Behaviors in Adolescents," October 13–15, http://consensus.nih.gov/2004/2004YouthViolencePreventionSOS023html. htm (July 16, 2007).

National Mental Health Information Center. 2003. "Children's Mental Health Facts: Children and Adolescents with Mental, Emotional, and Behavioral Disorders," April, http://mentalhealth.samhsa.gov/publications/allpubs/CA-0006/default.asp (February 20, 2008).

Nissen, L. 2006. "Effective Adolescent Substance Abuse Treatment in Juvenile Justice Settings: Practice and Policy Recommendations." *Child and Adolescent Social Work Journal* 23:298–315.

Northey, W., K. Wells, W. Silverman, and C. Bailey. 2003. "Childhood Behavioral and Emotional Disorders." *Journal of Marital and Family Therapy* 29:523–45.

Nottingham, W. 1978. "Drug Program Allegedly Used Coercive Tactics to Control Clients." *St. Petersburg Times*, February 12.

O'Connor, S. 2004. *Orphan Trains: The Story of Charles Loring Brace and the Children He Saved and Failed*. Chicago: University of Chicago Press.

Office of Justice Programs. 2006. *Drug Courts: The Second Decade*. Washington, D.C.: U.S. Department of Justice.

O'Hare, T. 2005. *Evidenced-Based Practices for Social Workers*. Chicago: Lyceum.

Ollendick, T. and N. King. 1994. "Diagnosis, Assessment and Treatment of Internalizing Problems in Children: The Role of Longitudinal Data." *Journal of Consulting and Clinical Psychology* 62:918–27.

Osterling, K. and A. Hines. 2006. "Mentoring Adolescent Foster Youth: Promoting Resilience during Developmental Transitions." *Child and Family Social Work* 11:242–53.

Palmer, T. 1996. "Programmatic and Nonprogrammatic Aspects of Successful Intervention." In A. Harland, ed., *Choosing Correctional Options That Work: Defining the Demand and Evaluating the Supply*, 131–82. Thousand Oaks, Calif.: Sage.

Pappenfort, D., D. Kilpatrick, and R. Roberts, eds. 1973. *Child Care: Social Policy and the Institution*. Chicago: Aldine.

Parsons, T. 1949. *The Structure of Social Action*. Glencoe, Ill.: Free Press.

Paul, C., J. Fitzjohn, P. Herbison, and N. Dickson. 2000. "The Determinants of Sexual Intercourse before Age Sixteen." *Journal of Adolescent Health* 27:136–47.

Pavuluri, M. and M. Naylor. 2005. "Multi-Model Integrated Treatment for Youth with Bipolar Disorder." *Psychiatric Times* 22:24–27.

Pelham, W., T. Wheeler, and A. Chronis. 1998. "Empirically Supported Psychosocial Treatments for Attention Deficit Hyperactivity Disorder." *Journal of Clinical Child Psychology* 27:190–205.

Philip, K. and L. Hendry. 2001. "Making Sense of Mentoring or Mentoring Making Sense? Reflections on the Mentoring Process by Adults Mentors with Young People." *Journal of Community and Applied Social Psychology* 10:211–23.

Platt, A. 1977. *The Child Savers: The Invention of Delinquency*. 2d ed. Chicago: University of Chicago Press.

Polonsky, M. 2007. "THE SEED: Behavior Modification for Adolescents in Fort Lauderdale, Florida." *Insider's View*, www.insidersview.info/theseed.htm (June 30, 2007).

Pumariega, A. 2006. "Residential Treatment for Youth: Introduction and a Cautionary Tale." *American Journal of Orthopsychiatry* 76:281–84.

Quinn, W. 2004. *Family Solutions for Youths at Risk: Applications to Juvenile Delinquency, Truancy, and Behavior Problems*. New York: Brunner-Routledge.

Quinney, R. 1970. *The Problem of Crime*. New York: Dodd, Mead.

Rai, A., B. Stanton, Y. Wu, X. Li, J. Galbraith, L. Cottrell, R. Pack, et al. 2003. "Relative Influences of Perceived Parental Monitoring and Perceived Peer Involvement on Adolescent Risk Behaviors: An Analysis of Six Cross-sectional Data Sets." *Journal of Adolescent Health* 33:108–18.

Rapp, C. and R. Goscha. 2006. *The Strengths Model: Case Management with People with Psychiatric Disabilities*. 2d ed. New York: Oxford University Press.

Rapport, M. 1992. "Treatment of Children with Attention-Deficit Hyperactivity Disorder (ADHD)." *Behavior Modification* 16:155–63.

Reamer, F. 1983. "The Free Will–Determinism Debate in Social Work." *Social Service Review* 57:626–44.

——. 2001. *The Social Work Ethics Audit: A Risk Management Tool*. Washington, D.C.: NASW Press.

——. 2006a. *Ethical Standards in Social Work: A Review of the NASW Code of Ethics*. 2d ed. Washington, D.C.: NASW Press.

——. 2006b. *Social Work Malpractice and Liability: Strategies for Prevention*. 2d ed. New York: Columbia University Press.

Reamer, F. and D. Siegel. 2006. *Finding Help for Struggling Teens: A Guide for Parents and the Professionals Who Work with Them*. Washington, D.C.: NASW Press.

Reinecke, M., F. Dattilio, and A. Freeman, eds. 1996. *Cognitive Therapy with Children and Adolescents: A Casebook for Clinical Practice*. New York: Guilford.

Reinecke, M., N. Ryan, and D. DuBois. 1998. "Cognitive-Behavioral Therapy of Depression and Depressive Symptoms during Adolescence: A Review and Meta-Analysis." *Journal of the American Academy of Child and Adolescent Psychiatry* 37:26–34.

Reynolds, W. and K. Coats. 1986. "A Comparison of Cognitive-Behavioral Therapy and Relaxation Training for the Treatment of Depression in Adolescents." *Journal of Consulting and Clinical Psychology* 54:653–60.

Rhodes, J. 2002. *Stand by Me: The Risks and Rewards of Mentoring Today's Youth*. Cambridge, Mass.: Harvard University Press.

Rhodes, J., R. Spencer, T. Keller, B. Liang, and G. Noam. 2006. "A Model for the Influence of Mentoring Relationships on Youth Development." *Journal of Community Psychology* 34:691–707.

Rivera, C. 1990. "Parents Protest Straight's Fate." *Los Angeles Times*, November 2.

Roberts, A. and K. Yeager, eds. 2004. *Evidence-Based Practice Manual: Research and Outcome Measures in Health and Human Services*. New York: Oxford University Press.

Roger, T. 2003. "Officials to Investigate 'Tough Love' Facility Here." *Tico (Costa Rica) Times*, January 17, www.ticotimes.net/archive/01_17_03_2.htm (July 1, 2007).

Roll, J., M. Prendergast, K. Richardson, W. Burdon, and A. Ramirez. 2005. "Identifying Predictors of Treatment Outcome in a Drug Court Program." *American Journal of Drug and Alcohol Abuse* 31:641–56.

Rome, E., S. Ammerman, D. Rosen, R. Keller, J., Lock, K. Mammel, J. O'Toole, et al. 2003. "Children and Adolescents with Eating Disorders: The State of the Art." *Pediatrics* 111:98–108.

Romi, S. and E. Kohan. 2004. "Wilderness Programs: Principles, Possibilities and Opportunities for Intervention with Dropout Adolescents." *Child and Youth Care Forum* 33:115–36.

Root, R. and R. Resnick. 2003. "An Update on the Diagnosis and Treatment of Attention-Deficit/Hyperactivity Disorder in Children." *Professional Psychology: Research and Practice* 34:34–41.

Rose, R. and K. Jones. 2007. "The Efficacy of a Volunteer Mentoring Scheme in Supporting Young People at Risk." *Emotional and Behavioural Difficulties* 12:3–14.

Rosenthal, R. 2004. "Overview of Evidence-Based Practice." In Roberts and Yeager, *Evidence-Based Practice Manual*, 20–29.

Russell, K. 2003. "An Assessment of Outcomes in Outdoor Behavioral Healthcare Treatment." *Child and Youth Care Forum* 32:355–81.

——. 2005. "Two Years Later: A Qualitative Assessment of Youth Well-Being and the Role of Aftercare in Outdoor Behavioral Healthcare Treatment." *Child and Youth Care Forum* 34:209–39.

Russell, K. and D. Phillips-Miller. 2002. "Perspectives on the Wilderness Therapy Process and Its Relation to Outcome." *Child and Youth Care Forum* 31:415–37.

Rutter, M. 1985. "Resilience in the Face of Adversity: Protective Factors and Resistance to Psychiatric Disorder." *British Journal of Psychiatry* 147:598–611.

——. 1987. "Psychosocial Resilience and Protective Mechanisms." *American Journal of Orthopsychiatry* 57:316–31.

Saleebey, D., ed. 2006. *The Strengths Perspective in Social Work Practice.* 4th ed. Boston: Pearson Education.

Sanders, W., ed. 1970. *Juvenile Offenders for a Thousand Years: Selected Readings from Anglo-Saxon Times to 1900.* Chapel Hill: University of North Carolina Press.

Santelli, J., J. Kaiser, L. Hirsch, A. Radosh, L. Simkin, and S. Middlestadt. 2004. "Initiation of Sexual Intercourse among Middle School Adolescents: The Influence of Psychosocial Factors." *Journal of Adolescent Health* 34:200–208.

Santisteban, D., J. Coatsworth, A. Perez-Vidal, W. Kurtines, S. Schwartz, A. LaPerriere, and J. Szapocznik. 2003. "Efficacy of Brief Strategic Family Therapy in Modifying Hispanic Adolescent Behavior Problems and Substance Abuse." *Journal of Family Psychology* 17:121–33.

Scheier, L., G. Botvin, and N. Miller. 1999. "Life Events, Neighborhood Stress, Psychosocial Functioning, and Alcohol Use among Urban Minority Youth." *Journal of Child and Adolescent Substance Abuse* 9:19–50.

Schemo, D. 2007. "Report Recounts Horrors of Youth Boot Camps." *New York Times,* October 11, www.nytimes.com/2007/10/11/washington/11report.html?_r=1&oref=slogin (March 10, 2008).

Schiraldi, V., B. Hollman, and P. Beatty. 2000. "Poor Prescription: The Cost of Imprisoning Drug Offenders in the United States." Justice Policy Institute, Washington, D.C.

Schmidt, U. 1998. "Eating-disorders and Obesity." In Graham, *Cognitive-Behaviour Therapy for Children and Families,* 262–81.

Scott, J. and M. Gutierrez. 2004. "The Current Status of Psychological Treatments in Bipolar Disorders: A Systematic Review of Relapse Prevention." *Bipolar Disorders* 6:498–503.

Sealock, M., D. Gottfredson, and C. Gallagher .1997. "Drug Treatment for Juvenile Offenders: Some Good and Bad News." *Journal of Research in Crime and Delinquency* 34:210–36.

Sells, S. 2002. *Parenting Your Out-of-Control Teenager.* New York: St. Martin's.

Sexton, T. and J. Alexander. 1999. *Functional Family Therapy: Principles of Clinical Intervention, Assessment, and Implementation*. Henderson, Nev.: RCH Enterprises.

Shekter-Wolfson, L., D. Woodside, and J. Lackstrom. 1997. "Social Work Treatment of Anorexia and Bulimia: Guidelines for Practice." *Research on Social Work Practice* 7:5–31.

Sheldon, W. 1949. *Varieties of Delinquent Youth: An Introduction to Constitutional Psychiatry*. New York: Harper.

Shireman, C. and F. Reamer. 1986. *Rehabilitating Juvenile Justice*. New York: Columbia University Press.

Silverman, W. and P. Treffers. 2001. *Anxiety Disorders in Children and Adolescents: Research, Assessment, and Intervention*. Cambridge: Cambridge University Press.

Skiba, D., J. Monroe, and J. Wodarski. 2004. "Adolescent Substance Use: Reviewing the Effectiveness of Prevention." *Social Work* 49:343–53.

Slicker, E. and D. Palmer. 1993. "Mentoring At-Risk High School Students: Evaluation of a School-Based Program." *School Counselor* 40:327–34.

Smith, C. 1995. "'I Feel Like I'm Going to Die': North Star Teen's Journal Charts His Own Demise." *Salt Lake Tribune*, May 28.

Smith, D., M. Marcus, and K. Eldredge. 1994. "Binge-Eating Syndromes: A Review of Assessment and Treatment with an Emphasis on Clinical Application." *Behavior Therapy* 25:635–58.

Sowell E., P. Thompson, C. Holmes, T. Jernigan, and A. Toga. 1999. "In Vivo Evidence for Post-Adolescent Brain Maturation in Frontal and Striatal Regions." *Nature Neuroscience* 2:859–61.

Sowell E., P. Thompson, C. Leonard , S. Welcome, E. Kan, and A. Toga. 2006. "Mapping Brain Maturation." *Trends in Neurosciences* 29:148–59.

Spencer, R. 2006. "Understanding the Mentoring Process between Adolescents and Adults." *Youth and Society* 37:287–315.

Springer, D. 2004. "Treating Juvenile Delinquents with Conduct Disorder, Attention-Deficit/Hyperactivity Disorder, and Oppositional Defiant Disorder." In Roberts and Yeager, *Evidence-Based Practice Manual*, 263–73.

Stanton, B., X. Li, R. Pack, L. Cottrell, C. Harris, and J. Burns. 2002. "Longitudinal Influence of Perceptions of Peer and Parental Factors on African American Adolescent Risk Involvement." *Journal of Urban Health* 79:536–48.

Stark, K., C. Vaughn, M. Doxey, and L. Luss. 1999. "Depressive Disorders." In Ammerman, Hersen, and Last, *Handbook of Prescriptive Treatments*, 114–40.

Stein, R., B. Saelens, J. Dounchis, C. Lewczyk, A. Swenson, and D. Wilfley. 2001. "Treatment of Eating Disorders in Women." *Counseling Psychologist* 29:695–732.

Stout, C. and R. Hayes, eds. 2005. *The Evidence-Based Practice: Methods, Models and Tools for Mental Health Practitioners*. Hoboken, N.J.: Wiley.

Straus, Martha B. 2007. *Adolescent Girls in Crisis: Intervention and Hope*. New York: Norton.

Strober, M., B. Birmaher, N. Ryan, D. Axelson, S. Valeri, H. Leonard, S. Iyengar, M. Gill, J. Hunt, and M. Keller. 2006. "Pediatric Bipolar Disease: Current and Future Perspectives for Study of its Long-term Course and Treatment." *Bipolar Disorders* 8:311–21.

Sutherland, E. and D. Cressey. 1966. *Principles of Criminology*. 7th ed. Philadelphia: Lippincott.

Swenson, C., S. Henggeler, I. Taylor, and O. Addison. 2004. *Multisystemic Therapy and Neighborhood Partnerships: Reducing Adolescent Violence and Substance Abuse.* New York: Guilford.

Szalavitz, M. 2006. *Help at Any Cost: How the Troubled-Teen Industry Cons Parents and Hurts Kids.* New York: Riverhead Books.

——. 2007. "The Trouble with Troubled Teen Programs." *Reasononline,* January, www.reason.com/news/show/117088.html (June 30, 2007).

Taffel, R. 2005. *Breaking through to Teens: A New Psychotherapy for the New Adolescence.* New York: Guilford.

Thompson, L. and L. Kelly-Vance. 2001. "The Impact of Mentoring on the Academic Achievement of At-Risk Youth." *Children and Youth Services Review* 23:227–42.

Thyer, B. 2004. "Science and Evidence-based Social Work Practice." In H. Briggs and T. Rzepnicki, eds., *Using Evidence in Social Work Practice: Behavioral Perspectives,* 74–89. Chicago: Lyceum.

Torgensen, K., D. Buttars, S. Norman, and S. Bailey. 2004. "How Drug Courts Reduce Substance Abuse Recidivism." *Journal of Law, Medicine and Ethics* 32:69–72.

Tourmbourou, J., T. Stockwell, C. Neighbors, G. Marlatt, J. Sturge, and J. Rehm. 2007. "Interventions to Reduce Harm Associated with Adolescent Substance Use." *Lancet* 369:1391–1401.

Traub, J. 2005. "The Moral Imperative." *Education Next* 1:21–33.

Turner, S., D. Longshore, S. Wenzel, E. Deschenes, P. Greenwood, T. Fain, A. Harrell, et al. 2002. "A Decade of Drug Treatment Court Research." *Substance Use and Misuse* 37:1489–1527.

Tyuse, S. and D. Linhorst. 2005. "Drug Courts and Mental Health Courts: Implications for Social Work." *Health and Social Work* 30:233–40.

Ungar, M., ed. 2005. *Handbook for Working with Children and Youth: Pathways to Resilience across Cultures and Contexts.* Thousand Oaks, Calif.: Sage.

U.S. Census Bureau. 2006. "Poverty: 2005 Highlights," August 29, www.census.gov/hhes/www/poverty/poverty05/pov05hi.html (July 18, 2007).

U.S. Centers for Disease Control and Prevention. 2006. "Youth Risk Behavior Surveillance—United States, 2005," *Morbidity and Mortality Weekly Report* 55 (June 9), www.cdc.gov/HealthyYouth/yrbs/index.htm (February 22, 2008).

U.S. Department of Health and Human Services. 1999. *Mental Health: A Report of the Surgeon General.* Rockville, Md.: U.S. Department of Health and Human Services.

Vandiver, V. 2002. "Step-by-Step Guidelines for Using Evidence-Based Practice and Expert Consensus Procedures." In A. Roberts and G. Greene, eds., *Social Workers Desk Reference,* 731–39. New York: Oxford University Press.

Vaughn, M. and M. Howard. 2004. "Adolescent Substance Abuse Treatment: A Synthesis of Controlled Evaluations." *Research on Social Work Practice* 14:325–35.

Vitousek, K. 2002. "Cognitive-Behavioral Therapy for Anorexia Nervosa." In C. Fairburn and K. Brownell, eds., *Eating Disorders and Obesity: A Comprehensive Handbook,* 308–13. 2d ed. New York: Guilford.

Vorrath, H. H. and L. K. Brendtro. 1985. *Positive Peer Culture.* 3d ed. New York: Aldine.

Waldron, H., N. Slesnick, J. Brody, C. Turner, and T. Peterson. 2001. "Treatment Outcomes for Adolescent Substance Abuse at Four- and Seven-Month Assessments." *Journal of Consulting and Clinical Psychology* 69:802–13.

Webster-Stratton, C. and M. Herbert. 1994. *Troubled Families—Problem Children: Working with Parents—A Collaborative Process.* New York: Wiley.

Weiner, T. 2003a. "U.S. Youths Rebel at Harsh School." *New York Times,* May 27, www.nytimes.com/2003/05/27/international/americas/27COST.html?ex=13700592 00&en=f34ede40f959adao&ei=5007&partner=USERLAND (June 23, 2007).

——. 2003b. "Plea for Inquiry on School Network." *New York Times,* November 5, www.nytimes.com/2003/11/05/national/05BRFS4.html?ex=1183435200&en=d62159 f19e979fcc&ei=507 (July 1, 2007).

Weiss, B., A. Caron, S. Ball, J. Tapp, M. Johnson, and J. R. Weisz. 2005. "Iatrogenic Effects of Group Treatment for Antisocial Youths." *Journal of Consulting and Clinical Psychology* 73:1036–44.

Weissman, M., J. Markowitz, and G. Klerman. 2000. *Comprehensive Guide to Interpersonal Psychotherapy.* New York: Basic Books.

Weisz, J. 2004. *Psychotherapy for Children and Adolescents: Evidence-Based Treatments and Case Examples.* Cambridge: Cambridge University Press.

Weisz, J., A. Jensen-Doss, and K. Hawley. 2006. "Evidence-Based Youth Psychotherapies versus Usual Clinical Care: A Meta-Analysis of Direct Comparisons." *American Psychologist* 61:671–89.

Weisz, J., C. McCarty, and S. Valeri. 2006. "Effects of Psychotherapy for Depression in Children and Adolescents: A Meta-Analysis." *Psychological Bulletin* 132:132–49.

Weisz, J., B. Weiss, S. Han, D. Granger, and T. Morton. 1995. "Effects of Psychotherapy with Children and Adolescents Revisited: A Meta-Analysis of Treatment Outcome Studies." *Psychological Bulletin* 117:450–68.

Wellford, C. 1973. "Age Composition and the Increase in Recorded Crime." *Criminology* 11:61–70.

Wells, K. and D. Whittington. 1993. "Child and Family Functioning after Intensive Family Preservation Services." *Social Service Review* 67:55–83.

Whittaker, J. and A. Maluccio. 2002. "Rethinking 'Child Placement': A Reflective Essay." *Social Service Review* 76:108–34.

Wilkinson, G., P. Taylor, and J. Holt. 2002. "Bipolar Disorder in Adolescence: Diagnosis and Treatment." *Journal of Mental Health Counseling* 24:348–57.

Wills, T., A. Yaeger, and J. Sandy. 2003. "Buffering Effect of Religiosity for Adolescent Substance Use." *Psychology of Addictive Behaviors* 13:327–38.

Wilson, G. and C. Fairburn. 1993. "Cognitive Treatment for Eating Disorders." *Journal of Consulting and Clinical Psychology* 61:261–69.

——. 1998. "Treatments of Eating Disorders." In Nathan and Gorman, *A Guide to Treatments That Work,* 501–30.

Wilson, G., C. Grilo, and K. Vitousek. 2007. "Psychological Treatment of Eating Disorders." *American Psychologist* 62:199–216.

Wilson, J. 1975. *Thinking about Crime.* New York: Basic Books.

Winters, K., R. Stinchfield, E. Opland, C. Weller, and W. Latimer. 2000. "The Effectiveness of the Minnesota Model Approach in the Treatment of Adolescent Drug Abusers." *Addiction* 95:601–12.

Wolfe, D. and E. Mash, eds. 2005. *Behavioral and Emotional Disorders in Adolescents: Nature, Assessment, and Treatment.* New York: Guilford.

Zarate, C. and J. Quiroz. 2003. "Combination Treatment in Bipolar Disorder: A Review of Controlled Trials." *Bipolar Disorders* 5:217–25.

Zibart, E. 1983. "Va. Jury Finds Drug Program Imprisoned Man." *Washington Post,* May 13.

Zimmerman, M. and R. Arunkumar. 1994. "Resiliency Research: Implications for Schools and Policy." *Social Policy Report* 8:1–17.

Zimmerman, M., J. Bingenheimer, and P. Notaro. 2002. "Natural Mentors and Adolescent Resiliency: A Study with Urban Youth." *American Journal of Community Psychology* 30:221–43.

Zimmerman, M., K. Steinman, and K. Rowe. 1998. "Violence among Urban African-American Adolescents: The Protective Effects of Parental Support." In S. Oskamp and X. Arriaga, eds., *Addressing Community Problems: Research and Intervention,* 78–103. Newbury Park, Calif.: Sage.